UNIVERSITY OF NORTH CAROLINA AT CHAPEL HILL
DEPARTMENT OF ROMANCE LANGUAGES

NORTH CAROLINA STUDIES
IN THE ROMANCE LANGUAGES AND LITERATURES

Founder: URBAN TIGNER HOLMES
Editor: MARÍA A. SALGADO

Distributed by:

UNIVERSITY OF NORTH CAROLINA PRESS
CHAPEL HILL
North Carolina 27515-2288
U.S.A.

NORTH CAROLINA STUDIES IN THE
ROMANCE LANGUAGES AND LITERATURES
Number 232

GIL VICENTE
AND THE DEVELOPMENT OF THE COMEDIA

Veronese, Paolo (Paolo Caliari): *Mars and Venus United by Love.* Oil on canvas, 81 x 63 3/8 in. (205.7 x 161 cm.). The Metropolitan Museum of Art, John Stewart Kennedy Fund, 1910. (10.189)

GIL VICENTE
AND
THE DEVELOPMENT OF THE COMEDIA

BY
RENÉ PEDRO GARAY

CHAPEL HILL

NORTH CAROLINA STUDIES IN THE ROMANCE
LANGUAGES AND LITERATURES
U.N.C. DEPARTMENT OF ROMANCE LANGUAGES
1988

Library of Congress Cataloging-in-Publication Data

Garay, René Pedro, 1949-
   Gil Vicente and the development of the comedia.

   (North Carolina studies in the Romance languages and literatures; no. 232)
   Bibliography: p.
   1. Vicente, Gil, ca. 1470-ca. 1536–Criticism and interpretation. 2. Portuguese drama–Classical period, 1500-1700–History and criticism. 3. Spanish drama–Classical period, 1500-1700–History and criticism. I. Title. II. Series.
PQ9252.G37   1988   869.2'2   88-24552
ISBN 0-8078-9234-3

DEPÓSITO LEGAL: V. 65 - 1989   I.S.B.N. 84-599-2572-2

ARTES GRÁFICAS SOLER, S. A. - LA OLIVERETA, 28 - 46018 VALENCIA - 1989

Para Amparo, pela força poética da memória que deixou.

CONTENTS

	Page
LIST OF FIGURES	XI
PREFÁCIO	XIII
PREFACE	XVII
ACKNOWLEDGEMENTS	XXI
INTRODUCTION: GIL VICENTE'S COMIC RENAISSANCE DRAMA	1

I. COMIC THEORY BEFORE THE SIXTEENTH CENTURY 9
   A) *Early Medieval Observations* 9
   B) *Late Medieval Observations* 22

II. THE DEVELOPMENT OF THE *COMÉDIA* FORM IN THE IBERIAN PENINSULA . 35
   A) *Dramatic Traditions of the Iberian Peninsula Before the Sixteenth Century* 35
      1. Comic Form and Expression 35
      2. Poetic Traditions in Peninsular Drama 37
      3. The Medieval Dance-Songs 48
      4. Later Manifestations 58
   B) *Comic Theory Before the Sixteenth Century* 60

III. THE SCOPE OF THE VICENTINE SECULAR PERSPECTIVE 75
   A) *Duality and the Binary Structure* 75
      1. "Pacíficas concordanças" 75
      2. Early Notions about Duality 79
   B) *The Vicentine Farsas, Comédias and Tragicomédias* 95

IV. THE *COMÉDIA DE RUBENA* 111
V. THE *COMÉDIA DO VIÚVO* 175
WORKS CITED 217

LIST OF FIGURES

		Page
1.	The *Comédia de Rubena* (Act I)	125
2.	Rubena's prayer to the Virgin Mary	129
3.	The *Comédia de Rubena* (Acts II and III)	161
4.	The *Comédia de Rubena*	173
5.	The *Comédia do Viúvo*	186

PREFÁCIO

Gil Vicente é, como se sabe, o maior dramaturgo da Literatura Portuguesa de todos os tempos. E mesmo se consideramos os demais países em que o Português é língua oficial, nenhum outro há que se lhe compare. Tal relevância ganha vulto quando nos lembramos de que a sua obra é mais do que um patrimônio português; é ibérico: a sua importância ultrapassa as fronteiras de Portugal: é ibérica. Nos quadros da poesia e do teatro peninsular do século XVI, é reconhecida a sua presença marcante, sobretudo como autor de *comédias*.

Faltava, porém, um estudo que desse conta desse papel fora do comun, que poucos escritores portuguesses ou espanhóis chegaram a desempenhar. O Professor René Pedro Garay resolveu em boa hora enfrentar o desafio, e o resultado aí está, nas mãos do leitor: uma densa obra de análise e crítica, que recomenda o seu autor e desde logo vem ocupar um espaço privilegiado na área dos estudos vicentinos.

Visando a Golden Age peninsular, o Professor Garay focaliza em primeiro lugar as raízes medievais da comédia no contexto europeu; a seguir, tendo a Renasçença por pano de fundo, faz uma avaliação das tradições dramáticas na Península Ibérica antes do século XVI e da teoria da *comédia*. Passa, depois, a discutir as idéias de Gil Vicente a respeito desse gênero e ao exame de suas *farsas*. E por fim aplica toda a sua notável erudição e cultura na análise e interpretação da *Comédia de Rubena* e *Comédia do Viúvo*, escolhidas não só por suas intrínsecas qualidades poéticas e teatrais, como ainda por terem sido escritas maiormente em Espanhol.

O Professor Garay sustenta a tese de que, no tocante à *comédia*, "Gil Vicente shares with his Spanish contemporary, Torres Naharro, the distinction of having given shape to the most important type of dramatic genre in the history of Hispanic theatrical literature", isto é, "he helped create a new genre which greatly influenced and oriented subsequent dramatic perspectives in the Hispanic Peninsula." Graças aos sólidos conhecimentos filosóficos, teológicos, literários e dramatúrgicos, e à acurada pesquisa nos textos vicentinos, a tese se torna de todo convincente.

As conclusões, umas genéricas, outras específicas, a que chega o Professor Garay, derivam da exaustiva investigação dos textos vicentinos e do aproveitamento oportuno das referências bibliográficas, tudo formando um auténtico silogismo. De um lado, diz ele, "It is in the two comedias examined here that the Portuguese dramatist supplied the most coherent formula for comic structure in the drama of the Iberian Peninsula"; de outro, acrescenta ele, pondo ênfase no aspecto poético, que acredita, com razão, ser nuclear da visão do mundo de Gil Vicente: "it was in the two comedies that we have seen that he poured his most important message of harmonization, one in which both worlds, the ironic and the romantic, come together to form, in realistic terms, the very texture and design of his poetic expression."

O modelo crítico adotado adequa-se com pertinência à tese proposta e à bibliografia manuseada, que vem desde Aristóteles até os mais recentes teóricos do teatro. Sem ser eclético, o Professor Garay afastou-se de um único e exclusivo modelo, preferindo, com acerto, fundir a investigação de tipo estructuralista e semiótico, mais propriamente greimasiano, à de tipo culturalista, sempre tendo em mira as peças de Gil Vicente como ponto de partida e de chegada.

O produto é uma obra de ensaísta agudo, atento às minúcias do assunto, mas que não perde de vista a demonstração da tese, de *scholar*, riguroso e sistemático. Além de repor Gil Vicente em discussão nos meios acadêmicos, com todo o aparato eruditivo à sua disposição, e uma visão moderna, o estudio situa o verdadeiro papel representado pelo autor português no âmbito das literaturas ibéricas e o seu valor como poeta e dramaturgo, precursor da comédia da Golden Age. É de notar a linguagem, ágil e vibrante, a persuasão constante e o apoio textual, invariavelmente a serviço do propósito em causa.

Compulsando a bibliografia mais recente em torno de Gil Vicente, e sempre com o mais apurado espíritu crítico, o Professor

Garay desfaz várias idéias feitas acerca das origens do teatro popular na Idade Média, bem como da comédia vicentina. O seu estudo se distingue, assim, não só pela luz nova e intensa que derrama sobre o autor português, como também sobre o teatro medieval, notadamente na Península Ibérica.

Em suma, o Professor René Pedro Garay elaborou um ensaio que se inscreve definitivamente na bibliografia vicentina como una das suas mais valiosas contribuições dos últimos anos: daqui por diante, torna-se praticamente impensável ampliar a pesquisa acerca do poeta e dramaturgo ibérico, sem ponderar as achegas e sugestões críticas contidas neste livro.

MASSAUD MOISÉS
Universidade de São Paulo

PREFACE

As is well known, Gil Vicente is the foremost dramatist in Portuguese literary history. Even if we consider the rest of the Portuguese-speaking world, there is still no other dramatist of comparable worth. His relevance takes on added significance when we recall that his works are more than just part of Portugal's national patrimony: his is an Iberian. His importance extends beyond Portugal's boundaries; it is Iberian in scope. His relevance is recognized within the parameters of sixteenth-century Peninsular poetry and drama, especially as author of *comédias*.

There has been lacking, however, a study accounting for Vicente's extraordinary role, one which few Portuguese or Spanish writers have succeeded in playing. Professor René Pedro Garay has finally taken on the challenge, and the result is now in the reader's hands: a work rich in critical analysis which speaks well of its author and immediately assumes a special place in the area of Vicentine studies.

Setting his sights on the Golden Age in the Iberian Peninsula, Professor Garay begins by focusing on the medieval roots of the *comédia* within its European context. With the Renaissance as a background, he undertakes an appraisal of the dramatic tradition in the Iberian Peninsula prior to the sixteenth century and the emergence of a theory concerning the *comédia*. He proceeds next to discuss the view of Gil Vicente with respect to this genre and to the farces. Finally, the author applies his scholarship and cultural formation to the *Comédia de Rubena* and *Comédia do Viúvo*, selected not only for their intrinsic poetic and theatrical qualities but also for having been written mainly in Spanish.

Professor Garay maintains the thesis that, with respect to the *comédia*, "Gil Vicente shares with his Spanish contemporary, Torres Naharro, the distinction of having given shape to the most important type of dramatic genre in the history of Hispanic theatrical literature." Accordingly, "he helped create a new genre which greatly influenced and oriented subsequent dramatic perspectives in the Hispanic Peninsula." Thanks to his knowledge of philosophy, theology, literature, and dramatic theory, and to his precision with the Vicentine text, his thesis becomes utterly convincing.

In the manner of a syllogism, the conclusions which Professor Garay reaches, some general and others more specific, come from his thorough investigation of the Vicentine texts and from his timely use of bibliographical references. On the one hand, he observes, "It is in the two comedies examined here that the Portuguese dramatist... supplied the most coherent formula for comic structure in the drama of the Iberian Peninsula." On the other hand, he goes on to add, while stressing the poetic aspect which he rightly believes to be central to Gil Vicente's view, "it was in the two comedies that we have seen that he poured his most important message of harmonization, one in which both worlds, the ironic and the romantic, come together to form, in realistic terms, the very texture and design of his poetic expression."

The critical method adopted is well suited to the proposed thesis and to the bibliography employed, extending from Aristotle to the most recent thinkers of dramatic theory. Although he is not eclectic in his approach, Professor Garay has avoided a single, exclusive method by wisely joining a structural and semiotic approach, more properly greimasian, to a cultural one; always maintaining a constant eye on Gil Vicente's plays as both point of departure and arrival.

The end result is the work of an incisive essayist sensitive to his subject's fine points while never losing sight of the need to demonstrate a thesis which befits a disciplined and systematic scholar. Besides returning Gil Vicente to the realm of academic discussion, setting forth the facts with scholarly and up-to-date information, the study points to the true role represented by the Portuguese author within the context of Iberian literature, his value as poet, dramatist, and precursor of the Golden Age

Comedy. One should also mention the language, agile and vibrant, with constant persuasiveness and textual support, invariably useful for the purpose sought.

Examining the most recent bibliography of Gil Vicente, and always with a critical eye, Professor Garay questions several ideas concerning the origins of popular theater in the Middle Ages, as well as of the Vicentine comedy. His study stands out, therefore, not only by the new and intense light that he projects on the Portuguese author, but also on medieval theater, especially that of the Iberian Peninsula.

In sum, Professor René Pedro Garay elaborated an essay which inscribes itself definitely in the Vicentine bibliography as one of the most valuable contributions in recent years: from now on, it will be pratically impossible to expand the research of the Portuguese poet and dramatist without pondering over the outline and critical suggestions contained in this book.

Translated by Richard A. Prêto-Rodas
University of South Florida

ACKNOWLEDGEMENTS

Without the kind assistance and encouragement of the following persons and institutions this study would not have been possible: The Fundação Calouste Gulbenkian in Lisbon, Portugal, who funded the original research, António José Saraira, Alexandrino Severino, Maria Correa for her patience and expertise in technical matters, the Simon H. Rifkin Center for the Humanities of The City College of City University of New York, Len R. Coleman who taught me much of life and aesthetics, Pedro Fonsêca who read and discussed with me many sections of the manuscript, Angel Sánchez who helped me with word-processing. My colleagues of the Dept. of Romances Languages of The City College who took the time and lent their experience, René Francisco Garay and Sindo Garay for their inspiration, Daniel Villarejo for his sound advice. Finally, this book owes much to James Richard Andrews of Vanderbilt University, my teacher and friend, who taught me the stuff of literature and whose contribution is incalculable in every single page.

INTRODUCTION

GIL VICENTE'S COMIC RENAISSANCE DRAMA

Gil Vicente, generally considered to be the founder of the Portuguese theater, has never fallen out of favor with drama critics. One of the more recent judgements about the sixteenth century dramatist comes from A. R. Milburn, Fellow of University College and University Lecturer in Spanish and Portuguese (University of Cambridge), who, in evaluating the playwright's aesthetic merit, observes that Gil Vicente was "the greatest [dramatist] in Europe before Shakespeare" (800).

This distinction has been recognized by many other critics; the list is long and the words of praise are even more abundant. Interest in the Portuguese sixteenth century dramatist, as witnessed by continuing publications and research, is just as strong today as it has been in the past. Even modern and contemporary writers (e.g., Lorca, García Márquez, etc.) still find in the Portuguese playwright some of the essential elements of Iberian traditionalism.

Earlier examinations of his work, however, have given little attention to the intrinsic value of Gil Vicente's aesthetic accomplishments. With few exceptions, more emphasis has been placed on centrifugal studies dealing with a whole gamut of character types, the place of the comic in his plays, and other a-dramatic topics which are illuminating and, indeed, important to an understanding of the author's works, but which have generally failed to define the immanent structure of the works that display Gil Vicente's dramatic genius.

As an imitator of, and also one of, the Iberian "primitivos" (i.e., Juan del Encina, Lucas Fernández, etc.) he has suffered from the false historical and critical perspectives of those censuring critics who, not content with examining the body of his dramatic production within the context of his own literary traditions and historical reality, would compare him with other dramatists who succeeded him (e.g., Shakespeare, Molière) and which, of course, were not participants of the same cultural setting that defines the Vicente dramaturgical perspective.

Often relegated to the category of imitator, Gil Vicente has been seen as an adept follower of the theatrical conventions of his contemporaries (e.g., Juan del Encina), not only in the use of the pastoral motifs borrowed from them, but also in adopting the distinctive *sayagués* dialect of the earlier conventional shepherd-types. That Mestre Gil, however, surpassed his fellow Peninsular dramatists in lyrical genius goes undisputed even today. It is in this respect that he first approaches the dramatic form that has been considered the genre *par excellence* of the Spanish Golden Age: the *comedia*. An investigation of this particular type of dramatic genre, as Gil Vicente envisioned and developed it, is the subject of this study.

Margaret Wilson *(The Spanish Drama of the Golden Age)* traces the beginnings of this traditional form of Hispanic theatrical literature. In considering several important aspects of that dramatic tradition, she arrives at the following important conclusion:

> ... various strains had proved their ability to survive, and were awaiting the genius who would blend them into a satisfying whole: the popular devotion of the religious drama and the humour of the *commedia dell'arte*, the *pundonor* of the Italian tragicomedy and the Senecan mode of the later tragedians, the lyricism of Vicente and the national themes of Cueva (19).

The *Comedia*, as the Peninsular mentality envisioned it in the Golden Age of Hispanic literature and as Gil Vicente helped to develop, is the subject of this examination. Perhaps a few words concerning this type of dramatic structure are in order before we begin our investigation. The *comedia*, as Wilson observed above, is a highly synthetic notion of a theatrical performance. Its essence is to disregard the dramatic conventions and theatrical precepts considered important in other areas of developing national theaters. With the exception of the unity of action (the only one that Aristotle actually insisted upon) the other two unities (place and time) were for the most part disregarded, or at least not given the consideration that these classic formulas received elsewhere.

As will be seen in the survey that follows, the highly theocentric notions of late medieval and *early* Renaissance drama, so characteristic of the Christian Humanist stage, may explain the aesthetic reasons for this attachment to conventional (often a-dramatic) rules of dramaturgical development as opposed to the neo-classic unities of later centuries. This is particularly true of the Iberian Peninsula which treasured its medieval past and transformed its new-found world vision (i.e., the Renaissance) within the dimensions of its national experience: historically, culturally, socially, aesthetically, philosophically, theologically.

Refusing to neglect the dramatic concerns of the past, the *comedia* appears before us, in its full realization, as a synthesis of old dramatic conventions and the new social realities of the Renaissance. Like the English popular theater that was to be crystallized in the Shakespearean dramatic forms, it too refused to confine itself to the strict rules of foreign impulse. As Bernard Beckerman notes:

> ... medieval and Elizabethan theater enjoyed a temporal and spatial magnitude unknown in classical Greece. From the thirteenth through the fifteenth centuries, playgoers were exposed to extended cycles of plays, frequently taking two or three days for a complete performance.... Such was the heritage of a sixteenth-century Englishman. To him the plays of the Elizabethan commercial theater, so extensive in comparison to classical drama, were of more limited magnitude than the cycle plays ... (156).

This drama critic admits that in Shakespeare "Monarchy is not merely an abstract idea, but a personified idea about which the populace has strong feelings" (143). Like the *comedia*, then, this type of popular entertainment depended on the audience response to the traditional forms of societal ceremonies: "In effect, the theater artist must eschew the background of the past" (144).

It is against the backdrop of these dramatic traditions that the first part of this study will observe the *comedia:* from its earliest ritualistic manifestations to the conventional and ideological synthesis developed by the Portuguese playwright. Relatively little has been written concerning this influential part of the Vicentine dramatic production (i.e., the *comédia*[1]), and yet, I. S. Révah has rightly considered the plays we will observe "l'essentiel de l'activité de Gil Vicente" (*Comédia* 33).

It is in the development of this specific form of theatrical activity that Gil Vicente shares, with his Spanish contemporary, Torres Naharro, the distinction of having given shape to the most important type of dramatic genre in the history of Hispanic theatrical literature. In his *Comédia de Rubena* (1521) and *Comédia do Viúvo* (1524), the Portuguese dramatist revised the dramatic techniques of the medieval past and helped create a new genre which greatly influenced and oriented subsequent dramatic perspectives in the Hispanic Peninsula. Structurally, these two plays are more significant than the dramatist's earlier production because they approximate, however slowly, the procedures and techniques of modern dramaturgy. Ideologically, they present a complex interplay of ideas, through a richly interwoven texture of symbolic associations that prelude a new age, the age of Christian humanism. It is hoped that the historical considerations of genre and the theoretical methods of its investigation may help not only to define the Vicentine *comédia* against the backdrop of its rich literary past, but also uncover the underlying beauty of these two works.

The second part of this investigation concerning theoretical applications, is a response to the need for an in depth analysis of the two Vicentine *comédias* in question: The *Comédia de Rubena* and the *Comédia do Viúvo*. The methodology used will be one that delves into the structure of the works in such a way as to uncover their semiological system of signification. The method itself is synthetic because it begins with the Aristotelian promise and incorporates those literary theories of analysis which reflect the Aristotelian notions of poetics.

An interpretive approach that focuses its attention on the literary text's immanency is perceived here as best suited for this type of genre investigation because it emancipates the semantic

---

[1] In this study, the word *comedia* will be written with an accent (i.e., *comédia*) when it refers to the Portuguese word in the context of its own aesthetic reality, and without an accent (i.e., *comedia*) when it refers to the Spanish type of comic drama leading to and reflecting the generic distinction of the Golden Age of Spanish theater.

properties of each work and also uncovers the structural principle that they may share. Although the orientation given in this part is theoretical (i.e., dictated by the intrinsic laws that govern the complex system of meaning in each text), some further attention will be given to the notion of genre as it relates to its place in the history of comic forms, and, more specifically, the history of comedy. Because it is more important to define the specific properties of each text, the historical considerations will be limited to those which clarify the generic import of the two texts. It is hoped, however, that the first three chapters of this study will guide the reader in making the necessary associations for that final diachronic emphasis. Both levels of interpretation, however – the synchronic (i.e., immanent) and the diachronic (i.e., historical) – are here considered essential and will receive due consideration.

The formalistic spirit that orients the following interpretive ideas is, then, based on a strictly Aristotelian approach. Aristotle provided the basic formulas of poetic analysis which may here serve as a foundation for further, more modern, speculations on the subject of comic drama. Any type of fictional discourse which purports to be "mimetic" (i.e., action as representation of circumstantial reality) is inspired by the precepts uncovered by the author of the *Poetics*. When considering the purpose of this study (i.e., comedy as a distinctive genre), the words of the Greek critic become all the more important. As Lauter points out:

> Theories of comedy focusing on the ends of the art run... more toward psychology and philosophy than toward literary criticism per se – a fact attested by the number of psychologists (e.g., Lipps, Freud) and philosophers (e.g., Schopenhauer, Bergson, Langer) who have written on the subject from this viewpoint. Another philosopher (Aristotle) provides the model for a more empirical approach to the subject. By examining a number of works of literary art, one may note certain features common to some, excluded from others. One then defines the genre in terms of the "parts," as they came to be called, which invariably occur in specimens of the genre (xx).

Furthermore, the intricate adaptation of the Aristotelian treatise on tragedy to comedy, as made by Lane Cooper in *An Aristotelian Theory of Comedy,* authorizes us to investigate the Vicentine comic formula as an imitation of a comic action that closely follows the

Aristotelian model for tragic action. That is, an organic mimesis which is disclosed through the technical poperties of the dramatic complication ("plot-making"), through the definition of the dramatic agents of the plot or, in more modern terminology, "actants"[2] ("charater delineation"), and finally through the stylistic embellishment which reflects a specific thematic notion ("thought and language").

Modern literary critics have defended and maintained the time-honored precepts of rhetorical investigation found in the *Poetics*. The Canadian "mythographer," Northrop Frye, has contributed much to the notions found in the Aristotelian document. His theory of literary genres, which Robert Scholes has labeled as "generic structuralism," (118) follows closely Aristotle's notions of genre definition and classification. As Frye explains in *Anatomy of Criticism*:

> A theory of criticism whose principles apply to the whole of literature and account for every valid type of critical procedure is what I think Aristotle meant by poetics. Aristotle seems to me to approach poetry as a biologist would approach a system of organisms, picking out its genera and species, formulating the broad laws of literary experience, and in short writing as though he believed that there is a totally intelligible structure of

---

[2] Carlos Reis observes that the concept of "actant" reflects the dynamic interplay of forces which structures the literary construct: "O conceito de actante se subordina ao princípio do desenvolvimento de acções, actores serão todos os elementos diegéticos que dinamizam essas acções (sobretudo personagens mas também animais, sistemas de idéias, valores morais, forças transcendentes, fenômenos atmosféricos, etc., etc.)..." (376). When A. J. Greimas observes that "... an actant is constructed from a bundle of functions..." (218), he means that the discrete units of a narrative (i.e., functions) coalesce into larger units of meaning (i.e., actants) producing a tension, an opposition of forces, that triggers the dialectical movement of literary discourse. Robert Scholes further explains that Greimas: "... postulates a level of thought prior to language, in which these rudimentary oppositions are given anthropomorphic shape, through which purely logical or conceptual oppositions become *actants* in a polemical situation that, when allowed to develop temporally, becomes a story. These actants, if they are given social or cultural qualities, become *rôles* in fictional actions. If they are given individuating qualities, they become *acteurs*, or, as we would say, characters. But in any case, this beginning of narrative in a semantic opposition leads to situations and actions which are characterized by this same opposition. The basic actions are disjunction and conjunction: separation and union, struggle and reconciliation. Narratives consist essentially in the transfer of a value or an object from one actant to another" (103).

knowledge attainable about poetry which is not poetry itself, or the experience of it, but poetics. One would imagine that, after two thousand years of post-Aristotelian literary activity, his views on poetics, like his views on the generation of animals, could be re-examined in the light of fresh evidence. Meanwhile, the opening words of the *Poetics*, in the Bywater translation, remain as good an introduction to the subject as ever, and describe the kind of approach that I have tried to keep in mind for myself (14).

Finally, the Aristotelian ideas as well as Frye's modern renditions and elaborations of those notions will be viewed in the light of more contemporary theories of poetic forms. These methods of literary inquiry seem, rather, to complement the former ideas. The formalists and structuralists have focused on the immanency of the literary text (i.e., formalism) as well as on a broader, more abstract, concept of mythic patterns of human thought (i.e., structuralism). They share, along with the Aristotelian model, the "biologist's" method of analysis; that is, they are meticulous and untiring in their attempt to place literary categories in a broader, more meaningful, human context while investigating the "universal" laws that govern the dynamics of the literary sign-system.

These "system-builders," as Scholes notes, bring to light and consummate, as it were, the Aristotelian vision of critical perspectives. Through their procedures the reader may perceive the inter-relation of various levels of literary discourse, thus facilitating the semantic apprehension of the entire range of the textual sign-system. Formalism and, later, structuralism are not to be confused, yet they both share the Aristotelian desire to be specific in analysis before formulating generic relationships and before telescoping the thematic materials into one organic perspective of literary discourse. When both are considered for analytical purposes, they help uncover the meaning of a text (whatever the semantic philosophy of the reader be) and, when seen in the light of archetypal criticism, they provide useful tools of analysis and comparison. In this respect, Frye has observed that "The structural principles of literature ... are to be derived from archetypal and anagogic criticism, the only kinds that assume a larger context of literature as a whole (134).

These ideas are shared by Scholes, who also understands the formal-structural method to be fundamentally a neo-Aristotelian procedure in modern critical approaches:

> In a sense, formalism has lasted until now mainly because we have been so slow in assimilating it and so feeble in improving it. But in another sense the achievement of the formalists, like that of Aristotle, will be permanent because it will have to be incorporated in any later poetics of fiction. Poetics is, in fact, the discipline par excellence of low structuralism (158).

The critical perspectives outlined briefly above may bring new light to bear on the Vicentine *comédias* that will be analyzed. It is hoped that these Aristotelian and neo-Aristotelian notions of poetics will illuminate the investigation of these dramatic texts and bring new light with which to reconsider the dramatic and poetic skill of Gil Vicente.

CHAPTER I

COMIC THEORY BEFORE THE SIXTEENTH CENTURY

A) EARLY MEDIEVAL OBSERVATIONS

With the downfall of the Roman Empire and the subsequent effect on the intellectual and cultural life of its citizens, Western European civilization moved slowly into a period of historical development known to us now as the Middle Ages. During this time, drama and other theater-related forms of entertainment appear to have entered a dreary void in which they seemed doomed to suffer great losses through the many restrictions and sanctions imposed by the Church.

According to Brockett, a letter written in 533 registers the last stage performance in Rome. He further emphasizes that while theatrical activity most likely continued after that date, it probably did not survive the Lombard invasion (586) after which the state refused to support and to encourage this type of popular divertissement. It must be remembered as well that church opposition was consolidated and strengthened only after Constantine (Emperor 324-337) made Christianity the official religion of the state. In addition to this, church authority had already greatly increased after Theodosius I abolished in 393 all other forms of religious worship in the Empire. The support of the state greatly helped in the church's attack.

Church resistance to theatrical practices was a decisive factor in its almost complete dissolution, for state activity could not endure, without a great loss, the additional pressures from within (e.g., the decay of an organized state and its subsequent lack of compensation for the arts) and from without (e.g., the barbarian invasions of the fifth century). Although many Roman citizens also resisted the licentiousness of theatrical activity, the church had, in addition to moral reasons, other grounds for oppositions; namely, its association, within the Roman governmental organization, with pagan festivals, and also its flagrant abuse and ridicule of Christian rituals – a tradition retained by stage actors and mimes:

> As a result, the break between church and theatre, was inevitable. Tertullian (c. 150-c. 220), the North African theologian, denounced the theatre in his *De Spectaculis,* arguing that Christians forswore the theatre when they were baptized. From about 300 A. D. on, church councils sought to dissuade Christians from attending performances, and in 398 the Council of Carthage decreed excommunication for anyone who went to the theatre rather than to church on holy days. Actors were forbidden the sacraments of the church unless they forswore their profession, a decree not rescinded in many places until the eighteenth century (Brockett 72).[1]

From this period in review to the painstakingly slow emergence and ultimate development of liturgical drama in the tenth century, the stage is silenced. Five centuries of inactivity passed by before the theater again emerged from the antiphonal songs of the church liturgy – its only hope for survival and established support. This theatrical "renaissance," insignificant at first, became nonetheless the seedbed for all subsequent European dramatic activity.

But if organized forms of comic performances failed to captivate the attention of the medieval audience, other forms of comic expression did not cease and, in fact, thrived in the revelry of pagan festivities, in the mimed dance songs (e.g., the dramatic, perhaps mimed, dialogues of the "cantigas de amigo" in Portugal and Spain), and much later in the ecclesiastical amusements

---

[1] Some reasons for church opposition reflect the charges that had already been made against the theater by the conservative sector of Rome. Brockett notes that "Some historians believe that it was as a concession to this group that no permanent theatres were erected prior to 55 B. C." (63). Actors too were considered inferior citizens and many of them were probably slaves: "It seems likely, therefore, that the social status of the actor varied considerably, although the majority always ranked low in public esteem" (68).

initially allowed by the church such as the Feast of Fools and that of the Boy Bishop (Tydeman 16).[2]

The Comic Muse could not, in fact, be silenced although punitive circumstances prevented its unfolding into the type of comic performance envisioned by the Aristotelian precepts and practiced on the Athenian stage. Neither could it develop significantly from the comic recitations of the impoverished mime tradition, whose antics and buffoonery were also denounced by church officials. Even in the Byzantine Empire where the Hellenic past was so carefully guarded, one notices these extreme measures imposed by the church:

> Mimes, acrobats, and ceremonial dancers appeared at banquets given by the emperor on state occasions; revels of various sorts were features of urban festivals; and wandering performers played at rural festivals and wine harvests. Foreign visitors to Byzantium often reported their amazement and delight at the variety and skill of its entertainments, which exceeded anything then known in Western Europe. But though actors may have been plentiful they seem to have been considered disreputable. Churchmen often denounced them, and in 692 the Trullan Synod sought to have all mimes and theatrical performances banned. According to ecclesiastical rules, both professional entertainers and anyone who married them were to be expelled from the church. The state also denied actors many civil rights. Clearly there were exceptions, however, for Justinian took a mime actress, Theodora, as his empress (Brockett 79).

This description of the dramatic practices in the Byzantine world clearly demonstrates the extent of the decaying Greek theatrical ideal.

The everchanging concept of comedy had, by this time, been stripped of its essential component – an organic representation of a

---

[2] Fernando Lázaro Carreter registers the festivities relating to the election of the Boy Bishop in the Hispanic Peninsula: "Sustancialmente consistía en la elección de un muchacho que, durante dos o tres días, ejercía funciones episcopales; lo que variaba en los distintos obispillos descritos en España y fuera de ella, eran los excesos y procacidades a que, con ese motivo, se entregaban clérigos y seglares" (22). Judging from the description given by a nineteenth-century Brazilian author, Manuel Antônio de Almeida, these festivities were equally as popular in Portugal and ultimately in colonial Brazil (59).

single action. It had to be cleansed by the moralism of the church before it could once again appear before its audience as an ethically acceptable form of entertainment. When it eventually re-surfaced, it did so to instruct men in the paths of virtue, or so it seemed. This didactic function of comedy, as expressed by the Roman commentators, appears to have been the only consistent element maintained in comic practice during the Middle Ages. As for comic theory, we must look to the rhetorical tradition of Rome, preserved now in the commentaries of the Latin grammarians, to find any semblance of analytical exposition concerning comedy. It is fortunate, however, that by employing dramatic texts (e.g., Terence) to illustrate oratorical principles these commentators preserved comic theory from the unfailing whip of Christian moralists.[3]

Of the Latin grammarians, Aelius Donatus appears to be the most influential source of comic theory during this period; his importance extends well into the sixteenth century. In his *De Comoedia*,[4] he preserved and elaborated upon comic theory, thus providing a sound basis for all subsequent commentaries. That this treatise on comedy was of primary significance to the development of comic drama, theory and practice, can be deduced from the immense popularity of his observations to later theorists. It was regularly attached to the editions of Terence that were made

---

[3] It is important to bear in mind that the formal pedagogical system was entirely in the hands of the church during the Dark Ages (c. 500-1100). Only churchmen possessed enough knowledge to instruct others, thereby monopolizing the content of education in these early monastic schools. The basic curriculum was, of course, the "seven liberal arts" – the Trivium (grammar, rhetoric and dialectic) and the Quadrivium (geometry, arithmetic, astronomy and music), but in fact, only the Trivium received any significant attention. The Quadrivium was a pseudoscientific branch of learning chiefly concerned with magical and otherwise esoteric definitions of celestial phenomena, etc. There was, as we have noted before, no formal study of poetics as we understand the term today. Grammar and its two sister arts of Rhetoric and Dialectic constituted the basic curriculum of education in the Middle Ages.

[4] We will, for the sake of simplification, refer to the following commentaries on comic theory as belonging to Donatus although modern scholars have attributed the compilations to two distinct authors, both grammarians of the fourth century, namely Donatus and Evanthius. The first section of the treatise, that which lays the historical basis for comedy (e.g., ritual beginnings) and compares it to tragedy, has been attributed more specifically to Evanthius. The second part, in which more details in less coherent exposition are accumulated, belongs to Donatus (Nugent 259-80).

available to (and became extremely popular in) the medieval monastic schools and universities.

Unfortunately, little attention has been given to the treatise due to the more pressing philological attention of establishing a true text. The actual contents of the exposition, however, present a wealth of theoretical principles which should be examined carefully. Marion Herrick summarized the uniqueness of the tract, noting that "Before the middle of the sixteenth century, Horace and Donatus were the principle authorities on dramatic poetry, and the common critical approach at the time was a comparison of the moral purpose and style of comedy and tragedy" (36).

We have already observed the importance of these two motivating forces – "moral purpose and style" – in shaping comic theory within dramatic traditions. It is my hope that a close examination of the commentary will provide a new light that will later clarify some questions related to the comic procedures and practices of the Portuguese comic genius, Gil Vicente.

The first section of the Donatan treatise – the one attributed to Evanthius by most scholars – begins with a historical account of comedy. It states that both comedy and tragedy have their origins in the religious festivals of thanksgiving practiced by the Greeks during the harvest.[5] Later, endeavoring to find the most remote link in the development of comedy, the author names Homer as the originator of comic expression, stating that the *Odyssey* was made in the image of comedy: "Ad imaginem comoediae." In this section, it is important to point out the distinction given to stylistic embellishment in the evolution of comic form. It is the elegant and polished diction, "decora atque levia," that molds comic form after Homer. The commentator notes that "clever" imitators abandoned the Homeric formula for it was rough and crude: "impolita" and "rudimentis." In the typical patristic fashion of the medieval compendium, the author attempts first to define his topic through etymological inquiry: "This name was composed, I think, from the phrase, *apo ton komon kai tes oides,* that is, from 'countryside' and 'sing'."[6]

---

[5] "Initium tragoediae et comoediae a rebus diuinis est incohatum, quibus pro fructibus uota solventes operabantur antiqui" (Nugent 277).

[6] "... ut opinor, a pagis et cantilena composito nomine *apo ton komon kai tes oides,...*" (277).

Having ended this survey of comic and tragic genesis, the Evanthian tract now focuses on comedy itself, and more specifically on the differences that separate Old Comedy from New Comedy. In Old Comedy the plots were not entirely fictional and real names were often used, whereas in the New Comedy the action did not directly reflect the lives of real men. Evanthius concludes that the Old Comedy was more profitable since it detected and corrected through ridicule the morals of its citizens.[7]

In these few remarks of the opening lines we already discover two important issues that will prove influential in future elaborations on this topic: first, the total disregard of the comic manner of presentation (Homer's epic is cited as an example), and second, the importance given to diction or the appropriate comic style. Although the ethical importance is discussed, the tract does not dwell on this issue. In this sense, that is, in presenting a predominantly critical discussion about comedy, the tract far outweighs the irregular and highly subjective opinions summarized in Horace's *Ars Poetica*.

The treatise continues by describing another type of comic form which stems from Old Comedy: satire. Again the commentator begins his discussion on this type of comic literature with an etymological explanation in which he relates the word satire to the riotous attendants of Bacchus – the satyrs:

> And from this then another type of play had its beginning: satire. It was named from satyrs, who are gods that we know are always engaged in joking and impudence. This is the origin of the name, even if some others mistakenly believe it to have another derivation. Now satire was a type of song that, although it entailed harsh and, as it were, crude jibes at the faults of the citizens, yet had no attribution of proper names. But this type of comedy was also harmful to many poets, since they came under suspicion with powerful citizens of having described the activities of those citizens (and made them worse

---

[7] "etenim per priscos non ut nunc ficta penitus argumenta, sed res gestae a ciuibus palam cum eorum saepe qui gesserant nomine decantabantur, idque ipsum suo tempore moribus multum profuit ciuitatis, cum unus quisque caueret culpam, ne spectaculo ceteris exstitisset et domesticio probro,..." (277-278).

COMIC THEORY BEFORE THE SIXTEENTH CENTURY   15

than they were) and having spoiled the genre by this kind of composition.[8]

As a result of the rage of these powerful citizens being held in ridicule, the poets now turn to New Comedy. This type of "new song" ("aliud genus carminis") is highly praised by the commentator who sees in the adoption of this comic pattern a more acceptable form of presentation than the satiric model:

> The poets, compelled by that difficulty which we discussed above to give up satire, discovered a new type of song, which is New Comedy. New Comedy, with its more universal story line, concerns in general all men who have moderate means. It produces entertainment, through its coherent plots, realistic characterization, useful sayings, clever witticisms, and harmonious meter.[9]

Once again we come across a concern with the rhetorical merit of comic drama and its ethical commitment – "utilis sententiis." In addition to this, however, the treatise introduces other topics of a structural nature – the plot arrangement and the realistic depiction of the comic characters who enter into scene.

In his elaboration of the final section, the commentator takes great care in defining the structure of New Comedy. He expresses his dislike of the Greek prologue where the gods relate the arrangement of incidents to the audience, preferring instead the Terentian formula.

As for the parts of comedy, the commentator states that:

---

[8] "et hinc deinde aliud genus fabulae id est satyra sumpsit exordium, que a satyris, quos in iocis semper ac petulantiis deos scimus esse, uocitata est, etsi (alii) aliunde nomen praue putant habere. haec satyra igitur eiusmodi fuit, ut in ea quamuis duro et uelut agresti ioco quod idem genus comoediae multis offuit poetis, cum in suspicionem potentibus ciuim uenissent, illorum facta descripsisse in peius ac deformasse genus stilo carminis" (278).

[9] "hoc igitur quod supra diximus malo coacti omittere satyram aliud genus carminis..., hoc est nouam comoediam, repperere poetae, quae argumento communi magis et generaliter ad omnes homines, qui mediocribus fortunis agunt, pertineret et minus amaritudinis spectatoribus et eadem opera multum delectationis afferet, concinna argumento, consuetudini congrua, utilis sententiis, grata salibus, apta metro" (278).

> Comedy is divided into four parts: the prologue, protasis, epitasis, and catastrophe. The prologue serves as a kind of preface to the play; it is the only part in which it is permissible to tell the audience something which is external to the plot, either for the sake of the poet or of the play itself or the actor. The protasis is the first act and the beginning of the play. The epitasis provides the growth and development of the complications and is, one might say, the knot of the whole problem. The catastrophe is the turning of events to a happy outcome through the discovery of the facts being revealed to all.[10]

We can readily see the importance of this treatise by the few remarks we have just summarized. The commentator has a keen eye for analytical observations, and knows the value of comparing and contrasting elements from both comic and tragic patterns of dramatic literature. Certainly he anticipates the value of verisimilitude in character portrayal when he observes that Terence, unlike those who preceded him, delineated his roles with great care and subtlety:

> And yet he [Terence] alone dared, even against the traditions of comedy, since he sought the ring of truth in his fictional plots, to introduce from time to time prostitutes who were not wicked. In these cases, however, there was both a reason why they might be good and a pleasure in the thing itself.[11]

Perhaps the most illuminating part of this section, certainly the one which proved to be most influentail in shaping the matter of comic focus, is the discussion on the differences between tragedy and comedy:

---

[10] "comoediae per quattuor partes diuiditur: prologum, protasin, epitasin, catastrophen. est prologus uelut praefatio quaedam fabulae, in quo solo licet praeter argumentum aliquid ad populum uel ex poetae uel ex ipsius fabulae uel actoris commodo loqui; protasis primus actus initiumque est dramatis; epitasis incrementum processusque turbarum ac totius, ut ita dixerim, nodus erroris; catastrophe conuersio rerum ad iucundos exitus patefacta cunctis cognitione gestorum" (278).

[11] "quin etiam solus ausus est, cum in fictis argumentis fidem ueritatis assequeretur, etiam contra praescripta comica meretrices interdum non malas introducere, quibus tamen et causa, cur bonae sint, et uoluptas per impsum non defit" (278).

> Although there are many differences between tragedy and comedy, these are the chief distinguishing features: in comedy the fortunes of men are ordinary, the onslaughts of difficulties minor, the outcomes of actions happy. But in tragedy everything is the opposite: the characters are outstanding, the fears great, the outcomes disastrous. Then again, in comedy the beginning is stormy, the end calm, but in tragedy the opposite holds true. In tragedy a life is portrayed which one must flee, in comedy a life which one ought to seek. Finally, all comedy deals with fictional plots, whereas tragedy is often sought in historical reality.[12]

Particularly interesting here is the part where comedy is defined by its beginning and ending. Gil Vicente, much later, will share the same views when he states categorically that all comedies must begin in sorrow.

By comparison to the first section of the Donatan tract, the second treatment of the subject, that is, the one ascribed to Donatus himself, lacks the coherent pattern of analysis observed in the first document. In an almost naive fashion, Donatus throws together an assortment of information which betrays a highly subjective interest in comic trivia. The miscellaneous catalog includes mention of a prize goat, "For a goat was given to these [writers of comedy] as a gift, because the animal was considered a nuisance to the vines,"[13] a preoccupation with the source of comic titles to which the commentator dedicates two sections, the hidden meanings of the "pilleus" [a felt cape], the costuming conventions of the Greek stage (including the colors traditionally worn by slaves, pimps and prostitutes and the use of masks), stage curtains, and a final section, disproportionately lengthy, on music; complete with instruments and even a recognition of the virtuoso himself:

---

[12] "inter tragoediam autem et comoediam cum multa tum imprimis hoc distat, quod in comoedia mediocres fortunae hominum, parui impetus periculorum laetique sunt exitus actionum, at in tragoedia omnia contra, ingentes personae, magni eimores, exitus funesti habentur; et illic prima turbulenta, tranquilla ultimam, in tragoedia contrario ordine res aguntur; tum quod in tragoedia fugienda uita, in comoedia capesenda extratragoedia saepe de histori fide petitur" (278).

[13] "...caper namque pro dono his dabatur, quia animal uitibus noxium habebatur" (278).

"The name of the person who arranged the music was put in the beginning of the play after those of the author and actor."[14]

Although the Donatan observations seem trite and a bit humorous at times when compared to the more coherent and, indeed, critical discussion of the Evanthian section, it is important to realize that Donatus' fascination with theatrical miscellanies reaveals an acute awareness of dramatic *representation*. That is, he recognizes the importance of stage activity in relation to comic expression. This may seem of slight significance to the modern theater-goer, who is confronted with a well-defined tradition of stage activity, but at this early age, any manifestations of interest in the representative elements of dramatic comedy must not be overlooked. One cannot help but see a relation between this concern and the subsequent theories and stage practices of medieval theorists and dramatists. In this respect, it is necessary to recall again the inorganic nature of comic expression in the Middle Ages, where the "dramatist" was ostensibly concerned only with the "happy" outcome of the story as prescribed; the manner of presentation was of little consequence to the definition given to comedy.

Whereas it is highly unlikely that the few medieval readers of Latin plays considered them solely as worthy examples of oratorical virtuosity, the fact remains that these scholars were apparently not inspired to see these plays represented on the stage. According to their system of values, this was not the most salient characteristic of comedy.[15] This seems to have had a continued impact even

---

[14] "eius qui modos faciebat nomen in principio fabulae post scriptoris et actoris superponebatur" (280).

[15] We have already observed this very important aspect of medieval dramaturgy. "Comoedia" was not a term necessarily associated with stage activity and was used instead to denote a poem with a fortunate outcome (e.g., Dante's *Divine Comedy*). In addition to this, more and more scholars are now affirming the narrative framework of medieval and humanist drama. Live acted drama and its structuring of incidents in such a way so as to produce a resolution of conflictive forces were not the end or purpose of theatrical activity at this time. Instead, as Tydeman emphasizes, the important focus was on narration and recitation in play performances. This modern scholar of medieval drama cites an excerpt from a commentary of Nicholas Trevet (c. 1258-c. 1328), in which the chronicler reiterates a common misconception about drama initially attributed to Isidore of Seville (c. 560-636): "The theatrum was a semicircular open space, in the middle of which there was a small house called the scena in which there was a platform on which the poet stood to recite his works. Outside the house were the mimi

as late as the sixteenth century. Bernard Beckerman has ventured a theory concerning the "irregular" and "haphazard" structure of Elizabethan drama that appears to be directly influenced by the medieval narrative tradition. This drama critic has observed that Elizabethan dramatists used popular romance and history as sources for their plays. In doing so, the dramatist was often faithful to his story at the risk of loosening the dramatic tension of the plot:

> On one hand there existed the impulse to complete the story, on the other there persisted the temptation to dilate upon the effect of the action upon the individuals. One reason why modern audiences suffer from "fourth act fatigue" in witnessing a Shakespeare play stems from the fact their interest in the play is disproportionate. They have a greater interest in the narrative line than in the dramatic (*Shakespeare* 35).

This notion of dramatic comedy might explain the "a-dramatic" intent of the later humanist playwrights. This appears to be the case with Gil Vicente who, as we shall see, is more interested in delivering an ethical message through poetic dialogue than in the "correct" dramatic depiction of the conflictive dilemma.[16]

Returning now to our immediate concern with the Donatan treatise, its value can be summarized by stating that other than the importance given to the representation of comic works, Donatus has little to say that does not overlap with Evanthius' more coherent vision. The strictly rhetorical value of comedy is not given any significance other than that inferred through the association he makes between comedy and the well-known Ciceronian state-

---

who performed bodily movements while pieces were being recited by adapting themselves to whatever character the poet was speaking of" (48).

[16] António José Saraiva, one of the foremost critics of Gil Vicente, sees in the Portuguese playwright a tendency which, although not in keeping with the classic dramatic formulas (e.g., the three unities), was nonetheless indicative of more modern theories of drama. Saraiva compares Brecht's *The Caucasian Chalk Circle* to plays of Gil Vicente who also staged the moral dilemma of a changing social setting: "Não é, como se vê, uma peça realista, tendo por objecto a imitação da realidade. Não é, também, uma peça de acção única, limitada no tempo e no espaço. É, repito, uma narrativa ilustrada no palco.... Entre um autor da Idade Média no extremo ocidental da Europa e uma autor contemporâneo no centro do Continente, descobrimos laços inesperados, um encontro surpreendente. Ambos cultivam um mesmo gênero: a narrativa posta em cena" (*Gil* 469, 475).

ment about the comic purpose. In this respect, he emphasizes Cicero's didactic definition so often quoted – "comoediam esse Cicero aut imitationem vitae, speculum consuetudinis, imaginem veritatis." Once again the social ideal far outweighs the structural categories of dramatic discourse.

Later, forgetting that Cicero had made this remark, Donatus explains that Livius Adronicus ("the first playwright") ". . . said, justifiably that comedy is a mirror of daily life. For, just as we easily grasp the outline of reality by means of the image when a mirror is held up to us, so through the reading of comedy we perceive the image of life and of daily habit without difficulty."[17]

Unlike Evanthius, however, Donatus appears more concerned with the ethical possibilities of comedy. From the very beginning his definition of comedy advocates the ethical relevancy of comic drama: "Comedy is a play that presents various manners of life of private citizens, from which one may learn what is useful in life and what, on the other hand, is to be avoided."[18]

This ethical stance is emphasized when Donatus relates the moral propriety of comedy with its etymology. This he does by stating that when the Athenians wanted to single out ". . . for reproach those who were living improperly, . . . they would congregate in the countryside and there, . . . high-spirited and zealous, they publicly proclaimed the faults of individuals – with their names. From this custom the name was created, so that it was called comedy."[19]

Donatus, like Evanthius, divided comedy into four parts: the prologue (to which he gives considerable attention), protasis, epitasis, and catastrophe. After stating the etymological source of the word prologue, he elaborates upon the four different kinds; namely, the introductory, the critical, the narrative and the mixed.

---

[17] "aitque [sic] esse comoediam cotidianae uitae speculum, nec iniuria. nam ut intenti speculo ueritatis liniamenta facile per imaginem colligimus, ita lectione comoediae imitationem uitae consuetudinisque non aegerrime animaduertimus" (278).

[18] "Comoedia est fabula diuersa instituta continens affectuum ciuilium ac priuatorum, quibus discitur, quid sit in uita utile, quid contra euitandum" (278).

[19] "huius autem originis ratio ab exteris ciuitatibus morisbusque prouvenit. Athenienses namque Atticam custodientes elegantiam cum uellent male uiuentes notare, in uicos et compita ex omnibus locis laeti alacresque ueniebant ibique cum nominibus singulorum uitia publicabant, unde nomen compositum, ut comoedia uocaretur" (279).

The introductory prologue recognizes the poet or recommends the play to the audience. The critical prologue addressess the audience or curses a rival playwright. The narrative prologue explains the plot. Finally, the mixed prologue combines all of these.[20]

These preceding remarks about the Donatan treatise may serve to introduce the basic notions about dramatic comedy that were prevalent in the early Middle Ages. We have observed that in spite of the impoverished state of theatrical practices, histrionic activity did survive. The importance of these fourth century statements become truly significant if one considers the remarkably theatrical basis of the document. It is no coincidence that it proved to be so influential in the history of Western European dramatic comedy.

No other Terentian commentator elaborated such a complete and conclusive theory of comedy. The only other noteworthy authority on this subject was Servius (c. 370), who reiterated the ideas mentioned above. In keeping with these principles, he too re-emphasized the stylistic importance that underlies a definition of comic and tragic actions. To Servius, comedy was a type of poem that dealt with a commonplace event; written in a humble style. He does not fail to mention, however, that with time the "humble" style gave way to a more artful rendition: ". . . and what was ordinary, gradually by means of certain merry conceits of speech and an artful kind of style, yet retaining its common and humble matter, they have developed [redigere] into an art, wherefore it has retained still its ancient name till this day" (Baldwin 66).

Like all the grammarians mentioned above, he too proposed that comedy both delight and instruct its audience, the *utile et dulce* principle proposed by Horace. We will have occasion to see that when the Terentian commentators of the fifteenth and early sixteenth centuries expound their theories about comic drama, they will retain this moral canon exacted by the grammarians of the fourth century. In fact, the zealous Renaissance commentators, when holding up the Ciceronian mirror of life, will only see the clouded reflections of a highly conventionalized and truly subjec-

---

[20] "Comoedia autem diuiditur in quattuor partes: prologum, [. . .] Prologus est prima dictio, a Graecis dicta uel antecedens ueram fabulae compositionem elocutio, [. . .] eius species sunt quattuor: . . . commendatiuus, quo poeta uel fabula comendatur; . . . relatiuus, quo aut aduersario maledictum aut populo gratiae referentur; . . . argumentatiuus, exponens fabulae argumentum; . . . mixtus, omnia haec in se continens" (279).

tive code of ethical standards. Just as many of the Aristotelian principles were codified during the eighteenth century (the three unities), so too was the Ciceronian notion of "truth" cast in the image of their own times.

B) LATE MEDIEVAL OBSERVATIONS

By the tenth century, theatrical elements were again developing from religious sources; especially in the annual church celebrations of Biblical events. This type of "theater" is known as liturgical drama because it evolved from a process called troping; that is, by inserting words into the choral sections of antiphonal songs written for specific religious ceremonies of the church liturgy. This practice was apparently perfected at the monastery of St. Gall (Switzerland) and later given definite dramatic form in the *Regularis Concordia* compiled in the second half of the tenth century by Ethelwold, Bishop of Winchester. According to Brockett the oldest extent Easter trope dates from about 925 and reads as follows:

> ANGELS: whom seek ye in the tomb, o christians?
> THE THREE MARYS: Jesus of Nazareth, the crucified, o Heavenly Beings.
> ANGELS: He is not here, he is risen as he foretold. Go and announce that he is risen from the tomb (91).

At about the same time, a nun at Gandesheim, Hroswitha (c. 935-1001), was writing and perhaps performing her own plays modeled after those of Terence. Although scholars differ as to the significance of Hroswitha's work in the course of medieval drama, her position in the development of comic activity is unique and must be acknowledged. Hroswitha's work is the only known group of plays which links the classical world of drama to medieval dramatic practices. In *Dulcitius*, for example, she brings together all of these influences: the comic elements modeled after Terence, the farcical antics of the buffoon, and the theological focus; all are here to form a most entertaining and highly theatrical composition. This is, as far as I can discover, the first secular or strictly non-liturgical instance of comic expression cast in representational form after the classical period. One has to wait until the comic episodes of liturgical drama are completely severed from their religious sources before again observing any significant signs of the development of comic drama.

To be sure, secular theatrical activities persisted; especially those involving the seasonal festivities of a whole community, but the idea of dramatic representation could not take root without the support of influential citizens and the church. And so we must again turn to the liturgy for any real evidence of theatricality. Although the entire Christian ritual can be seen as a "sacred drama," it is very unlikely that comic form would develop directly from the serious matter of the Christmas and Easter tropes only. Severe restrictions and moralistic adherence to decorum prevented any genuine expansion of these tropes into anything resembling a coherent comic episode.

The unfolding of comic drama, however, appears to stem in part from the insignificant scenes of Biblical and non-Biblical (e.g., Apocryphal) events which depicted the strictly secular aspect of man on earth. These episodes written in the vernacular and deliberately comic in nature were not forbidden, at first, by churchmen. It is very possible that they provided just the right amount of comic relief to sustain the attention of an otherwise unruly and disinterested crowd of believers. In time, these portions of the action would gain significance as autonomous playlets which were often banished from the inner sanctity of the church interior.

With the rise of universities and the establishment of the guild system and other organizations capable of sustaining theatrical interest outside the church, later developments continued this secular tendency of the Middle Ages. By the fourteenth century the church's role in society had come to be somewhat disputed by other temporal institutions, a tendency that will culminate in the secular views of the Renaissance. But in spite of this very gradual secularization we have observed in the transference of theatrical activity form the interior of the church to areas located beyond the limits of its domain, the nature of these plays remained highly religious in inspiration, even in spite of the flourishing secular elements that in later years give way to the farce and other modes of comic expression assimilated into the formation of comedy as we know it today.

The long and elaborated plays of this period depicted the whole history of man as related to God – from the creation to the last judgement. This fact alone may account for their a-dramatic quality, for how could a playwright give any unity to such an extensive saga? "Dramatic unity," therefore, is rarely present in these representations, and it is doubtful that adherence to this aesthetic principle of theatrical elaboration was of any consequence to the writer or to his audience.

This observation cannot be emphasized enough, for it determines a peculiarity of medieval theater that will have serious effects on later observations about comic drama. If unity was not a product of the dialectical tensions produced in the dramatic compositions themselves, then it must follow that the medieval playwright and his audience embraced another concept of unity in theatrical entertainment; another manner of consolidating all of the material represented on stage so as to appear as one whole and complete action to them. One must, therefore, discard the modern (not necessarily contemporary) concept of dramatic unity if one is to find any semblance of homogeneity in these plays. Instead, one must look elsewhere, to the governing (dramaturgical) principles that extend beyond the limits of the representation itself. In short, onw must look at the thematic unity of these medieval performances, for it becomes quite clear that thematic "unity" (as opposed to the classical notions of organic unity, the unity of a single action) was the orienting principle at the time in question.

Furthermore, the narrative demands imposed by the playwright's source (e.g., the Bible, the novels of chivalry, etc.) far outweighed his desire to stylize in any personal way the original text. Given the general respect for authoritative sources by medieval writers, it is not surprising that the playwright's concern lay more in emphasizing the correct sequence of events so as not to falsify the historical validity of the source. This may account for the very loose and episodic nature of medieval drama. Once again, these plays did not observe the same plot conventions we take for granted in modern theatrical practice. It is important to know these conventions in order to better understand and appreciate the structure of these compositions.

Although these performances revolved around the church calendar (e.g., Nativity, Easter, Corpus Christi, etc.) and were, as stated earlier, religious in nature, many comic scenes did in fact develop as a means of providing comic relief from the very serious matter at hand:

> In spite of their essentially, religious purpose, many plays contain extended comic scenes usually involving devils, villains, or buffoons. Most of the comic episodes depended upon the juxtaposition of reality with the ideal, of human failings with divine commandmants, of the fashionable with the eternal, and thus remain relevant to the play's didactic purpose. But, though always in part didactic, the plays were also highly effective theatrical entertainments (Brockett 103-4).

This double aspect that Brockett emphasizes is typical of the struggle that later persisted, on a more artistic level, in the late medieval morality plays where, for the first time, a conflictive framework was developed resembling the dynamic exchange of modern dramaturgy. Instead of juxtaposing contrasting forces (e.g., the secular and the spiritual in this case), the morality play allegorized these forces and staged the ensuing struggle within a humanized context, psychologically more intricate than the preceding models of theatrical realization. Still later, when the conflictive situation is totally secularized, allegory gives way to a more realistic depiction of man's dilemma on earth, to a depiction of the struggle with others as well as with himself.

The morality play, then, was the last manifestation of medieval religious drama. In its basic plot arrangement – the dialectical opposition of two contrastive elements – one can see the rudimentary genesis of modern dramatic compositions. When it adapted its basic dramaturgical formula to the changing social realities (i.e., the "mirror of life") of the Renaissance, this type of performance nourished a new concept of drama: "The morality play thus became the chief dramatic link between the medieval stage and the Shakespearean" (Bevington 795).

Although the morality plays remained close to the vernacular religious cycle, they often included comic interludes and a great deal of spectacle with song and dance. In general, however, one must look elsewhere to find the development of other forms of comic expression. The comic interludes that, more and more, invaded the realm of liturgical drama soon became autonomous playlets in their own right. Those that developed a more independent structure based on the antics and buffoonery of the comic situation, became known as farces.

While the religious plays focused on man as he related to God, the farce (totally secular), emphasized instead man's most naturalistic aspect. In these short pieces, humour is achieved at the expense of very low comic principles which in a simple expository fashion, mirrors the worst vices in man (e.g., adultery, cheating, hypocrisy, excessive pride, etc.). Given the limitations of this popular form of comic expression, (e.g., irregular plot structure, inadequate characterization, common usage of foul language and obscene gesticulations, etc.), we can readily see why it was destined in the history of comedic forms to remain dwarfed by other, more reputable and transcendent forms of dramatic compositions.

As to other forms of secular theatrical activity, (e.g., interludes, tournaments, mummings, disguisings, royal entries, and other types of courtly entertainment) it is safe to assume that their influence on the structure of comedy was minimal due to the a-dramatic spirit that gave rise to these activities. Mainly spectacle, with an occasional lyrical dialogue, these court revelries never achieved the literary status that comic drama later enjoyed.

Although the more elaborate court entertainments held the attention of a minority (i.e., the reduced court audience), it was an adherence by the common man to the histrionic church rituals and their comic possibilities that contained the germ of medieval drama. It is safe to assume that the Middle Ages, as a period of dramatic fomentation in Western Europe, was regulated by a Christian world view which was founded on the belief that man, through the redemption of Christ, could attain salvation and eternal bliss. All of man's efforts and talents, from the heart-felt rendition of a saint's confession to the construction of a Gothic cathedral, were guided by this motivating principle. To those who adhered to this pattern of Christian ethics, life itself was a drama, a "sacred drama" with felicitous results. This is crucial to the definition of comedy which the medieval mind discerned from the past.

We note this interpretation of the comic Christian vision in the twelfth century commentary of John of Salisbury who, in a bitter moment, anticipating the secular notions of the Renaissance, warns that "The life of man appears to be a tragedy rather than a comedy in that the end is almost invariably sad." He goes on to say that "It is surprising how nearly coextensive with the world is the stage on which this endless, marvelous, incomparable tragedy, or if you will comedy, can be played; its area is in fact that of the whole world" (qtd. in Robertson 208).

In this respect Dante (1265-1321), whose *Divine Comedy* became the measure of comic excellence in later theories of comic development, explains in the prefatory remarks to his *Commedia* that the ultimate purpose of his divinely inspired poem ". . . is to remove those living in this life from a state of misery, and to bring them to a state of happiness" (qtd. in Robertson 274).

From these remarks we must conclude that unlike the modern attitude, the medieval poet was interested more in the mystical truth of his discourse than in the aesthetic principles that shaped its form. That is to say, that the thematic material shaped his aesthetic vision of dramatic activity. It is within this conceptual framework that we must examine the medieval versions of comedy, lest we mistake their moralistic point of reference for an uncritical stance.

The reasons given above may serve as an introduction to the absence of any significant corpus of analytical material on the subject of comedy during the Middle Ages. Horace's *Ars Poetica* and the Donatan treatise remained the most important documents about comedy during this period. We shall see that the other incidental remarks on this topic were concerned with the thematic approach to comic expression; that is, comedy as a reflection of man's moral dilemma as he advances, in a fashion reminiscent of the moralty play structure, toward a desired end.

The first evidence of any coherent statement about the subject of comedy comes from the Byzantine poet and grammarian of the twelfth century, John Tzetzes (c. 1110-1180), who collected in his very short interpretation some of the stock ideas about comedy. Tzetzes' statement reflects the interest in classical drama that never completely ceased in the Eastern Empire. These Byzantine scholars not only preserved the classical manuscripts from destruction, but also maintained an interest in the Greek plays, eventually introducing them into the Western World:

> Regardless of what one concludes about Byzantine performance, Constantinople is important in theatre history for

another reason: its perservation of classical Greek manuscripts. Byzantine scholars were interested in classical drama especially during the final centuries of the empire, and when Constantinople fell in 1453, many fled to the west taking with them the manuscripts on which our texts of the Greek plays are based. Without the efforts of these scholars, many Greek plays would have been lost forever (Brockett 80).

Some of these ideas handed down from classical antiquity bridge the earlier views about comedy (i.e., as a didactic medium of expression) to later opinions. They continue a pattern of critical discussions about comedy that will reinforce the earlier notions as well as influence later commentators.

The merits of the Tzetzian document are, however, incidental, for he does little more than collect stray ideas handed down from antiquity. In his *First Proem to Aristophanes* he betrays an interest in various Aristotelian sources, especially the *Coislinian Tractate* from which the author copies, almost verbatim, the causes in drama that lead to comic laughter. As Lane Cooper notes: "The inconsistency of Tzetzes need not detain us; he put together his scraps of information in his own uncritical way" (86). Other than these observations about the causes of laughter and the development of comedy, Tzetzes gives a definition that reinforces the ethical approach of these times and the approach that will be adapted by the poets of the Iberian Peninsula. The Platonic notion that the ludicrous originates in (self) ignorance[21] and must, therefore, be corrected through the purgative effects of laughter is retained here. But whereas Plato uncovered the problem and Horace made it a precept for the comic poets in general, Tzetzes, in the typical fashion of the early Middle Ages, adapts it to the

---

[21] The following conversation between Protarchus and Socrates complements the Platonic ideas concerning the source of comicity which influenced later commentators:

> Socrates: Generally the ridiculous is a certain kind of badness; it gets its name from a certain state of mind. It is that part of badness in general which is the opposite to the state of which the inscription at Delphi speaks.
> Protarchus: You mean "know thyself," Socrates?
> Socrates: I do. And the opposite of that, in the inscription's language, would plainly be "Do *not* know thyself" (Lauter 6).

castigating spirit of the age: ". . . and to the pleasure of comedy he [Cratinus] added profit, attacking evil-doers, and chastising them with comedy as with a public whip" (Lauter 34).

Tzetzes does not appear too concerned with the actual dynamics of drama (e.g., stage performance) other than what might be inferred from his definition that "Comedy is an imitation of an action." This comment, however, can readily be applied to non-dramatic literary genres as well. Nowhere does Tzetzes mention the ever-important aspect of representation in his document. This aspect of comedy – dramatic representation or, as the Spanish (Renaissance) playwright Torres Naharro defined it, "por personas disputado" – had been ignored for many years and now continued to be an accidental element of the comic mode of expression. At this time the intrinsic difference between a tragedy and a comedy concerned the nature of the story told:

> Tragedy differs from comedy in that tragedy has a story, and a report of things that are past, although it represents them as taking place in the present, but comedy embraces fictions of the affairs of everyday life (Lauter 33).

How these "affairs of everday life" were presented to an audience (readings, recitations, representation) was not the important issue. It became more pressing to define the story in terms of its verisimilitude (i.e., a copy of circumstantial reality), so that it might serve as a positive model of instruction. This may explain Radulfus de Longo Campo's statement where he notes that:

> Although fable and argument [i.e., comedy] are fictitious, they are directed toward the contempt of vice and the appetite for virtue. Thus poetry expels vices and inspires virtue, sometimes through history, sometimes through fable, and sometime through argument (qtd. in Robertson 287).[22]

---

[22] In this discussion of tragedy and comedy, Nicholas Trivet, a fourteenth-century English Dominican, complicates the issue of comic presentation: "They [comedies] were written by the poets in three ways. They might be narratives in which the poet alone speaks, as in Vergil's *Georgics;* or they might be in dramatic form so that the poet never speaks, but only the persons introduced. This method is proper to both tragedies and comedies. The third method is a mixture of the first two, where both the poet and the persons introduced speak, as in the *Aeneid*

Dante's *Divine Comedy* reiterates this purpose of comic expression when he relegates this "poetical narration" to the realm of moral philosophy. This, along with the motivating principle of his poem betrays an interest in the ethical approach to poetic elaboration.

In the Middle Ages the distinctions between dramatic and other forms of poetic discourse were blurred by the more important moral concern of the story being communicated. Fiction, when divorced from the realistic depiction of virtuous conduct, had to be justified in terms of its relevance to reality and this was often done through allegorical exegesis. Dante expresses this as follows: "Inasmuch, then, as the being of such things depends upon something else it follows that the truth of these things likewise depends upon something else..." (qtd. in Robertson 272).

It was Dante, in fact, who consolidated all the previous notions concerning comedy into one coherent statement with far reaching consequences. In his explanatory letter to the Can Grande della Scala, he stated one of the most salient precepts of comedy, one that even Aristotle suggested when he observed in the *Poetics* that in comedy former enemies walk off as friends: "... and no one slays or is slain" (Aristotle 77).

This concept, which was never abandoned by any of the commentators discussed above, became the very soul of comedy for it reflected the basic conceptual framework of the Middle Ages. In this respect, comedy ran parallel to and reflected the history of man, from the initial fall from grace to the final victory of virtue over the forces of evil. This, I believe, explains the title with which Dante's "sacred poem" became known to posterity: *Divina Commedia*. It was not a concern with genre distinctions, therefore, that gave this poem the title "commedia," for, as Ernst Robert Curtius explains, "The antique system of poetic genres had, in the millenium before Dante, desintegrated until it was unrecognizable and incomprehensible" (358).

---

of Vergil" (Robertson 287). The commentator recognizes here the dramatic manner of presentation but apparently does not consider it an essential element of dramatic comedy. By the time Dante develops his definition of comedy, the manner of presentation becomes a rhetorical issue: "The form or manner [note the use of these two terms as synonyms] of treatment is poetic, fictive, descriptive, degressive and figurative; and further, it is definitive, analytical, probative, refutative, and exemplificative" (Robertson 273).

Dante himself assigned the *Commedia* to the branch of philosophy dealing with morals or ethics for it was written ". . . not for speculation, but with a practical object." That "object," as he states in another passage of the *Accessus*, is ". . . to remove those living in this life from a state of misery, and bring them to a state of happiness" (Robertson 274).

Hence it becomes more understandable to us why Dante chose the happy ending as the prime element of his comic vision:

> For if we consider the subject matter, at the beginning it is horrible and foul, as being Hell; but at the close it is happy, desirable, and pleasing, as being Paradise (Robertson 274).

When this formula is applied to comic drama in particular, the other structural elements of the genre as we know it today become of secondary importance. Unity, therefore, becomes primarily a thematic concept; for Dante, this thematic interpretation is a reflection of the Christian comic view: the harmonious resolution of a discordant world. The structure of imaginative discourse for Dante, as well as for other comic poets of the Middle Ages, was a peripheral idea concerning layout or general format, a mechanical division of the parts from the whole that often betrays an interest in the symbolism of numerology:

> The form of the treatise is threefold, according to the threefold division. The first division is that whereby the whole work is divided into three *cantiche;* the second, whereby each *cantica* is divided into *cantos;* and the third, whereby each *canto* is divided into rhymed lines (qtd in Robertson 273).

It is interesting to note that very often, even the "structure" or, better, the external division of the text reflected the Christian world view which we have observed as the motivating principle of medieval literature. It was not by coincidence that Dante chose the threefold division. Frederick Mayer notes that:

> This mysticism [The Pythagorean worship of numbers] had a lasting impact upon the ancient world and it continued throughout the Middle Ages to modern times. The number three, for example, was regarded as divine by scholastic writers

and even by Dante, who divided the *Divine Comedy* into three parts: hell, purgatory, and paradise" (28).

Dante's comic narrative ("poetice narrationes"), like most medieval forms of discourse, emphasized the felicitous outcome of an initially unfortunate chain of events. Unity, then, depended on the moral outcome of the story being told and the surface "delights" (e.g., stylistic embellishment, etc.) should not overshadow this ultimate truth of the text. These are basic principles of medieval aesthetics inherited from the Augustinian tradition. In Spain, Gonzalo de Berceo refers to this tradition in his *Milagros de Nuestra Señora* when he invites his readers to look at the allegorical amenities of his garden of delights:

> Sennores e amigos, lo que dicho avemos,
> Palabra es oscura, esponerla queremos:
> Tolgamos la corteza, al meollo entremos,
> Prendamos lo de dentro, lo de fuera dessemos (Berceo 11).

The other important governing principle of comic action that Dante uncovers is the style. It was important to Dante's concept of comedy that the poet choose the appropriate rhetoric for comic expression. The Florentine poet continues here the rhetorical traditions of earlier theories on comedy – from Plato's inference about comedy, to the elaboration of these ideas in the treatises of the Latin grammarians. There is little doubt that Vergil's stylistic categories – Mediocrus Stylus, Humilis Stylus, Gravis Stylus –were influential; especially if one considers the importance of Vergil in Dante's narrative: "O de li altri poeti onore e lume, vagliami 'lungo studio e 'l grande amore che, m'ha fatto cercar lo tuo volume. Tu se'lo mio maestro e 'l mio autore, tu se' solo colui da cu'io tolsi lo bello stilo che m'ha fatto onore" (qtd. in Singleton 8-9).

These stylistic divisions become very important in later theories of comic form. It was Horace who, continuing an earlier tradition, emphasized this principle of comic drama in his *Ars Poetica:*

> A comic subject is not susceptible of treatment in a tragic style, and similarly the banquet of Thyestes cannot be fitly described in the strains of everyday life or in those that approach the tone

of comedy. Let each of these styles be kept for the role properly alloted to it (Dorsch 82).

Dante, in an apparent attempt to justify the sometimes overly polished eloquence of his *Commedia*, mentions that although the style of comedy should be humble and commonplace, it sometimes uses the elevated language of tragic expression. In this respect, he quotes, in his prefatory letter, the rest of the Horatian definition: "Yet even comedy at times uses elevated language, and an angry Chremes rails in bombastic terms while in tragedy Telephus and Peleus often express their grief in prosaic language..." (Dorsch 82). In general, however, the style of comedy in Dante's preferred use of the term is "... unstudied and lowly, as being in the vulgar tongue, in which even women-folk hold their talk" (qtd. in Robertson 274).

This twofold definition of comedy that Dante offers us – the happy conclusion and the use of decorum in the stylistic embellishment of the text – becomes the standard rule for comic dramatists before the recovery of the Aristotelian document in the Renaissance. Certainly Gil Vicente adhered to this standard in his own definition of comedy, and from the evidence elsewhere, it would appear that others too were greatly influenced by these remarks.

After the comments made by Dante about comic expression, comic drama became, like the earlier (French) *débats* and later (English) *Chambers of Rhetoric*, a visual and rhetorical means of conveying the poet's stylistic virtuosity; a secularized vehicle of humanistic expression which still reflected the past – the medieval past – as it ventured into the refined conventions of the Renaissance spirit.

CHAPTER II

THE DEVELOPMENT OF THE *COMÉDIA* FORM
IN THE IBERIAN PENINSULA

A) Dramatic Traditions of the Iberian Peninsula Before the Sixteenth Century

1. *Comic Form and Expression*

We have already observed in the introductory section the main principles of comic theatrical activity that were passed on to later theorists, from the beginnings of comic drama in the Latin Middle Ages to the unfolding of a more coherent dramatic theory in the late Middle Ages. We noticed in that summary that the medieval concept of comedy and comic drama was quite different from the notions that were based on the Aristotelian principles and that are so often an integral part of our modern dramatic perspectives.

The adaptation of these ancient ideas about comedy within the scope of the medieval modes of perception, however, becomes the foundation upon which any critical analysis of these forms should be viewed. Such an intricate ordering of the ancient and medieval views as a reflection of a new social reality are therefore of great import to the study of sixteenth century drama.

The ideas that filtered down from earlier theorists about comic expression are of special interest to the student of Peninsular dramatic literature due to the overwhelming significance of the Middle Ages in the development of the "modern" Iberian frame of reference. It cannot be denied that this historical fact has influenced the literary conventions and ideological perspectives of

Spain's and Portugal's later literary accomplishments. What is essential to the literary trends that followed the medieval period, what, in fact, distinguishes the Iberian concept of the Renaissance and the post-Renaissance or baroque, is precisely this coalescence of the Iberian medieval tradition and the new European literary trends of the Renaissance. Unlike France who, much later, rejected the past in its acceptance of the neo-classical ideas, Spain and Portugal experimented with these new forms, adapting them instead within the scope of their national traditions:

> Vernacular literature begins in Spain considerably later than in France. The Latin culture of the twelfth century reaches there quite belatedly too. Hence Spanish literature, down to the end of the seventeenth century, preserves medieval characteristics which give it a physiognomy of its own.... Spain's cultural "belatedness" of course in no sense signifies a "backwardness," in the sense either of the old or the new progressivism. Rather, it brought to the Spanish period of flourescence the rich content of the Middle Ages, and insofar was productive (Curtius 541-42).

What has been said about this very important aspect of the Iberian historical reality can certainly apply to its concept of theater as a whole; especially if one recognizes that theater is the most apt mode of aesthetic expression to reflect a true and complete vision of its society. The moralistic aspect, as we have seen, was the prevailing concept of theatrical activity that the Middle ages inherited from the earlist times. In this emphasis on the moral propriety of literary compositions and its relation to real life situations, one can hear the distant echoes of Cicero's time-honored definition of comedy: "Comedy is an imitation of life, a mirror of custom, an image of truth."[1] The "comedia," more than any other theatrical development in Western Europe, is a manifestation of this fact for, in many ways, it is a sociological document in which the prevalent ideas of its society are not only reviewed but are also integrated within the popular preferences of its past traditions in such a way as to mirror the contemporary reality.

---

[1] "Comoediam esse Cicero aut imitationem vitae, speculum consuetudinis, imaginem veritatis." (qtd. by Cooper 91).

The "comedia," then, owes its very existence to the specific historical reality of the Iberian Peninsula before the sixteenth century. It is there that one must search in order to find its roots. The following summary of the most important dramatic manifestations that occurred before the sixteenth century may help identify those multiple elements that differentiate the "comedia" from related forms of dramatic literature elswhere.

2. Poetic Traditions in Peninsular Drama

Although it is the opinion of Humberto López Morales that too much emphasis has been given to the theory about the development of Peninsular theater from lyric texts, it is with these texts that our summary must begin, for no other evidence has been uncovered to prove other possible sources. Liturgical drama is no longer considered the seedbed of medieval drama in the Iberian Peninsula as it was in other European nations. López Morales notes that one reason for the lack of liturgical texts of dramatic significance may be due to the peculiar historical reality of the Iberian Peninsula at this time (i.e., the ninth and tenth centuries): "La presencia árabe durante siglos y los complejos sucesos de la Reconquista son fenómenos *sui generis* que no sólo la condicionan de forma diferente, sino que en mayor o menor grado le han dejado huella indeleble" (44). For reasons not well defined, there has been a tendency to overlook the histrionic possibilities of the Mozarabic (i.e., Hispano-Gothic) ritual which was, until the implementation of the Roman rite by the Cluny monks, the accepted and offical order of worship in Peninsular churches: "A pesar de que éste [the Mozarabic ritual] poseía ceremonias con elementos de representación y música en su liturgia, nunca se practicaron los tropos, ni ninguna otra forma literario-musical análoga que sirviera de basamento al drama" (47). Gilbert Chase in *The Music of Spain* does not agree with López Morales concerning the dramatic quality of these liturgical rituals. His comments, instead, focus on the "dramatic quality" of these early religious chants:

> Dramatism and the incorporation of popular elements were the outstanding traits of the Hispano-Gothic liturgical chant. The dramatic quality arose above all from the participation of the

people in the prayers and hymns, alternating in their responses with the officiant. The device of *centonization*, that is, the expansion of the regular liturgical phrases by interpolations or additions, was widely practiced by the arrangers of the Hispanic liturgy and this had the effect of giving fuller scope to the dramatic element. For example, the *Pater Noster* – whose Hispanic melody is one of the oldest in Europe, dating perhaps from the fourth century – was sung with an "Amen" interposed by the congregation after each petition of the prayer. The effect must have been not only dramatic, but also highly artistic and profoundly religious (22).

López Morales also rejects the possibility of liturgical developments after the entrance into the Iberian Peninsula of the Cluny order with its *Lex Romana* because, as he states, ". . . en Cluny no existió el teatro litúrgico" (50).

In addition to this, he is perhaps too severe in his denial of poetic origins when he states that "La teoría del origen litúrgico no cuadra bien en el teatro de Castilla, pero buscar sus raíces únicamente en la lírica trovadoresca es arbitrario" (111). Although the author does not totally deny the lyric influence – "Que estos cancioneros ofrecen en sus debates y otras formas dialogadas elementos teatrales de importancia es cosa innegable" (110) – it would appear that his argument is weakened by the use of the word "arbitrario," for few indeed are those specialists of medieval Peninsular drama (and of the later *comedia*) who deny this type of dramatic literature its overwhelmingly lyrical significance. Although López Morales admits a formal debt to the poetic traditions that shaped the theater in Castille, he fails to elaborate on other levels of possible lyric influences. In fact, he ends the section of his book concerning "La herencia trovadoresca" with a short paragraph that is most revealing and suggestive in terms of what has just been stated:

> No sorprende, tras semejante deuda formal, encontrar en estas piezas influencias temáticas de los cancioneros. Los debates amorosos con sus requiebros y sus reproches, y otras situaciones, como la del escudero que por amor de la pastora se hace pastor, son esquemas calcados de la lírica cortesana medieval (119).

In this last statement, the author very clearly uncovers other possible poetic sources for the development of later theatrical forms. It is with this statement that we must begin our survey of the poetic traditions that gave rise to the ensuing dramatic manifestations of the Iberian Peninsula.

The thematic (i.e., "escudero" vis-à-vis "pastor") and formal (i.e., metrical) influences which López Morales suggests are only part of the overall importance that dramatic forms in the Iberian Peninsula owe to the lyric past. Furthermore, the critic does not see the importance of this tradition in the early theatrical developments in other countries: "La teoría es totalmente inoperante para Francia, Italia e Inglaterra, y válida sólo en parte para Castilla" (110). It will be shown that the poetic tradition is indeed important in Iberian dramatic conventions, and that López Morales' statement does not appear to be applicable for the other European countries as well.

For some time now scholars have generally agreed that throughout Western Europe many of the earlier secular songs of the Middle Ages were often written with a dramatic intent in which two or more speakers performed; sometimes a chorus was implied. Donald Gout describes this theory of dramatic evolution from song:

> There are simple ballads and ballads in dramatic style, some of which require or suggest two or more characters. Some of the dramatic ballads evidently were intended to be mimed; many obviously call for dancing. Often there is a refrain which, at least in the older examples, must have been sung by a chorus (31).

For their part, Jacques Roger and Jean-Charles Payen have also observed the influence of the lyric tradition on the development of secular theatrical forms in Western Europe:

> Il est possible que le théâtre français ait aussi été influencé par les productions mi-narratives, mi-dramatiques des jongleurs. J. Rychner a montré que, recitant une épopée, le jongleur 'jouait sa chanson comme un acteur son rôle'. Lorsqu'il mimait une action et contrefaisait sa voix pour animer un dialogue, il ne faisait pas à proprement parler du théâtre; mais on peut penser que ces efforts d'interprétation mènent a la représentation

théâtral. Sans qu'il soit possible de l'affirmer avec certitude, il paraît probable que notre théâtre comique doive beaucoup aux traditions de métier des jongleurs (90).

It would appear, then, that these dramatic style compositions were not restricted to any one particular geographic location in Western Europe. Samplings of these lyric songs have been found throughout the European continent. From the "cantigas" of the Iberian Peninsula to the "Trouvère" and "Troubadour" songs of the French minstrels, as well as the "Minnesingers" and "Meistersingers" of Germany, have come to us the texts of many lyrical songs that often reveal a dramatic intent in an era when drama, as we think of the term today, was not an aesthetic possibility.

One case in particular may serve to illustrate this point. Among the "troubadour" and "trouvère" traditions in medieval France there existed a very popular type of lyric song called the "pastourelle" which was imitated and assimilated into the lyric tradition of the Iberian Peninsula in the repertory of the "cantigas de amor." It is important to consider this transitional stage of comedic form not only because it reflects the Iberian focus on the antagonism between two distinct social castes (and its subsequent significance to the developing concept of "honra" in the Iberian Peninsula), but also because of what it signifies in the structural development of comedy (i.e., from poetic sources).

Grout describes the development of a full length dramatic composition from this type of medieval song:

> A favorite genre was the *pastourelle*, one of the class of dramatic ballads. The text of a pastourelle always tells the following story: a knight makes love to a shepherdess who usually, after due resistance, succumbs; alternatively, the shepherdess screams for help, whereupon her brother or lover rushes in and drives the knight away, not without blows given and received. In the earliest pastourelles, all the narration was monologue; it was a natural step, however, to make the text a dialogue between the knight and the shepherdess. Later, the dialogue came to be acted as well as sung; if one or two episodes were added and if the rescuing shepherd appeared with a group of rustic companions, and the performance were decked out with incidental songs and dances, the result was a little musical play. One such play, in fact, is the famous *Jeu de Robin et Marion*, written by

Adam de la Hale [sic], the last and the greatest of the trouvères, about 1284 (31).[2]

This process whereby lyric motifs are later dramatized and given more specific generic definition can also be evidenced in the Iberian Peninsula. It is tenuous in Portugal, where dramatic manifestations of human emotion are characteristically veiled by the subjectivity of lyric expression, but still the dramatic evolution described above is observable. The medieval Portuguese "pastorelas," which Joaquim Nunes classifies as "Cantigas de amor," exhibit, in embryonic form, some of the same dramatic elements as the French "partourelles" which Grout described above. In addition to this, António Bragança has noted that the same lyric vein of dramatic development is observable, much later, in the works of Bernardim Ribeiro (1481?-1545?): "Alguns séculos depois haveriam de encontrar [as pastorelas] apropriados e suaves acentos nas *éclogas* do suavíssimo Bernardim Ribeiro" (110).

Much less introspective than Ribeiro but no less poetic in intent was the contemporary Spanish poet and dramatist, Juan del Encina (1469-1529?), who in his "églogas" dramatized similar pastoral situations. Encina's eminence as "Patriarca del Teatro Español" seems to have been subordinated to poetic interests and exhibits the dramatic peculiarity which J. Richard Andrews has already observed: "The Spanish Theater, as secular literary form, came into being as a persuasive defense for poetry and poetic ability. It was an instrument placed at the service of poetic creation" (*Encina* 98-101).

These opinions appear to contradict those of López Morales for whom, as stated earlier, the poetic tradition added little to theatrical developments in the areas of the Iberian Peninsula not influenced by the liturgical tradition; that is, outside of Catalonia.

---

[2] Some scholars have suggested a more specific evolution of this dramatic form. Peter Dronke notes that some have considered the "alba" a generic precursor of the later "pastourelle" in which dialogue is added to the woman's soliloquy of the earlier [?] lyric composition. This later form, in turn, is further dramatized through the introduction of a third character, the "gaita." The English critic emphasizes the "alba's" dramatic quality when, in comparing one of the earliest surviving love-lyrics (sixth century B.C.), he states: "In this it foreshadows, in astonishing detail, one of the most moving *albas* in western literature, the farewell of Shakespeare's Romeo and Juliet." Dronke is not exaggerating when he states that the points of comparison are "astonishingly" similar (168-69).

Perhaps the discrepancies between the words of López Morales and those of Andrews, Grout and others may be explained by the differing opinions that these individuals hold about drama and theater in general. As late as the sixteenth and seventeenth century, dramatic productions, or "drama" if you will, in Iberian Peninsular theater dispense, as we have stated before, with all the classic unities of dramatic structure that define the better part of modern dramaturgy.

It is erroneous to think of theater only in terms of these disciplined notions of drama; even much of our contemporary theater turns its back on these ideas about dramatic literature (cf. Brecht, Weiss, Ionesco, Anton Arrufat, etc.) in favor of less restrictive dramatic conventions. If by the term "drama" we look back at the very rigid formulations of the French neoclassic school, we will find it difficult to define much of what is truly Peninsular in dramatic output; from the "autos" and "comédias" of Gil Vicente to the "dramas estáticos" of Fernando Pessoa. Drama, then, is a term that should be used with great care when applied to the Iberian theatrical reality, from its very beginning to its contemporary manifestations.

It is my opinion that, whereas it is a specific genre of fictional expression, drama shares with other literary forms an element of conflict whether it be lyrical, dramatic or narrative. It is true that conflictive interaction performed before an audience defines what is generically essential to theatrical performance, but theater as an art form has always tended to be a much more inclusive type of activity, allowing spectacle, poetic recitation, and other "a-dramatic" forms of entertainment to enter the stage inter-action. Conflict, as such, cannot define dramatic art nor any other type of fictional literature.

Theater, then, must not be considered a totally exclusive form of fiction. Like the novel it shares a narrational level of communication in that it attempts to tell a story, and like poetry it intensifies or crystallizes a fundamental human truth through the use of highly symbolic language. Different types of dramatic works will emphasize one or the other quality. Unlike a poem or a narrative, however, theatrical activity must be enacted, roles must be impersonated, directly before an audience. This fact (i.e., the creation of a "persona" in a three dimension setting) is the very essence of theatrical activity.

It appears that Peninsular drama owes a great deal to both the narrative and the poetic traditions that preceded it; from one it chose its basic plots as did other European countries (e.g., biblical accounts and, much later, the very popular novels of chivalry), and from the other its metaphorical and symbolic mode of expression.

The poetic tradition, however, was by far the more important aspect of the two motivating principles of theatrical development in the Iberian Peninsula. This can best be exemplified by the work of Calderón (1600-1681) who as late as the seventeenth century uses poetic utterances in much the same way that Juan del Encina or Gil Vicente had done earlier; at times the stage action is in fact interrupted for highly lyrical moments of poetic recitation. Although the style (Gongorism) is by Calderón's time different from that of Encina and Vicente, the opportunity to offer lyrical commentary about the action is done in much the same fashion. This great poet and dramatist is still guided in the seventeenth century by the lyrical spirit (i.e., the poetic tradition) that gave rise to the earlier Peninsular dramatists.[3]

Many more examples could be given to support the extraordinary weight and depth of the poetic background that oriented the development of Peninsular dramatic activity. Margaret Wilson sees in this development an unusual proportion of popular elements which are absent or relatively unimportant in other cultures:

> A tradition related to the communal lyric past and which appears to have been much more highly developed in Spain as a

---

[3] In *El Alcalde de Zalamea*, one of the more often quoted of the Calderonian plays, the dramatist often suspends the stage action to deliver, in its place, a poetic rendition of that action in terms of the action represented. In one instance he is driven to an excessive image that almost becomes ludicrous. This occurs in scene VIII of act III where Pedro Crespo is imploring the Captain to marry his now dishonored daughter: "de rodillas y llorando sobre estas canas, que el pecho, viendo nieve y agua, piensa que se están derritiendo." In another lyrical moment, Calderón renders a poetic speech which has often been considered contradictory to the *ethos* of the character pronouncing it (i.e., el capitán): "En un día el sol alumbra y falta; en un día se trueca un reino todo; en un día es edificio una peña; en un día una batalla pérdida y victoria ostenta...." As this passage proves, at times, the poetic energy contradicts the characterization of the dramatic agent in the same work. Further evidence of popular lyric conventions in dramatic development may be observed in the songs that "La Chispa" often sings to reflect the action of the play.

whole is that of dramatic ritual, whether religious or secular. It seems certain that there were frequent representations marking some season or occasion, in which song and dance played a more important part than any written text, and in which the audience were involved as worshipping or rejoicing participants, rather than remaining apart as detached observers of an aesthetic performance. The influence of this popular tradition is strong in the dramatic text of the Golden Age, in which song and dance often play an important part (6).[4]

These activities are essential aspects of comedy. The *comedia* is a genre that relies heavily on spectacle, having inherited from the past these ritualistic tendencies. As a genre, then, it depends on the lyric communal past for its total definition. One of the characteristics of this dramatic development is precisely the use it makes of a variety of lyric metres. Unlike the preferred English iambic pentameter or the often used French alexandrine, the *comedia* utilizes a great variety of lyric metres from other poetic sources, a procedure which underlies the importance of rhetorical forms and poetic sources of the national past.

In the Golden Age of drama in Spain and Portugal these sources responded to the Italianate rhythms in vogue (e.g., the heptasyllable and the hendecasyllable), but the long-admired eight-syllable *romance* was native to the Peninsula and was consequently cultivated as an autochthonous form of expression. This was the metre of the *romance*, or ballad. The a-temporal quality of these ballads as well as their inherent dramaticity underlines their essentially poetic nature. Gil Vicente often used this form as well as others of the late Middle Ages to synthesize the dramatic stage

---

[4] This ritualistic aspect of the Spanish theater can be seen in the observations made by visitors to Spain during the period in question (the Golden Age). In one account written by a Dutchman, Francis van Aerssen, it is observed that: "The King... after mass, returns with a torch in his hand, following a silver Tabernacle, in which is the Holy Wafer, attended by the Grandees of Spain and his several Councils... The two companies of Players that belong to Madrid at this time, shut their theatres, and for a month represent these Holy Poems: this they do every evening in publick [sic] on scaffolds erected to that purpose in the streets before the houses of the Presidents of several Councils" (Brockett 207). This observation may also serve as an example of how little the religious or communal approach to dramatic activity had actually changed since the time of the Dionysian theatrical offerings in Greece.

action: "... no cultiva Gil Vicente un solo metro que escape a la escuela del Cancionero de Resende," admits López Morales (119).

But there is more than just formal influence in the development of the *comedia* as a dramatic genre from the *cancioneros* and other earlier poetic sources (e.g., the *kharjahs, cantigas,* etc.). We must also consider the general importance of figurative language in the development of the *comedia* as a specific generic type. Bruce W. Wardropper sees in the dramatic technique of the *comedia,* "the reproduction in a play's plot of imagery originating in its poetry" (189). For his part A. A. Parker has spoken of the unique concept of verisimilitude in the *comedia.* Human truth, he adds, is not a product of the realistic depiction of an action on stage, but rather of the poetic significance of that action "independent of space and time" (55).

Causality in dramatic plot construction is minimized here in favor of a characteristically Iberian dramatic law – the law of Poetic Justice, an interest in the righting of wrongs as dictated by socially acceptable moral norms. This harmonizing principle, as the term implies, seeks a logic which is essentially nonrealistic, preferring instead the idealistic truths and universal values of a highly moralistic society. The relationship of the individual with his or her social reality appears to be the main interest of Iberian drama. Generally, this social relationship is expressed in a highly subjective, lyrical, mode. Wardropper elaborates on this idea when he adds that a technique of the Spanish theater often depends on the "... employment of the 'means of lyric poetry' to enhance dramatic effect and to intensify meaning" (190).

The implications of this statement, in which the critic emphasizes the poetic origins of plot construction in Peninsular drama, go beyond the mere formal and thematic influences suggested by Humberto López Morales. These critics have noticed that formal dramatic conventions are superseded by a direct cause-effect relationship between the stage fiction and its (poetic) source. Naturally, the "movement-of-spirit," which according to Dante constituted dramatic action, will respond to a lyrical impulse or to a narrative one. This undoubtedly influences the nature of the dramatic action, often defying the laws of drama with which we are most familiar today.

A. A. Parker's interpretation supports these ideas when he emphasizes that "the theme of a play is the human truth expressed metaphorically by the stage fiction" (44). His evaluation of the *comedia* emphasizes the importance of thematic unity over unity of action, that is, whether or not the incidents of the play are "realistically" depicted in a causally related sequence or not, the heterogeneity of plot construction which is often expressed in the duality of a dramatic situation, is a generic quality of the Peninsular *comedia*. It invites the audience to make the symbolic associations that complete the "action" on stage, in a manner similar to the reader who ponders over the intricate and hidden meanings of a poetic text. If, as Parker states, our historical sense is offended by the flagrant (yet intentional) "abuse" of factual material which distorts historical sources in the play's story, we have not understood the poetic principle that guides the *comedia* form, nor its artistic excellence.

The Vicentine *comédia* shares with these later dramatic forms many qualities that are essentially Hispanic in comic structure. This alone allows the intentional comparisons that have been elaborated here. Calderón's *El mágico prodigioso*, for example, is just as "unrealistic and remote" as Gil Vicente's *Comédia de Rubena* which, as we will observe, contradicts all the laws of conventional dramatic unity. They both share, however, the dramatist's desire to explicate a universal (often moral and, ultimately, theological) truth. This, once again, is not accomplished through the principle of causal unity, but rather through poetic associations of a highly symbolic nature. The Peninsular *comedia*, as understood by Gil Vicente and his Spanish contemporary Torres Naharro, constitutes a unique dramatic concept of comedy; one which seeks final harmony through poetic truth. It is, as it was in the Middle Ages, an ultimately theological (i.e., ritualistic) approach to dramatic construction.

Perhaps it is the poetic quality of the Vicentine texts, rather than their situational context, which makes them "modern" or, better, universal in appeal. Be that as it may, it remains a fact that Gil Vicente's contribution to Peninsular dramaturgy was essentially lyrical and not "dramatic." That, after all, was the reality of his age as well as of his national tradition. We will have occasion to observe that our dramatist envisioned and, at times, grasped the skills of dramatic art, but fell short of evolving those post-Medieval dramaturgical techniques significantly. According to M.

Romera-Navarro that task would be left to his contemporary, Torres Naharro:

> Encina, Lucas Fernández y Gil Vicente muestran ingenio en el diálogo e inspiración lírica – sobremanera el último –, pero no talento dramático. ... Y, como no existe movimiento dramático, tampoco hay caracteres propiamente dichos, puesto que en la escena, como en la vida, no podemos concebir la existencia de un agente que no obra (51).[5]

From these statements it becomes very clear that neither unity of action nor character delineation are the most important elements of the Peninsular notion of comedy. One must not judge the efforts of these early playwrights, therefore, within the dramatic parameters of another age as has been done often with Gil Vicente. It is extremely important, instead, to analyze the dramaturgical skill of these "primitivos" (i.e., Gil Vicente, Juan del Encina, Lucas Fernández) in light of the historical and national realities in which they wrote. In this respect we must agree with O. B. Hardison when he observes that the danger to the (immanent) aesthetic appreciation of earlier ("primitive") forms of dramatic expression surfaces when they are considered as mere Darwinistic stages in the development of modern drama:

> In sum, the standard historians of medieval drama [Chambers, Young, and Craig] have followed the procedure used by early evolutionary anthropologists in connection with the study of myth. They have attributed present concepts and attitudes to a culture of the past. They have assumed that medieval man thought like nineteenth-century man, or ought to have done so. The result has been serious distortion. History has become teleological, interpreted both intentionally and unconsciously in terms of what texts anticipate rather than what they are (33).

Although Torres Naharro helped shape the *comedia*, perfected later by Lope de Vega and his contemporaries, one must look further back in time to find the true evidence which gave rise to

---

[5] Romera-Navarro admits, however, that the Vicentine characters are more well defined than those of Lucas Fernández and Juan del Encina: "... los [personajes] de Gil Vicente, infinitamente más animados, más activos..." (51).

this literary form. An understanding of the aesthetic principles that preceded such a well-defined tradition of dramatic activity should be the first step in defining the true elements of the *comedia*.

In the following section an attempt will be made to uncover the essential dramatic activities in the Iberian Peninsula that gave rise to this dramatic form. In addition to this, a section is included that will review the theoretical documents in which comic expression is considered, from the earliest times (e.g., Isidore of Seville, seventh century) to the time of Gil Vicente. It is hoped that the following summary will further elucidate the significant events of Peninsular theatrical history, as well as clarify the theatrical tradition which helped shape the Vicentine plays. The summary of these dramatic manifestations and ideas might clarify the dramaturgical principles which gave rise to the Peninsular concept of *comedia* that Gil Vicente inherited, elaborated upon, and transmitted to later playwrights.

3. *The Medieval Dance-Songs*

The most remote example of lyrical texts that give way to future theatrical developments appear before the eleventh and the twelfth centuries in Moslem Spain. These early songs or Romance language refrains that accompanied the lengthier Arabic or Hebraic *muwashshahah* were songs in which a young woman lamented a lost love or expressed the joy (or shame) of an amorous encounter. Although they are, without doubt, the earliest manifestation of a genuinely lyrical mode of expression in the Peninsula (and also in Western Europe), these woman-voiced love songs often revealed a truly dramatic quality which the poets projected through the creation of a "persona," a dramatic technique closely resembling that of Stanislavski's method known as "identification": the total immersion of the actor (i.e., implied author, in the case we are considering) in his fictional circumstances.[6]

---

[6] Hardison notes the importance of this method in dramaturgical practices when, in consulting the words of actors and theater experts, he registers the dramatic significance of this process: "It was the subject for an early (1888) psychological study by William Archer, in which actors were asked to describe their attitudes toward their roles. By far the greatest number agreed that 'contagion' (i.e., identification) was necessary for successful acting. 'In this sympathetic contagion,' concludes Archer, '... the poet – say Shakespeare –

This is not to say that the fictional elaboration of a "persona" is true drama, but rather, that the dramatic intent was made manifest through this procedure of authorial impersonation (i.e., identification), a fact made especially significant when one considers that these early songs, in which the speaker is always a woman, were written by men.

Later, in the Galician *cantigas de amigo*, lengthier renditions of a *kharjah*-like expression were most likely mimed and perhaps even represented "en scene" by amateur "actors" who, much as in regular playlets, enacted improvised versions of these lyrical "scripts." The quality of impersonation, of donning the mask, lends to these Galician songs an air of dramatism found earlier in the *kharjahs*. Peter Dronke poignantly examines the possible context of these early songs:

> Are these brief verses [the Spanish *kharjahs*] fragments from larger lyrics, the rest of which is lost? Not necessarily: as Joseph Bedier showed with regard to the Old French *refrains*, often of precisely similar length and scope, the context to envisage for such lines may well be a dance rather than a longer poem: there they could be built out by repetition, instrumentation and mime, or, in a longer dance-play, each *kjarcha* [sic] or *refrain* could have acted as a focal point for one scene (88).[7]

In these early *kharjahs* and *cantigas*, the affective moment of lyric expression often gives way to the more dramatic mode of recitation which objectifies and distributes the conflictive situation among those involved. This is brought about by the problematic conversations about love (e.g., mother-daughter, knight-shep-

---

fecundates the imagination of the actor – say Salvini – so that it bodies forth the greatest passion-quivering phantom of Othello. In the act of representation, this phantom is, as it were, superimposed on the real man ... the passion of the moment informs him to his fingertips, and his portrayal of a human soul in agony is true to the minutest detail. His suffering ... cannot be called other than real.' Stanislavsk's "method" has similar elements. Assuming that "the actor must first of all believe in everything that takes place on stage," Stanislavski designed his famous 'method' exercises to facilitate generation of this belief" (33).

[7] Dronke's words become all the more resounding when we consider the validity of his interpretation concerning the "refrain" or popular motif in the development of the Peninsular concept of *comedia* (cf. *El Caballero de Olmedo*, *Peribañez*, *Fuenteovejuna*, etc.).

herdess, etc.). At times, this is accomplished through the (elliptical) rhetorical question, in which the poetic voice assumes the presence of another entity, human or not (e.g., "Ondas do Mar de Vigo"). The dialogic quality of these compositions welcomes a dramatic context from the reader which, as Dronke suggests, assumes the role of the audience.

Unlike the purely lyrical compositions aimed at the intensely personal and contemplative exposition of an action, these improvised mini-dialogues reflected the popular folk tradition of comic expression associated with the carnival spirit. One must assume that the ritualistic tendencies of these communal gatherings would not (necessarily) discourage secular theatrical activities in which exuberance and frolic abounded. As George Santayana observed: "The clown is the primitive comedian" (Lauter 414).

Further evidence of the pervasive carnival atmosphere and its impact on the creation of popular communal activities that often lead to representation may be observed in the sexual symbolism of these dance-songs. The references to "cervos do monte," "avelaneiras frolidas," "o laranjedo." etc., have been associated with the fertility rituals of these early village entertainments. They reflect, as it were, the ceremonial vestiges of the carnival festival in which seasonal renewal was manifested through comic expression in a conventional form of sexual symbolism. In his discussion of the *cantiga* "Bailemos agora, por Deus, ai velidas" written by the Galician minstrel Joan Zorro, Dronke notes that:

> The song turns on the age-old association of hazelnuts with fertility and erotic fulfilment. It is under the hazelnut tree that love has the best chance of being returned, even by those who have shown no love elsewhere. In a wide range of proverbial expressions going into the hazelnut trees ("In die Haseln gehen", "aller aux noisettes avec un garçon") is synonymous with love-making; already in the ancient world sterile women were beaten with hazel twigs to make them fertile, and hazelnuts were given to the bride and bridegroom on the wedding-night. Whether consciously or simply following a tradition whose meaning they barely surmise, the girls in their dance are invoking the tree's power (194).[8]

---

[8] For a more extensive account of the sexual symbolism of trees see James George Frazer's abridged version of *The Golden Bough: A Study in Magic and Religion*,

The natural vitality of these improvised games or "playlets" (i.e., histrionic activities) often took the form of songs, dances, mimes, and even contests (cf. "La Batalla de Don Carnal y Doña Quaresma" in the *Libro de Buen Amor*) which depicted and reenacted the ritual of seasonal changes. Although the structure and spirit of these songs is undeniably more lyrical than dramatic, it still announces a pre-theatrical or para-theatrical intent which would, at the very least, require a deliberately dramatic recitation of the text (i.e., the changing of voice quality and/or intonation, gestural accompaniment in the oral delivery, perhaps even symbolic attire, etc.).

Andrée Crabbé Rocha has observed this same dramatic quality of the lyrics in the *Cancioneiro Geral* (1517) written by Garcia de Resende. It is interesting to note that even at this late date there is influence of the earlier *cantigas* on these "formas primitivas de representação":

> Aliás, uma poesia dita em voz alta, para animar um serão, não podia deixar de viver, em parte, do esforço de bem dizer, da acentuação de certas intenções dos textos, da mímica ou dos jogos fisionómicos. O sistema de perguntas e respostas, bem como o das ajudas, instaura insensivelmente um "diálogo." Em certas contendas célebres, como a do "Cuidar e Sospirar," chega mesmo a haver distribuição de papéis, cabendo a este o de acusador, àquele o de defensor, àquelotro o de juiz, etc. O treino adquirido na observação dos ridículos e fraquezas do semelhante contribui, não pouco, para o adestramento nos meios de dominar todas as formas do cómico (57-58).

Even in the earlier *cantigas* where self-revelation in a conflictive context is the central issue, there is still a dramatic quality which produces an implicit tension; one which is often resolved not (necessarily) through external action, but rather through an inward operation of symbolic associations of a highly poetic nature. In the Iberian Peninsula, this procedure is not soon forgotten in later developments of comic expression.

---

especially chapters IX and X ("The worship of Trees" and "Relics of Tree-Worship in Modern Europe").

Besides the dramatic quality of these "lyrical" texts, that is, the quality that makes them virtual drama or objectified depictions of human action, there is also a degree of anonymity about them that places them within the legacy of traditional or oral literature. This allows and even invites elaboration and experimentation with other types of literary forms; as in the case of the traditional ballad, where narration often gives way before poetic and dramatic modes of expression. In any case, the dramatic quality of the songs is also made manifest through their communal (i.e., ritualistic) nature which insures their viability as representational art forms.

Dronke recognizes this in other cultural settings (e.g., the Latin *Winileod* and the Anglo-Saxon *Wulf and Eadwacer*):

> In its own way this song [*winileod*], like *Wulf and Eadwacer,* is an essentially dramatic creation. It is deeply personal, but in lyric this implies not (or not necessarily) the revelation of a *persona*, that is, the attainment of a certain dramatic objectivity. If the personal element here were only subjective, the result would be less a work of art than an embarrassment: the authenticity lies not in "the spontaneous overflow of powerful feeling" (which may or may not be present), but in the strength of the imaginative projection (93).

If we recall that Aristotle's definition of "action" encompassed also the motivation from whence it was derived (i.e., as literary discourses and/or as stage actualization), these *cantigas* become all the more dramatic in intent. That is, they become potential germs for the development of later dramatic activity. The ambiguity of symbols and implicit motifs (e.g., sexual symbolism) which pervades their texture invites further elaboration and further commentary from the reader or spectator; a fact which is evidenced by the traditional nature of these dance-songs. Later, when authorial pride substitutes the medieval sense of anonymity, the poet will take his pen to gloss (and even imitate the style of) these early lyrics. And the more popular ones, those entrenched in the national past, will ultimately become the "movement-of-spirit" that will give rise to the *comedia*.

Dramatic intent in these early compositions, then, is a product of what in modern literature is called authorial point of view. When Dronke remarks that the medieval poet objectified his sentiments and, thus, created a *persona*, he is referring to this process. Furthermore, when we consider that the fictional masks of these *kharjahs* and *cantigas* are deliberately divorced from the actual authorial "gender" (i.e., they are female voices created by the male poet), the dramaticity becomes all the more inspired. In an attempt to uncover the deepest recesses of the feminine psyche, these poets must be objective; especially if they are to disclose the true nature and psychological repercussions of the love relationship. This authorial impersonation is an inherently dramatic technique.

The importance of the medieval dance-songs is felt in the later developments of Iberian literature as well. Renaissance *cancioneros* collect them, imitate them, and even adapt them to the popular elements and motifs (e.g., courtly-love motif) preferred by humanist poets of the aristocratic Renaissance courts. Gil Vicente, for example, dramatizes in the *Comédia do Viúvo*, the courtly-love metaphor – lord (i.e., lady) and servant (i.e., lover) – of the early lyric tradition, thus exhibiting a marked interest in the dramatization of earlier poetic conventions. The characteristically lyrical note of the more "dramatic" compositions in these sixteenth century poetic collections is never lost, and it is not unusual for a modern writer to inherit the same traditional spirit and popular lyric vision of life.[9]

J. R. Andrews has pointed out the peculiarity of Portuguese theater when considered in light of the very lyrical beginnings of Peninsular drama:

> Fidelino de Figueiredo suggests, along with Gil Vicente, three men, "António Ferreira com a *Castro*, D. Francisco Manuel com a *Fidalgo Aprendiz* e Garrett com o *Frei Luiz de Sousa*", as worthy of attention in the theatrical literature of Portugal. Yet when we read these plays it is not the dramatic power and

---

[9] "[el] resultado de este redescubrimiento [de la poesía tradicional cancioneril] será el neopopularismo de poetas como García Lorca o Rafael Alberti, que van a inspirarse, por ejemplo, en el arte de un Gil Vicente" (Del Río 170). Ángel Del Río repeats this idea when he states in a section dedicated to Gil Vicente that "... algunos poetas contemporáneos, como Rafael Alberti, se han inspirado en el lirismo popular del poeta portugués, el más perfecto de todos los cultivadores de la lírica tradicional en el siglo XVI" (214). A more contemporary example of the Vicentine (poetic) influence on modern literature can be found in Gabriel García Márquez's *Chronicle of a Death Foretold*. The Nobel Prize recipient (1982) narrates a story prefaced with the following words: "'the pursuit of love is like falconry' Gil Vicente."

development which stand out, but the poetic conception and elevation, the underlying lyrical feeling. Within this lyricism which graces Portuguese literature, whether it be in form or in spirit, as the authentic and functional expression of their particular structure of life, Gil Vicente was able to create a superbly lyrical theater (*Artistry* 62).

One must not forget these remarks concerning the *cantigas* as they relate not only to the motivating spirit (cf. Dante's "movement-of-spirit") of the *comedia*, but also to its structural categories as a dramatic genre. The lyric note, as a formal (i.e., metrical) as well as a functional element, is a well recognized fact in Peninsular literature. In the works of Gil Vicente this lyricism has been defined as his most important contribution to Peninsular drama.[10]

Jack Horace Parker admits the inherent importance of these lyric compositions in the delineation of the dramatic action, although he fails to bring out the true nature of their dramatic purpose in the Vicentine theater:

> Many of the songs in Gil Vicente's plays have been called "traditional," in that some familiar theme has been picked up by the dramatist, and developed by him for his purpose. That purpose is usually to employ the lyrics as part of the dramatic action, but once in a while, as an interruption, for variety's sake, one finds a kind of sung interlude (122).

It is doubtful, however, that our playwright injected the popular songs (or wrote original ones) gratuitously, "as an interruption ... for variety's sake" alone. The purpose of these songs in the Vicentine *comédias* in particular is not only to advance and complete the dramatic action through symbolic associations, but also to provide comic spectacle (e.g., music, dance, appropriate attire, etc.) that complements that action. If we recall Wardropper's remark that the *comedia* dramatizes in the plot the imagery originating in its

---

[10] Among those who have dedicated attention to this very important aspect of the Vicentine plays, are Audrey Bell, Bowra, Dámaso Alonso, Joaquim Mendes dos Remédios, Pierre LeGentil, Eugenio Asensio, Albin Eduard Beau, Thomas Hart, and James Richard Andrews.

poetry, we quickly notice the significance of these dance-songs within the structure of the later, more extensive, Vicentine *comédia*.

The *cantigas*, as mentioned earlier, often achieve their dramatic tension through poetic oppositions. The dramatic possibilities, however, were very often checked by the dissipation of the narrative thread into the ambiguous poetic world of these symbolic associations. Although the mechanics of parallelism allowed for an unfolding of the story-line, the *cantigas* do not show dramatic conflict but rather suggest the conflict and (perhaps) its resolution through these poetic juxtapositions. When integrated into the structure of the Vicentine dramatic compositions, the traditional *cantigas*, or their popular and (later) artistic re-elaborations, provide the embryonic synthesis of the conflict enacted on stage. In this respect, the Vicentine play is structurally more a poetic reading of an action, than a dramatic presentation of that action as such.

In addition to the literary text itself, therefore, it is also important to consider the music, the choreography of the dance-songs, and even the costuming, if one is to apprehend the global poetic vision which completes the semantic context of the Vicentine comic plays. Although, unfortunately, lost to us now, we must assume that these non-literary theatrical sign-systems complemented the dramatic action presented on stage in a much more profound manner than has heretofore been considered, mainly through lack of documentation. The importance of considering the total performance of the theatrical work has been pointed out by Keir Elam:

> Every aspect of the performance is governed by the denotation-connotation dialectic: the set, the actor's body, his movements and speech determine and are determined by a constantly shifting network of primary and secondary meanings. It is an essential feature of the semiotic economy of the theatrical performance that it employs a limited repertory of sign-vehicles in order to generate a potentially unlimited range of cultural units, and this extremely powerful generative capacity on the part of the theatrical sign-vehicle is due in part to its connotative breadth. This accounts, furthermore, for the polysemic character of the theatrical sign: a given vehicle may bear not one but *n* second-order meanings at any point in the performance continuum (a costume, for example, may suggest socio-

economic, psychological and even moral characteristics). The resulting semantic ambiguity is vital to all but the most doggedly didactic forms of theatre, especially so to any mode of "poetic" theatre [!] which goes beyond "narrative" representation, from the medieval mystery play to the visual images of the Bread and Puppet Theater (11).

The problematic question of interpretive focus (i.e., the performance text and/or the literary text) makes it difficult, if not impossible, in this case, to speculate on the total theatrical significance of the Vicentine plays. Still, we cannot disregard these aspects as complementary to the stage activity. It is unfortunate that we cannot reproduce the texts of performance as they were enacted before the royal Portuguese court of the sixteenth century; and yet all is not lost, for the highly "poetic" nature of Gil Vicente's drama demands an interpretation that goes beyond audio and visual signification. It is in the critical interpretation of the poetic symbolism imbedded within the dramatic dialogue that we find the real significance of these plays.

Let us consider, for example, the talented "Rosvel" of the *Comédia do Viúvo*, who disguised as "Juan de las Broças" states his musical talents: "ya persoy medio guaitero; hago notas y plazeres a las moças" (Vicente 140). It is significant that one of the widower's daughters, Melicia, is first romantically attracted to Rosvel by this lyrical spirit: "O, como es tan plazentero!," she remarks. The disguised Prince later sings an inspired and symbolically revealing song: "Arrimárame a ti, rosa, no me diste solombra," announcing early in the play and in capsuled form the conflict of the dramatic action. His next song: "Malherido me ha la niña; no me hazen justicia" is enriched with the ambiguity typical of the *cantigas*. The plural verbal inflection of "hacer" does not correspond to the noun "niña" which not only universalizes the dramatic situation by the use of the generalized "hazen" appeal, but also points to the dramatic complication: his love for two "niñas," that is, the two daughters of the widower. Rosvel's plight, crystallized in these two songs, is later unfolded and given a comic resolution through the unexpected appearance of his brother. The ensuing nuptials celebrate the happy conclusion.

Spectacle and song appropriately complete the action which the author has complemented with lyrical elaboration. In these songs and dances Gil Vicente bestows a wide range of semantic possibilities that he dramatizes throughout. We must, therefore, consider the significance of music and dance as genuine theatrical sign-systems; we must also recognize the aesthetic pleasure and cultural significance that these popular songs and dances held for the viewing audience: "... the theatrical sign inevitably acquires secondary meanings for the audience, relating it to the social, moral and ideological values operative in the community of which performers and spectators are part" (Elam 10).

One might relate the "secondary meanings" in the Vicentine wedding scenes, for example, to the communal festivities mentioned earlier. This, after all, was the social context of the original ritualistic dance-songs. The *comedia*, which depends to a large extent on these communal occasions for its final configuration (i.e., fertility rituals and festivals of the wedding occasions), utilizes this folkloric, lyrical tradition of the Middle Ages to identify the significant social changes defined by the dramatic (comic) action. As Tydeman reminds us, "Any account of medieval stage conditions must acknowledge the presence of these and similar ceremonies, stemming from primitive pagan rites..." (21).

Comedy, then, more than tragedy depends on the communal ceremony – identified here with the spontaneous joy of song and dance – because, as Susanne K. Langer has written, "to maintain the pattern of vitality in a non-living universe is the most elementary instinctual purpose" (328). It has often been stated that the "Comic Rhythm" is inherently communal while the "Tragic Rhythm" is individual. For this reason "Comedy is an art form that arises naturally wherever people are gathered to celebrate life, in spring festivals, triumphs, birthdays, weddings, or initiations" (331). Langer explains that comic action, as an organic and/or structural pattern, seeks to perpetuate the species in much the same way that the biological process of life is endless in concept. This fact is the underlying principle which not only motivates the dramatic *cantigas*, but also the later, more well-defined, forms of the theatrical activities derived from the poetic tradition of the Iberian Peninsula. The shape of these dramatic manifestations is conditioned, of course, by the social reality of the times, but the essence of the "comic rhythm" underlies all of these manifestations of human joy. That is, the *comedia* as a literary genre is a concept closely allied to its communal function.

4. Later manifestations

Later theatrical manifestations continue this lyric vein that has been discussed in the previous section. The early dance-songs and other poetic forms (e.g., planctus, debates, literary contests such as the "Cuidar e Suspirar," "tensós," etc.) become the viable models for later dramatic forms of literary exposition. In the Portuguese *Cancioneiro Geral* (1517) there are several compositions which must be definitely considered rudimentary forms of theatrical activity. Andrée Crabbé Rocha sees in the "Farsa do Alfaiate" (1496?) a perfect example of this type of composition: "... [Anrique da Mota] deu a sua peçazinha uma movimentação, uma fantasia e um lastro de verdade permanente que a tornam ainda perfeitamente representável" (59). This "farsa" has been considered of extreme importance in the history of Portuguese theater, as well as very influential in the dramatic activity of Gil Vicente who is believed to have collaborated in one of these semi-dramatic compositions (cf. "Processo de Vasco Abul"). Luiz Francisco Rebello observes that it represents a genuine dramatic accomplishment before the Vicentine plays:

> Situada [a "Farsa do Alfaiate"] a meio do caminho que dos arremedilhos jogralescos e dos entremezes intercalados nos momos palacianos conduz aos autos e as comédias vicentinas, a obra sumária de Henrique da Mota dá-nos a impressão – como justamente observa Andrée Crabbé Rocha – de "uma criança que balbucia primeiro e depois articula" (Rebello 67).

Another form of a pre-Vicentine type of theatrical activity that we must consider because of its poetic inspiration are the *momos*. These aristocratic court masques were elaborate spectacles whose importance is well documented.[11] While they were, no doubt,

---

[11] In Portugal, reference to the non-literary "momo" appears first in 1256 when the Infanta D. Maria, daughter of Sancho I, wills to her brother, D. Pedro, a "momum quadratum." In this instance, the term apparently designates a kind of mask used on festive occasions. Later references appear in the *crónicas* (*Crónica da Tomada de Ceuta* of Gomes Eanes de Zurara, *Crónica de D. João I* of Fernão Lopes, and *Crónica de D. João II* of Rui de Pina), in the *Cancioneiro Geral*, and also in other (epistolary) sources; the most important of these belonging to the year 1500 in Lisbon when "momos" were celebrated on Christmas Eve. The Spanish ambassador to Portugal (Ochoa de Ysasaga) registered the events of that evening (Révah *Manifestations* 91-105), (Rebello 45-58).

most influential in the scenic conception of some Vicentine plays (e.g., *comédia sobre a Divisa da Cidade de Coimbra, Frágua de Amor, Triunfo do Inverno, Nau de Amores, Cortes de Jupiter*, etc.), they do not reflect the structural reality of the *comédias* nor the comic formula that our playwright envisioned. We should recall that Gil Vicente emphasized the popular element of the *comédia* which, according to him, had to be "chaa," (i.e., lowly) although not quite as "chocarreira" (i.e., scurrilous) as the earlier "farsas." The only two comedies (i.e., "comédias romanescas," for those who object to the term "tragicomédia") which exhibit the aristocratic spirit of the earlier *momos* are Gil Vicente's *Amadis* and *Dom Duardos*. These plays not only reflect the aristocratic ideology of the earlier pageants, but also the adventurous gallantry of the novels of chivalry which are the inspiration of the *momos* as well as of the two plays mentioned.

We have seen in this section that the major stimulus to secular theatrical activity before Gil Vicente (i.e., to the early forms of comic expression that point to the development of the *comedia*) was predominantly popular, reflecting the influence of the traditional lyrics and other histrionic festivities of folk (and later aristocratic) rituals. This popular spirit when conjugated with the lyrical preferences of the Iberian dramatists and, more specifically, Gil Vicente and his contemporaries, will define the major elements of the Peninsular concept of comedy.

For reasons which have been considered by others [12] but which escape the scope of this study, dramatic manifestations stemming from liturgical sources in Spain and Portugal before the sixteenth century are extremely few, especially when we compare them with the rich (contemporary) theatrical practices of Medieval England and France. The lack of documentation and of dramatic texts remains an obstacle to anyone interested in this area of Peninsular literary history. With this in mind, let us now review the few statements about comic theories in the post-classic period that contributed to the ideological and rhetorical configuration of this dramatic type: the *comedia*.

---

[12] The most thorough study to date in which the obstacles to dramatic activity in the Hispanic Peninsula are considered is that of Humberto López Morales in his book, *Tradición y creación en los orígenes del teatro castellano*, especially in the sections "El escenario histórico" and "Cluny y los textos litúrgicos de Toledo."

B) Comic Theory Before the Sixteenth Century

The post-classic concept of comedy which Renaissance theorists held was largely based on the comic theories of Donatus. But prior to the re-discovery of the Donatan document in 1433 other ideas about comic form and expression prevailed which were not found in the fourth century treatise. Surprisingly enough, however, some of the classical concepts were transmitted to later theorists. Some were passed on with objectivity, others with elaborations reflecting the spirit of the Middle Ages. It is important, therefore, to turn now to these sources in an attempt to uncover the prevailing notions about comic development before the sixteenth century.

Before the availability of the Terentian commentary written by Donatus, the only sources of information concerning comic drama or comic expression (the distinction, as we have already observed, was not always recognized by medieval rhetoricians) were made available through second-hand statements that were often quoted in support of a thesis, that is, to lend authoritative significance to their treatises. Most of this information, in fact, is found in the writings of the medieval compilers of universal knowledge who, in an attempt to underline the prominence of their written materials, often quoted and interpreted the classical authorities. This practice was continued, much later, by the humanists of the fifteenth and sixteenth centuries. The earlier statements about comedy are extremely rare due to the fact that the classical world was viewed negatively by church officials and was, therefore, more likely to be condemned as immoral rather than objectively represented. Nevertheless, there remained on record some interesting comments about comic expression which can give us an idea of the evolving concept of comedy in the earlier part of the Middle Ages, in the Dark Ages. Edwin Webber notes the importance of these medieval encyclopedias when he states that "The encyclopedic dictionaries, the standard reference works of the Middle Ages, probably supplied the most widely known bits of knowledge" (192).

Before reviewing this type of material, however, it may be well to remember that these early encyclopedists were men who were less interested in the structural categories of comic drama – the interest that orients our attention – than in the moral and/or immoral qualities of the classical authors. This is important in defining the significance and subsequent influence on comic theory of these early commentators as compared to the more formal conjectures of the humanist critics of the fifteenth and sixteenth century, that is, after the Donatan treatise was made available: "The humanist point of view, in regard to poetry, was of a more practical and far-reaching nature than that of the Middle Ages" (Spingarn 9).

This moralistic attitude of the medieval commentators should not be attributed exclusively to the apologetic church tradition with its sanctions against pagan theatrical activity. Instead, it would be well to remember the authoritative reputation of an earlier document, the Horatian *Ars Poetica*, in which the didactic element was also considered of vital consequence in the poetic tradition of the classical period. The continuing importance given to this treatise during the Middle Ages and the early Renaissance has already been pointed out. Spingarn notes the influence of the Horatian treatise in later writers of the Middle Ages when he states that "At no period from the Augustan Age to the Renaissance does the *Ars Poetica* seem to have been entirely lost. It is mentioned or quoted, for example, by Isidore of Seville [*Etymologiae*, viii,7,5], by John of Salisbury in the twelfth century, and by Dante in the fourteenth" (11).

The first of these early "critics" that Spingarn mentions as important in Western European theatrical traditions is Isidore of Seville (c. 560-636). It is interesting that in the history of Peninsular literature and, especially, dramatic literature, Isidore of Seville has been given very little consideration. Yet, his voluminous compendium (*Etymologies*, also known as *Origins*) reviews a vast amount of knowledge which, although marred by the uncritical observations of a typical medieval encyclopedist, still includes some important information about the prevailing notions of poetics in the post-classic period. In terms of dramatic theory, this encyclopedic treatise written by the "Spanish" bishop, however faulty its method of inquiry, has the merit of having gathered and interpreted several classical ideas about comedy which were influential in later medieval and Renaissance studies about comedic form.

The knowledge which filtered from the Hellenistic period into the Middle Ages concerning Aristotle's definition of tragedy and, by opposition, comedy becomes especially interesting when we consider these earlier views. By doing so, one notices the original transformations of the classical ideas, prior to the humanist notions that changed these earlier ideas about comedy into modern renditions. By observing these first definitions we begin to notice how the medieval (Peninsular) mind perceived the concept of decorum in comic form, the appropriate structure and function of comic action, characterization, and language.

There are two observations concerning comedy in Isidore of Seville's *Etymologies* which Spingarn emphasizes and which are of special importance in our survey. In the first of these the Iberian encyclopedist of the seventh century reminds us that "Comic poets treat of the acts of private men, while tragic poets treat of public matters and the histories of kings; tragic themes are based on sorrowful affairs, comic themes on joyful ones" (viii,7,6). The other passage of interest to us repeats the two opposing notions about characterization and adds that comedy's thematic function is concerned with illicit love relationships: "in another place he speaks of tragedy as dealing with the ancient deeds and misdeeds of infamous kings, and of comedy as dealing with the actions of private men, and with defilement of maidens and the love affairs of strumpets" (xviii, 45 and 46).[13]

These scant remarks about comic development can hardly be expected to revolutionize seventh century theories about comedy nor, for that matter, advance any dynamic hypothesis about comic drama; yet, its importance cannot be minimized when we consider how close these notions remained to the classical sources. We may take as a first example the division between tragedy and comedy based on the moral and/or social rank of the characters. This may be considered (somewhat) Aristotelian, especially if we may interpret the statement about this subject in chapter four of the *Poetics* as such: "Tragedy is an imitation of persons who are above the common level..." (82). In this respect, Spingarn holds that the:

> ... conception of the rank of the characters as the distinguishing mark between tragedy and comedy is, it need not be said,

---

[13] "Tragoedi sunt que antiqua gesta atque facinora sceleratorum regum luctuosa carmine spectante populo concinebant."; "Comeodia sunt que privatorum hominun acta dictis aut gestu cantaban, atque stupra virginum et amores meretricum in suis fabulis exprimebant" (Lindsay 65-6).

entirely un-Aristotelian. "Aristotle does undoubtedly hold," says Butcher, "that the actors in tragedy ought to be illustrative by birth and position. The narrow and trivial life of obscure persons cannot give scope for a great and significant action, one of tragic consequence."[14]

Certainly this seems to be the case in subsequent definitions on comedy which maintained, emphasized, and elaborated the Aristotelian statement. Theophrastus (c. 372-c. 287 B.C.), who continued the Peripatetic tradition, was purported to have included in his definition the rank distinction which was so popular in the Middle Ages and which, as seen above, St. Isidore raised to primary importance. The re-discovery of the Donatan treatise in 1433 served to underscore the importance of this distinguishing category (Spingarn 64-65).

In the Middle Ages, St. Isidore's influential statement concerning comedy was apparently given considerable attention by other (non-Iberian as well as Iberian) medieval writers:

> In the *Catholicum* of Johannes Januensis de Balbis (1286) tragedy and comedy are distinguished on similar grounds: tragedy deals only with kings and princes, comedy with private citizens; the style of the former is elevated, that of the latter humble; comedy begins sorrowfully and ends joyfully, tragedy begins joyfully and ends miserably and terribly (Spingarn 66).

Because different aspects of comic drama were emphasized, often to the exclusion of other elements, no systematic theory of comedy can be expected before the sixteenth century. Dante, as one may recall, distinguished his sublime concept of comedy in terms of its diction and its felicitous ending in Paradise. Still, what one author infers another emphasizes; and so medieval theories about the comic, like the oral tradition of medieval literature, was passed on and elaborated as new ideas entered the critical repertoire of these early critics. Before the sixteenth century, however, all of these ideas had been collected and were reflected in the structure of literary manifestations.

---

[14] Spingarn does admit, however, that "... a similar distinction can be traced, throughout the Middle Ages, throughout classical antiquity, back almost to the time of Aristotle himself" (64).

An interesting aspect of comedy which St. Isidore observes deals directly with the contemporary interpretations of classic comic action. In book eighteen, paragraph forty six, the bishop of Seville notes that the comic playwright mainly dealt in his plots with illicit love affairs and prostitution: "atque stupra virginum et amores meretricum in suis fabulis exprimebant." This thematic principle is diametrically opposed to the less ordinary and historical "antiqua gesta" which he observed in the tragic action. The medieval distinction between invented plots (of comedy) and historical plots (of tragedy), a differentiation one notices in Johannes Januensis de Balbis' definition above as well as in later definitions on comic drama (e.g., Torres Naharro), fits quite well within the limitations of comic action expounded by St. Isidore. When he tells us that the comic actions deal largely with the lives of private men as opposed to public matters and the history of kings ("regum"), he is reflecting a dichotomy in dramatic action that opposes an imitation of a historical action to that which reflects the daily activities of the everyday citizen ("privatorum hominum"). That is, one registers the heroic deeds of great men ("gesta") while the other *invents* (i.e., "in suis *fabulis*") and associates the lowly rank of individuals with the base concerns of the common.

If, as logic demands, we deduce from the comments above that St. Isidore also considered stylistic categories of differentiation to fit the decorum of the dramatic agents and the dramatic action, although not explicitly stated in his observations, it would be feasible and, indeed, well to credit St. Isidore with a short yet weighty theory of comedy. Furthermore, his influence as quotable authority to later critics and writers, Iberian or not (cf. Balbis), is of no small consequence. In St. Isidore's remarks, as Spingarn suggests, we discern for the first time an important contribution toward a comprehensive theory of comedy before the entry of the (Aristotelian) Renaissance theories:

  i. The characters in tragedy are kings, princes, or great leaders; those in comedy, humble persons and private citizens.
  ii. Tragedy deals with great and terrible actions; comedy with familiar and domestic actions.
  iii. Tragedy begins happily and ends terribly; comedy begins rather turbulently and ends joyfully.

iv. The style and diction of tragedy are elevated and sublime; while those of comedy are humble and colloquial.
v. The subjects of tragedy are generally historical; those of comedy are always invented by the poet.
vi. Comedy deals largely with love and seduction; tragedy with exile and bloodshed (66-67).

This, then, was the tradition that shaped the un-Aristotelian conception of the distinctions between comedy and tragedy. This idea persisted throughout and even beyond the Renaissance.
All of the above divisions of comic drama given by Spingarn are either stated or implied by the bishop of Seville in the seventh century. Whatever their theoretical merit or degree of influence, St. Isidore's remarks about the subject of comedy remain the only concrete evidence of the transmission of classical knowledge concerning comic development. Certainly it can be perceived as a valuable document, especially when one considers the lack of documents attesting to a tradition of theatrical manifestations in the Iberian Peninsula before the Renaissance. In addition to this, St. Isidore's knowledge of genuinely *theatrical* activity (cf., "aut gestu [!] cantabant") is, as I have already noted, quite unusual for this period of dramatic desintegration.
In the Iberian Peninsula, before the re-discovery of the Donatan commentary (1433) in Europe, the few remarks made about Roman comedy were totally unenlightened by first-hand observation. In the *Primera Crónica General* (late 10th century), for example, Webber has observed that Terence was placed in the distinctive category of "Philósopho" (193-95) although his influence on comic theory appears much earlier, in Garcia de Toledo's *Garcineida* (1099?). With the exception of sparse allusions to classical drama quoted by the humanists of the fifteenth and sixteenth centuries, little can be said about the formulation of a truly systematic approach to comedic form until the appearance in 1517 of Torres Naharro's dramatic treatise included in the *Propalladia*.
Faced with such a lack of theoretical literature about comic drama during the time after St. Isidore and before the Renaissance, critics have traditionally turned to other forms of historical documents for further evidence of dramatic activity in the Iberian Peninsula. The most often quoted example of this method of investigation concerns Alfonso el Sabio's statement in *Las Siete*

Partidas (ca. 1256), a compilation of ancient Gothic statutes. Partida I, ley xxiv, título vi, is a law prohibiting "juegos de escarnio" or other types of profane "representations" on church grounds and/or participation by the clerics in such activities.[15]

In Portugal, indirect testimonies such as these are extremely rare. There is a twelfth century document, however, which has been the subject of great controversy in discussions about the history of the Portuguese theater before Gil Vicente. Although this twelfth century letter proves little more than the existence, however meager, of secular theatrical (or, at least, histrionic) activity at this early date, it would be well to review it in relation to the developing notions of comic drama in the Iberian Peninsula.

The letter, presently found in the Torre de Tombo building in Lisbon, confirms a gift of land made to the "jogral" Bonamis and to his brother, Acompaniado, by the King D. Sancho I in 1193 for their services of entertainment in the court. This was done in exchange for a handsome gift ("hum casal em Canelas com seus termos e direitos"). It has been pointed out by some critics (e.g., Oscar de Pratt) that the substantial amount offered by the King to the entertainers may be evidence of the dramatic significance (i.e., length and literary merit) of this type of performance, but history teaches us that royal favours, for whatever the reason, have sometimes been distributed without due cause.

Still, the relevance of this "genre" as an evolving form of comic literature is important. The letter includes the following note in which the entertainers agree to the performance of an "arremedilum": "Nos mimi supranominati debemus Domino nostro rege pro roboratione unum arimidulum" (Picchio 149). The generic attributes of this "arimidulum" (also transcribed as "arremedilum," "arremedilho," etc.) has been the subject of much literary controversy. Some critics see this embryonic form of comic drama as a genuine dramatic genre (e.g., Oscar de Pratt, et. al.), while others (e.g., Picchio) relate the entertainment to the troubadour antics belonging to the lyric repertoire of the medieval minstrels. In

---

[15] Humberto López Morales refutes this type of evidence and warns that Alfonso el Sabio's redaction of the ancient laws in no way reflected the Hispanic reality of the times. He believes, instead, that the thirteenth century Spanish monarch and poet, was simply organizing and registering the legal statutes of other European nations: "Las *Partidas* son, por lo tanto, una obra de síntesis y no un reflejo de la realidad de su momento" (68-70).

Viterbo's *Elucidário* (1865), for example, one finds "Arremedilho" defined as a "Entremez, farsa, comédia [!], ou representação jocosa" (150).

Although Viterbo's definition invites the reader to associate the "arremedilho" with later, more well-defined dramatic genres, it appears to have exaggerated the dramatic qualities of the "genre" and has, consequently, confused many critics. The comprehensive category into which the term *comédia* is here placed distorts an otherwise intriguing hypothesis about the development of comic drama in the Iberian Peninsula. Little was needed after the nineteenth century critic's affirmation, for Teófilo Braga, Carolina Michaelis and others to re-construct a genre of the "arremedilho" from this twelfth century document. From these generalizations, an entire generic and even evolutionary theory of comic expression was begun. More recently, the Portuguese critic, Luiz Francisco Rebello, has once again defended the theory when he states that:

> Seria assim o arremedilho a célula orignária do teatro português, a partir da qual se formuou – no dizer de Teófilo Braga – "o fio da tradição" entre nós, juizo praticamente adoptado por todos os estudiosos, com a excepção única de Luciana Stegnagno Picchio, que o não aceita como gênero dramatico português específico, equiparando-o à imitações jogralescas, comuns a toda a Europa medieval (25-6).

Although Picchio is probably correct in equating the "arremedilho" with the popular antics of the troubadour (poetic) tradition, there is no reason why that activity should be necessarily divorced from a theory of dramatic origins, nor should we assume, whatever the generic design of the "arremedilho" be, that it did not reflect a contemporary (Portuguese) reality. It is in this sense that Rebello's remark gains critical importance: "Seria assim o arremedilho a célula originária do teatro português. . . ."

Nonetheless, Luciana Stegnagno Picchio has rejected, as Rebello declares above, the hypothesis defended by most other critics on this issue. In the course of her studies on this subject she has undertaken an exhaustive investigation into this matter and has uncovered much useful information about the term "arremedilho" and its proper place in the dramatic literature of the Middle Ages. In her findings Picchio has come to adopt a theory which, although apparently conflicting in terms of the accepted views about dramatic genesis in Portugal, and perhaps too stern in its non-acceptance of the dramatic possibilities of this early comic form, adds a great deal to the previous notions discussed here concerning the affinities between the lyric traditions of the Middle Ages and the origins of comic drama.

In this respect, she has observed that the "arremedilho" is a comic form which obeys the spirit and rhetorical pattern of the medieval minstrels who in turn inherited their repertoires from the travelling "histriones" or mimes of the late Roman theatrical tradition. Picchio's denial of the dramatic possibilities inherent in the early "arremedilho" points to the fact that she apparently sees no relationship between the minstrel's art of the Middle Ages and the development of later theatrical forms.

Not so restrictive in his interpretation but equally well documented in his opinion about these primitive forms of comic expression is Ramón Menéndez Pidal who had already made an observation about the early court entertainers which proves the affinity of these minstrels with the histrionic art, adding, in that respect, that ". . . a los que contrahacen e imitan les dicen *remedadores*" (18).

We note here, in addition to the etymological affinities between the words "remedadores" and "arremedilho," that Menéndez Pidal's definition quite clearly opens the way for a dramatic or, at least, an histrionic notion of these "remedadores'" art form; especially if we note the strong dramatic connotations of his definition in the word "imitar." Yet, we are still admittedly far from a concrete example, as Picchio states, of a modern notion of a dramatic genre.

These court comedians, distinguished by Menéndez Pidal from both the "cantores de lírica" and the "juglares de poesía narrativa," specialized in mocking others through impersonation, a satirical function which cannot be totally divorced from the burlesque and even scatological contents of the thirteenth century *cantigas,* the "cantigas de escarnio e de maldizer." Although it escapes the immediate scope and purpose of this study, one cannot help but point out that the same affinities that were found between medieval lyric forms and later dramatic manifestations (e.g., the *pastourelle* vis-à-vis the *égloga*) are also witnessed in these early lyric satires. Like the Greek Old Comedy invectives, the "cantigas de escarnio e maldizer" placed emphasis on ridicule and even slander as as source of comic laughter. Their possible association with the development of secular theatrical activity and, more specifically, the *farce* has been already considered by other critics: "C'est a l'origine un intermède comique dont on 'farcit' les représentations serieuses, puis la *Farce* devient un genre autonome" (Lagarde and Michard 79). That the "cantiga de escarnio e mal dizer" ("un intermède comique"[?]) may well have developed a more well-defined dramatic form (i.e., the "arremedilho") which in turn could have developed into the stuctural pattern of the *farce* is something that should not be entirely overlooked as a potential possibility in the development of the *comedia*.

Nonetheless, it is unlikely that the word "imitar" in Menéndez Pidal's definition amounted to anything more than an improvised mockery of some court personage lacking structural (literary) significance, or a humorous "slice-of-life" situation performed hurriedly before the royal audience and maybe rehearsed previously in a public area. Still, given the affinities between the early dramatic manifestations and the histrionic repertoire of the post-classic mimes or minstrels, and considering, in addition to this, the persistence of the term "arremedilho" in later developments of dramatic forms [16] it would be well to give the "arremedilho" an important place in the history of dramaturgical practices in Portugal before the more conclusive theatrical activity of Gil Vicente. These early forms of imitative entertainment, as the playwright Oscar Mandel observes, were undeniably a theatrical reality of the Middle Ages; their importance in later dramatic activities is a probability that is strong indeed:

> Even without surving texts, and even forgetting the origins of minstrelsy in the Roman theatre, we can be fairly confident that throughout the Dark Ages, and to the fifteenth century when texts begin to abound, the art of the minstrel included the performance of simple skits.... And what would we make of the art of puppetry, which is amply documented for the twelfth

---

[16] Luiz Francisco Rebello notes that "...em pleno século XVI, o autor da anónima *Obra da Geração Humana* (Gil Vicente?), na cena introdutória, e Chiado (no *Auto da Natural Invenção*) designam por "arremedi(i)ação" uma modalidade cénica que, na obra do último, se da também como sinónimo de comédia, representação, auto or prática" (27).

century? Were the puppeteers inventing skits independently of ordinary minstrels? This is most unlikely. Whenever and wherever men have made puppets perform, they have imitated the material of the "real" theatre. In the twelfth century, and most probably long before, these materials must have come from the "pitiable farce," as E. K. Chambers has called it, of street and market place (13-14).

In the Iberian Peninsula, Menéndez Pidal expresses this view about the existence of secular theatrical activity among the minstrels in the post-classic period of European development when he observes that:

> Los escritores eclesiásticos desde la más remota Edad Media no cesan de usar los términos de la antigüedad clásica: *mimi, histriones, thymelici*, para indicar gentes de su época actual que practicaban espectáculos indecorosos y condenables. Los tres nombres designan tipos procedentes del teatro romano, que luego extendieron su acción por las plazas, las calles y las casas para divertir a un público más reducido, o se establecieron en los palacios de los reyes como hombres de placer" (Menéndez Pidal 14).

It is highly probable, then, that the "arremedilho" was at least a species of the "pitiable farce" that Chambers had in mind. In this respect, we must not lose sight of the dramatic impact that the farce had on later, more serious and sustained, comedic forms. Whether or not we consider the "arremedilho" a dramatic type, however, depends on the differing opinions about drama and theater that were discussed earlier in this chapter. For now, it is important to underscore the significance of this Portuguese "genre" vis-à-vis the development of other literary types of theatrical activity.

This is not to say, however, that Picchio's rejection of the "Portuguese dramatic genre" hypothesis is totally unfounded, nor, on the other hand, that her critics are necessarily at fault in their eager affirmations. Such allegations are not necessarily contradictory; especially if one accepts the frontier of influence that existed between medieval poetry and the ensuing dramatic developments, a correspondence that is especially significant in the Iberian Peninsula. Although it is safe to say with Picchio that the "arremedilho" did not constitute a fixed generic type of drama *per se*, it is also true that her rejection of its influence on later dramatic forms is somewhat unsubstantiated, for it seems that she is determining the parameters of medieval theatrical activity within a modern perspective of theatre. She concludes, therefore, by stating that ". . . é noutra direcção que será preciso procurar as primeiras manifestações do teatro português" (Picchio 165).

For his part, Luiz Francisco Rebello emphasizes the influence of the "arremedilho" on later playwrights and later forms of comic expression in the Portuguese theater: "É, pois, com o gênio de Gil Vicente que se opera a mutação qualitativa do arremedilho em verdadeira e auténtica criação dramática" (31).

Given the affinities already discussed between poetic traditions and dramatic origins, and the continued use of the term in later, more well-defined forms of dramatic activity, one would have to give preference to Rebello's remark that the "arremedilho" was indeed a generating influence on the development of later forms. Although we can only conjecture about the specific thematic contents of the "arremedilho," it is safe to assume that these playlets contained a more well developed and/or extensive structural pattern of motifs than the simple "cantiga de escarnio e de mal dizer." It is unlikely that the ecclectic nature of the art these medieval "jograis" practiced (i.e., storytelling, juggling, dancing, singing, puppeteering, etc.) would necessarily exclude any of the thematic material of the earlier songs, nor the "representational" or oral means of rendering these forms of entertainment.

In spite of the suggestive implications of the twelfth century Portuguese document, however, comic theory did not progress in a systematic fashion until the humanistic endeavors of later centuries. Documentation proving the existence of interest in comic theory is lacking in Portugal but in Spain there are several references to comic expression which reflect an awakening interest in the classical ideas.

In the fifteenth century, during the epoch of the *cancioneros* in the Iberian Peninsula, we come across some opinions about comic drama which will later complete the theoretical position of Torres Naharro. The comic formulas prescribed before the activity of the Spanish playwright, however, were still somewhat based on legendary material about the classic period of comic development. These learned men of the Spanish and Portuguese Renaissance still remained attached to the basic precepts stipulated by the medieval scholars, even to those opinions about comic drama already studied in the work of St. Isidore of Seville. It is interesting, therefore, to see how these opinions differed from previous ones, and how they were amended by the influential critics of the late Middle Ages.

The first of these observations about comic form belongs to Don Iñigo de Mendoza, Marquis of Santillana (1398-1458), in whose works we observe, apparently for the first time, a marked influence of the new Italian spirit in Peninsular literary development. This humanistic vent not only led him to experiment with new Italianate forms (e.g., sonnet) and allusions to the precursors of the new Italian literary conventions (e.g., Dante, Petrarch, Boccacio, etc.), but also to thematic motifs of the type found in Dante's *Commedia*. With this change in the historical perspective leading to the new-age spirit came also a learned approach to the study of the classical writers of comic drama.

In his *Comedieta de Ponza* (1440) Santillana, an early humanist of Renaissance Spain, expresses these new concepts in comic development. George Ticknor has observed that the *Comedieta* itself approaches a structure which is similar to dramatic composition (Ticknor 395), but the real reason for its name appears to be derived from Dante who, as the Spanish poet of Juan II's court reminds us, had formerly prescribed the happy ending for the comic plot. In his "Little Comedy of Ponza" the felicitous conclusion is, in fact, a beatific vision reminiscent of the Florentine poet, in which Fortune, allegorized, consoles the grieving Spanish royalty, after their defeat at Ponza, with the grandeur of the Spanish past and prophecies of future glories. The interesting thing to note about the comic interpretation that Santillana gave to his work is the pragmatic interpretation of comedy in which the author incorporates the contemporary (national) reality within the scope of his comic vision.

Here the happy ending, a determining criterion for comedy, is not a product of individual resolution of conflict, but rather of the national or of the collective welfare. The Peninsular concept of *comedia* often depicts individualized human actions as "allegories" of societal norms (e.g., *Fuenteovejuna*), a concept which, similar to Dante's vision but perhaps not as encompassing theologically, emphasized the common well-being as it is related to accepted moral standards and orthodox theological truths. This notion of comedy, as we have seen before, is characteristically medieval in motivation and scope. It presents a moral and/or theological foundation for the thematic materials of later theories of comic drama (i.e., honor vis-à-vis social norms and Christian virtues), and also assumes that its audience shares this ultimate goal which is here manifested through the "cathartic" principle that Parker has called "poetic justice."

Although the humanistic definitions of comedy differ little from the former notions already discussed, it is the practical application of these comic rules within the framework of national preferences that will ultimately characterize and define the Peninsular *comedia*. Still, the classical definitions of these learned men of the early Spanish and Portuguese Renaissance were clearly echoed in later literary circles and their importance is considerable in forging the patterns of comic drama that were later chosen.

In the *Comedia* Santillana offers the following definition of comedy:

> Comedia es dicha aquella cuyos comienzos son trabajosos e después el medio e fin de sus días alegre, gozoso e bien aventurado: e de ésta usó Terencio peno [sic] e Dante en el su libro, donde primero dice haber visto los dolores e penas infernales, e después el purgatorio, e alegre e bien aventuradamente después el paraiso... (Sánchez Escribano and Porqueras Mayo 54-55).

A similar opinion is found in Juan de Mena (1411-1456) who, like Santillana, was a favorite (a "poet laureate") in the royal court of Juan II. In is *Coronación* (1438) which the poet dedicated to his literary patron Santillana, the Cordoban poet envisions the coronation of his patron on Mount Parnassus by the Muses and, in typical Peninsular orthodoxy, by the Virtues. The work itself is reminiscent of Dante's *Comedia* in certain passages and follows closely the definition given by the fourteenth century Italian poet. Not forgetting the commonplace comic formulas made famous by the Florentine author and other humanist scholars (e.g., Santillana), Mena repeats them adding a note about the comic style which the reader has already observed in the discussion about Dante's influence: "el tercero estilo es comedia, la cual trata de cosas bajas y pequeñas y por bajo y homilde estilo, y comienza en tristes principios y fenece en alegres fines, del cual usó Terencio" (53). This observation attests to the importance given to the beginning and ending of the comic plot in the early Renaissance.

These remarks about Terence (and Plautus) in the developing theories about comedy appear to have placed this dramatic form wihin its proper generic perspective (i.e., of comic drama) but these observations are not always reliable, for the true classic spirit was not often given due consideration. Generally, the early Renaissance writers still paid little attention to the genre distinctions so clearly respected in the Aristotelian document. This was especially true in the Peninsular theatrical tradition.

In fact, the above definitions offer little more than the cliché statements about comedy which had circulated in the post-classic period. Webber even doubts that the scholarly allusions to the classical writers of comic drama were founded on first hand knowledge, although he admits the possibility that these "gentlemen-scholars" had *some* acquaintance with the Roman playwrights.

From these Spanish interpretations, however, we can only assume that the bookish addition of classical authors in no way affected the medieval notions about comedy that had been so pervasively accepted in the Iberian Peninsula. It is entirely appropriate to agree with Webbler when he writes that "... the selection of Terence in a definition of comedy was then so conventional that nothing can be proved on the strength of it" (Webber 197-98). Familiarity with Terence and, to a lesser extent, with Plautus was a fact, especially after the awakening of the scholarly interests of the humanists which led to the rediscovery of the Donatan commentaries (1433), but the classical appreciation of the Roman playwrights had remained, for the most part, close to legendary sources, at least in the Iberian Peninsula. The essentially dramatic qualities of the pagan authors went unnoticed as the medieval outlook continued to impose its own interpretations about *comedy* well into the sixteenth century.

CHAPTER III

THE SCOPE OF THE VICENTINE SECULAR PERSPECTIVE

A) DUALITY AND THE BINARY STRUCTURE

1. Pacíficas concordanças

In an often quoted letter dedicated to D. João III concerning a devastating earthquake that occurred in Lisbon (1531) Gil Vicente complains to the king about the clergymen of Santarém who, according to our dramatist, needlessly and supersticiously scared the populace of that city into believing that God had stricken the sinful (especially the Jews and the New Christians) with this awful catastrophe. Anselmo Braamcamp Freire describes the situation in Lisbon:

> Estava ao tempo o nosso poeta dramático em Santarém. Foi esta uma das povoações mais afligidas pelo terremoto, e todos perderam a cabeça, principalmente os frades. O ódio aos cristãos novos, já bem patente nas Cortes de 1525, irrompeu exterminador. Do púlpito começaram os religiosos, "com mais soma de ignorância que de graça do Spírito Sancto", não a pregar, mas antes a praguejar, afirmando que o fenómeno sísmico não proviera de uma comoção natural dos elementos, mas da ira de Deus pelos grandes pecados em Portugal cometidos, os quais nomeavam, apontando a demasiada tolerância havida com os "estrangeiros na nossa fé", os Judeus e cristãos novos (280).

Gil Vicente was of the opinion that such a display of supersticious behavior on the part of the clergy was due to ignorance of the natural order of things. He was not able to tolerate the abuse and deception of the people and tried to avoid a pogrom of the sort that left many Jews dead in Lisbon years before (281). Will Durant decribes this massacre of 1506 in Lisbon: "... for three days massacre ran free; 2,000 Jews were killed; hundreds of them were buried alive. Catholic prelates denounced the outrage, and two Dominican friars who had incited the riot were put to death" (219). Gil Vicente gathered the priests at the convent of São Francisco and delivered a sermon to them which began with the now famous words: "Os frades de cá não me contentarao...."

In this sermon, not only did Gil Vicente repudiate the ideas of the clergymen by placing the catastrophe within the dimensions of natural phenomena, but he also reprimanded them for their lack of insight and charity. More important than the historical circumstances, however, is the fact that we find in this valuable letter, the only non-literary evidence in which Gil Vicente was able to set down his own philosophical perspectives. These ideas, when considered in relation to his works, clarify the ideology which penetrates them. It is here that one must turn to find the motivating principle that oriented Gil Vicente's structural notions of drama in general and the *comédia* in particular.

The sermon, which Gil Vicente included in the letter, begins with a discussion of the two worlds ("dous mundos"), a concept which brings to mind the Augustinian division in the *City of God*. This philosophical world view opposed the *City of God* to the *City of the World,* a dichotomy which, at least in its binary concept, reflects the ideological framework of the age in which Gil Vicente wrote. Although the interpretations given to these oppositions may differ somewhat in theological perspectives both men (i.e., St. Augustine and Gil Vicente) shared the opinion that natural or created phenomena was intrinsically good and had a purpose, including an aesthetic purpose, in the Divine plan.[1] That is, if

---

[1] J. Richard Andrews, who first emphasized the importance of the *Carta* of 1531, observes that "The Augustinian source which has seemed implicit to so many in 'o altissimo e soberano Deos nosso tem dous mundos' is immediately dissipated by the words 'o primeiro *foi* de sempre e pera sempre'. It is surprising that only I. S. Revah has seen that, 'Il est imposible d'attribuer une origine augustinienne a une cosmologie qui postule la coéternité de Dieu et du séjour de gloire et limit la création au monde terrestre. Il faudrait oublier tous les passages sur la création de ce que Saint Augustin appelle le 'ciel du ciel'.' But whether this

everything including matter is the product of God's Will (cf. "Creatio ex nihilo" of St. Augustine), then it follows that the imperfect world of man is fundamentally good and serves a divine purpose also. In his sermon Gil Vicente explains that God had created the world of imperfection to reflect the excellence of the eternal spheres: ". . . pera que por estes contrayros sejão conhecidas as perfeyções da gloria do segre primeyro." The ultimate harmonious union of these opposing elements in accordance with God's providential guidance he called "pacíficas concordanças" (*Copilaçam* fol. cclvii). These oppositions, then, were not only a teleological necessity for God's divine scheme but also harmonious when considered in light of His divine will. There was a moral lesson to be learned in this conflict of forces too, one which is represented in the ideological views as well as in the artistic conception (e.g., the structural patterns of dramatic action, rhetorical techniques, etc.) of the age.

In the analysis of the Vicentine *comédias* to follow, an attempt will be made to locate and explain the structural and ideological significance of Gil Vicente's theology of the two worlds ("dous mundos"). This highly spiritual notion of secularization was, as we shall observe, an important aspect of the Portuguese dramatist's brand of humanism: Christian humanism. The inherited medieval patterns of perception, especially those historical notions about comedy that have already been discussed, when considered in light of this new age of economic growth and social mobility, will help define the Portuguese playwright's comic vision.

It is necessary first, however, to define more specifically the philosophical implications of the earlier views on comedy as they persisted from earlier times and later influenced ensuing dramatists like Gil Vicente and his contemporaries. The philosophical notions they inherited and the ideological framework in which these humanists produced their works is important in defining the struc-

---

had been the case or not, it would seem that any conclusion based on such a facile correlation would have been, a priori, a very faulty one, for the idea of God having two worlds, created or not, neither begins nor ends in St. Augustine; not only is it found in Plato and in the Talmud but also in Sabunde and Maimonides. It is one of the commonplaces in the thought of man. Even if we disregard Revah's valid objection, this 'fala' could still not be reconciled with an Augustinian source, for there is nothing in the tone nor in the content which points in that direction" (Andrews "The Artistry" 15-16).

tural categories of comedy that they envisioned and ultimately staged.

The earlier classic views of man and his world were once again given consideration in the spirit of renewal that Humanism brought to the civilization of the Renaissance. One must first remember that at the end of the Middle Ages a new economic pattern (i.e., capitalism) was altering the social and political dimensions of Western Europe. The traditional structure of society was being seriously questioned by the humanist scholar who, unlike his ascetic predecessors, asserted the innate value of individual expression in the new-found economic freedom of his society. He welcomed the classic ideal, the gentleman of *virtù*, that had once been rejected in favor of the more celebrated pious monk of the Middle Ages. And yet, although secularization pronounced the triumph of man's self assurance (his ability to reason without the servile dependence on the medieval appeal to authority), it is entirely erroneous to think that the humanist impulse toward secularization was exclusively directed to worldliness alone. Christian ethics was still the foundation of this secular trend, and it is not surprising to find the pious scholar of the early Renaissance along side the "Machiavellian" prince of the age of despotic absolutism. The medieval legacy, particularly strong in the Iberian Peninsula, was not forgotten, but the secular trends altered its former vision of man significantly.

In the arts, this dualistic struggle of old and new produced exciting alternatives to the static notions of the past. In literature, for example, the antithetical patterns of medieval poetry such as the *debate* and the *disputatio* were incorporated into new dramatic conventions that could express the new vision of man. Duality was an important concept in the artistic tradition of drama, and was especially accomodating in this period of synthesis, of the alliance of Christian morality and pagan ideals. These medieval patterns of perception as well as the expression of new ideologies within their structures can be seen in the works of Gil Vicente who never totally disavowed the medieval conventions while seeking new forms of artistic expression. The historical background of this ideological and rhetorical perspective in the development of medieval poetry vis-à-vis dramatic forms may lead to a better understanding of this type of dialectical pattern of thought. In order to do this, however, it is essential to see briefly how these notions developed from antiquity, and how they were interpreted by the playwrights of the Middle Ages and the Renaissance.

2. *Early Notions about Duality*

Before Heraclitus (c. 544-484 B.C.) and Pythagoras (sixth century B.C.), philosophical explication was generally restricted to speculations about the permanence of primary matter. For the Pythagoreans the structure of reality as a dynamic concept of opposites was numerical, that is:

> All things had numbers and their odd and even values explained such opposites in things as one and many, square and oblong, straight and curved, rest and motion. Even light and dark are numerical opposites, as are male and female and good and evil" (Stumpf 12).

It was Heraclitus, however, who penetrated the very essence of change and its philosophical implications. Samuel Stumpf observes that for Heraclitus "the conflict of opposites is not a calamity but the permanent conditions of all things." He goes on to say that ". . . what appear to be disjointed events and contradictory forces are in reality intimately harmonized" (16).

When one compares these dynamic ideas of matter and their ideological implications with those of Gil Vicente in his letter, it becomes apparent that, although no direct influence can be found, the Portuguese poet and dramatist firmly believed in this type of world view. Joseph E. Gillet has traced the importance of this philosophical stance in Hispanic literature (58-62). He finds evidence of it in the disjunctive rhetorical devices of Juan Ruiz, Santillana, Jorge Manrique, Juan del Encina, Torres Naharro, Lucas Fernández and Gil Vicente. Many more names could be included, of course, but one classic work is decidedly missing from the list: Fernando de Rojas, the author of the *Celestina* (1499). This influential Spanish classic, the *Comédia de Calisto y Melibea* (i.e., *Celestina*), is the primary literary source not only for later models of dramatic works, but also for the type of antithetical ideology, the conflict between old and new, that is being considered here. It is in that work that the most significant statement about the duality of Renaissance thought in Iberian literature is brought to the foreground.

In the *Prólogo* to the 1502 edition (Sevilla) Alonso de Proaza, who is also credited with having added five new acts and the new title of *Tragicomedia* [!] *de Calisto y Melibea* to the *Celestina*, discusses the ideas he learned in Petrarch's *De Remediis utriusque fortunae* (1354-60) concerning this binary principle: "Todas las cosas ser criadas a manera de contienda o batalla, dize aquel gran sabio Eraclito en este modo: Omnia secundum litem fiunt. Sentencia a mi ver digna de perpetua y recordable memoria" (Rojas 15-16).

In these observations as well as in other comments about the dynamic Renaissance interaction of opposing forces, Proaza does not forget the venerable words of the fourteenth century Florentine Humanist and adds:

> Hallé esta sentencia corroborada por aquel gran orador e poeta laureado, Francisco Petrarcha, diziendo: "Sine lite atque offensione nihil genuit natura parens ... Sic est enim, et sic propemodum universa testantur: rapido stellae obviant firmamento; contraria inuicem elementa confligunt; terrae tremunt; maria fluctuant; aer quatitur; crepant flammae; bellum immortale venti gerunt; tempora temporibus concertant; secum singula, nobiscum omnia." (17).

Although there are definite words and even phrases that attest to the influence that this prologue and its source possibly had on Gil Vicente (cf. Vicente's "a tempestade dos ventos" vis-à-vis Petrarch's "bellum immortale venti gerunt"), it would be better to leave this problem unanswered for now, and discuss instead the more interesting philosophical import of these statements on the literary conventions of the age. It appears that Heraclitus' theory of opposites was fundamental not only in explaining the rationale of the incoming Renaissance spirit as opposed to the static scholastic tradition – the concept of "natural philosophy"; the line of thought that proceeds from human reason and not from faith or authority – but also the patterns of thought and, thereby, the structure of many works of literature that were influenced by this type of ideology.

In Rojas' *Comedia*, for example, one sees the underlying conflictive dualism that is conditioned by this type of philosophical concept. Stephen Gilman has already observed the importance of

Heraclitus's cosmology in his elaboration of the *Celestina*'s artistic structure and thematic significance:

> The best defense for this attempt to define the theme in terms of the *Prólogo* is that such a definition seems to work. Since Rojas does not permit any direct invocation of his authority, we must be consoled by the fact that the shopworn quotation from Heraclitus almost invites us to return to the text in a final attempt to summarize and integrate our several aspects of thematic art. In awareness of dialogue, the two major antagonists and causes are the alien universe which limits and destroys life and the sentiment of love which attempts to create from life autonomous significance (150).

In other words, the duality of thought that we find in the philosophical beliefs of Heraclitus and later Christian interpretations of his views is cast into a binary form when applied to a particular literary work. That is, the structure of the literary text is conditioned by this dualism that, at the same time, becomes the motivating principle of an artistic conception: the binary pattern. The specific outcome or resolution of the tensive elements at work in the literary text is a matter that, of course, belongs to either the comic vision or the tragic vision of life. In the humanistic period in question, the Christian vision of drama, as in Dante's *Commedia*, was comic; human reason had not yet made the empirical leaps that would eventually jeopardize the orthodox views of the Church.

From this comic, Christian perspective, the conflictive forces that battled in the natural world of phenomena, the imperfect world (cf. Vicente's "todolos movimentos... são litigiosos") are brought into peaceful unity through a harmonious plan designed by God (cf. Vicente's "pacíficas concordanças"). To the Neo-Platonic humanists this was identified with love or the light that emanates from the Divine.

This philosophical stance conditioned dramatic conventions as well. Humanist drama, in its attempt to depict the obstacles to social harmony, dramatized the socio-political upheavals of this feverish age of exploration and growth of secular activities. In doing so, these "learned men," fused the dynamic ideology of the new age with the Christian principles inherited from the past. By the same token, they did not forget the traditional literary conventions of the Middle Ages (cf. the "debate") which provided the basic structure for the new ideological "battles." It was an age so pregnant with the economic energy of capitalism, and so quick to adopt the new social categories imposed by the new order that only the dynamic philosophical views of Heraclitus could explain it's paradoxical turmoil. It was not by chance that the Greek philosopher was quoted often at the time. His philosophical ideas, as they were later interpreted by Christian theologians (e.g., St. Thomas Aquinas), allowed for the co-existence of reason and faith. A closer look at his ideas and their eventual reconstruction in the hands of later writers may help elucidate the harmonious viewpoint that guided the secular perspectives of Gil Vicente and his contemporaries.

As was suggested above, Heraclitus' views were not subordinated to the principle of chaos. In his metaphysical system, there was a supreme element (i.e., the *logos*) which governed the ever-changing course of natural phenomena. Although the *logos* doctrine was only later given theological significance, the moral implications of this "divine wisdom" *(logos)* became of special interest to the Humanist writers who dramatized their social problems by using categories in which peace and harmonious co-existence were the result of opposite values. One is here reminded, for example, of John Heywood's *Play of the Weather* (1525-33) or of Gil Vicente's *Cortes de Jupiter* (1521), in which the same judge-figure (Jupiter), representing the interests of his respective monarchy, imposes law and order as the statutes of Divine Justice would require. David Bevington has observed that the *Play of the Weather* is a prime example of this philosophical concept. He notes also that the influence of Boethius (c. 480-524) on this subject is made manifest in the Englishman's play:

> This medieval world view of order and degree sees an essential analogy between kingship and divine control of the four elements, earth, fire, air, and water. As in the great vision of Boethius, these elements, and the four corresponding qualities of cold, heat, wind, and rain, conspire to destroy one another until brought under the rule of God as the embodiment of harmony, dance, pattern, and Platonic being (991).

The author of the *Consolationis Philosóphiae* was not only a prominent figure in Christian thought, but also a very influential source for this type of philosophical theory of dualism. Boethius' writings retained the classic concepts of Heraclitus while giving special attention to the new Christian interpretation on the *logos* theory. In addition to his profound influence on the literature of the Middle Ages, Boethius seems to have been a favorite literary model for Gil Vicente, who, as Carolina Michaelis de Vasconcelos notes, was an avid reader of the earlier writer: "Creio bem que Gil Vicente a conhecia [i.e., *Consolationis*]. Não somente de fama, mas por leituras repetidas . . ." (252). She adds that Boethius' *Consolation of Philosophy* was well represented in the royal libraries of the Middle Ages, including that of Portugal: "Encontramo-lo pelo menos registado em todos os Catálogos de livrarias medievais, e citado em todas as obras filosóficas do século XV. (Por ex., no do *Condestável*, nos. 39 e 84, e no de *D. Manuel*, pag. 34 e 41)" (357).

It becomes clear, then, that the importance of Heraclitus' ideas to late medieval philosophy depended on its metaphysical possibilities of interpretation, on Neo-Platonic exegesis. That is, the integration of Christian ethical and moral theories to the philosopher's world view:

> The function of the logos in Heraclitus' world-scheme is manifold. The logos provides for order and for a definite outline of the cosmic structure. It sees to it that bounds are kept and chaos does not prevail. The logos has a moral meaning as well, for, according to Heraclitus, heavenly bodies are governed by moral laws, especially by the dictates of justice. In every way the world of nature and the world of morality can be identified. The result is that nature obeys the dictates of equity, that it is rational and law-abiding, not chaotic and tyrannical. If we want to understand the universe, Heraclitus advised, we must turn our minds to the logos. It is the measure of perfection and the criterion for human legislation. It is true that man's world is imperfect and quite inadequate, but when man sees the entire structure of the universe, Heraclitus thought, he understands the majesty and perfection of the world process (Mayer 37-38).

These words seem to echo those of Gil Vicente in his *Carta* of 1531. There too, as we noted earlier, the harmonious resolution of opposites allows for a poetic vision of "majesty" and "perfection" in the "entire structure of the universe." It directs attention to the basic idea that orients the patterns of thought in this age as well as of the new structural systems of comic drama. It is entirely within the orthodox views of the later Christian Church and, at the same time, reflects the secular ideas of the Humanist endeavor: social reform through (divinely inspired) justice. The humanistic return to wisdom (i.e., reason) through classical learning, as well as the new economic prosperity that ultimately defined and fixed the secular perspectives of this age, did not, as stated earlier, disregard the old order all together. Like Heraclitus' cosmological interpretation for his times – that the universe is governed by a dynamic process of thesis, antithesis, and synthesis of opposites – this humanistic age tried to integrate diverse modes of perception into a unified whole. As Harry E. Barnes reminds us, "Erasmus of Rotterdam (1466-1536), one of the greatest of humanists, occupied a position midway between extreme piety and frank secularism" (557). The protestant "synthesis" may be a clear example of this type of dialectical attempt at the resolution of an inherited pattern of thought in conflict with a new framework of existence.

Heraclitus, alone, however did not define the philosophical parameters of this age. The Greek philosopher from Ephesus may be the source for this ideology, but many are the writers who followed his thinking and adapted them into their own philosophical beliefs. We have already observed the influence of Boethius who saw a Divine purpose in the conflict between the four elements. The consolation that Lady Philosophy offers him, in fact, is greatly based on the principles of natural philosophy already observed in Heraclitus. The Christian metaphysical focus, however, differentiates the two world views radically. In the *Consolation of Philosophy*, which Boethius wrote while awaiting execution, the author relates to Lady Philosophy his own views on "the way the world is governed"; his explanation is reminiscent of the Vicentine idea:

> This world could never have achieved its unity of form from such different and contrary parts unless there were One who could bring together such diverse things. And, once this union was effected, the very diversity of discordant and opposed natures would have ripped it apart and destroyed it, if there

were not One who could sustain what He had made. Nor could the stable order of nature continue, nor its motions be so regular in place, time causality, space and quality, unless there were One who could govern this variety of change while remaining immutable Himself. This power, whatever it may be, by which created things are sustained and kept in motion, I call by the name which all men use, God (70).

Boethius knew, however, that God's divine plan was not comprehensible to man whose mind was capable of finite knowledge only. His subdivision of the Heraclitean unity of opposites (i.e., *logos*) into the spheres of Providence and Fate, so very popular from the Christian era to our own times, became the standard theological response to seemingly irreconcilable temporal disorder. Later, Lady Philosophy explains the inner workings of divine governance when she explains to the author that "When this government is regarded as belonging to the purity of the divine mind, it is called Providence; but when it is considered with reference to the things which it moves and governs, it has from the very early times been called Fate" (91). Lady Philosophy further explains this very important concept about the "order of chaos" in the universe when she states that ". . . Providence is the unfolding of temporal events as this is present to the vision of the divine mind; but this same unfolding of events as it is worked out in time is called fate" (90).

In his letter to the king, Gil Vicente is strong in his conviction that what appears to be a chaotic conflict of opposites to us on earth is, in fact, God's calculated design: ". . . e porque [Deus] nam quis que nenhua cousa tivesse perfeyta durança sobre a terra, estabaleceo na ordem do mundo que huas cousas dessem fim aas outras, e que todo o genero de cousa tivesse seu contrayro" (*Copilacam* fol. CCLVII). The intensity and force of the transitive verbs "querer" and "estabalecer" reflect the direct influence of God's will in implementing His divine plan. There is no room for doubting that such a conviction on the part of our dramatist was indeed a heartfelt reality which conditioned his world-view and, ultimately, the ideological premise of his dramatic design. If we consider the spiritual ideal that motivated Christian humanism (i.e., that all human powers of reason are directly dependent on God's will), it should not surprise us that the playwright of this period would preferably base his own structural pattern of dramatic presentation on that of the divine architect Himself. It is in this sense that Renaissance theater is true to the ritualistic impulse of all dramatic activity. This highly theological perspective of dramatic design is, I would propose, not only based on medieval rules of comic design (cf. Dante) but also the justification of the demonic world (i.e., devils, witches, and the forces of evil in general) as vehicles for the apocalyptic plan, a design that is far too complex for man's comprehension. An apparent paradox of the period, then, on an "actantial" level of the dramatic plot construction, also observable in Elizabethan drama, is thus perfectly tenable as an ironic device used by these Humanist playwrights to explain this highly theocentric type of world view. That is, the characters of the demonic world very often present themselves, unknowingly, as purveyors of the Divine Will.

In the period we are observing, the ideological and philosophical backgrounds for dramatic composition receive major emphasis from other classic thinkers as well. The theory of opposites, as a reflection of the binary pattern of reality that Heraclitus had exposed in his philosophy was also given attention by other philosophers that were influential in this age. We have already mentioned St. Augustine, supreme exponent of the duality principle in Christian theology (i.e., the unity of the two natures – divine and human – of Christ). Before discussing his very important thoughts about duality and its artistic impact, as well as his influence on Christian writers of the early Renaissance (especially, Gil Vicente), it would be well to consider another classic philosopher who is not only mentioned by Gil Vicente in the *Comédia de Rubena,* but who also exercised a profound influence on Renaissance versions of the dualistic process being considered here: Plato.

With the recovery of the classical literature that gave further impulse to the humanistic drive for reasoned patterns of behavior, Plato was to replace Aristotle, the principle source for scholastic dialecticians of the Middle Ages, as the model of philosophical (and literary) appeal. Especially important was the Christian synthesis of the Platonic ideas attempted by the Neo-Platonists (e.g., Plotinus, c. 204-270) who believed that matter "emanated" from the (divine) spirit in much the same way that man was related to his soul. The Christian interpretation saw man's soul struggling for the liberation from matter in its attempt to regain unity with God.

Artistically, these ideas mirrored an aesthetic concern that reflected the refined propensity and transcendent qualities of literary discourse in this age of humanistic endeavor. The concept of Beauty as a metaphysical Form or Idea was an immutable absolute to Plato and his followers, not an existential abstraction of form, shape, or other temporal category. Like the human soul, then, it inhabited the realm of the eternal and, as a corollary to that notion, artistic expression ideally sought the eternal sphere of pure essence. Platonic thought and later Neo-Platonic elaborations on those metaphysical notions of reality were, therefore, an important influence in the literary manifestations of the age.

Especially important to the idea of duality, however, is Plato's own concept of opposites which he expressed in his time-honored metaphor of the cave dwellers. This dichotomy between the world of light and the world of shadows is yet another expression of the duality in human existence. Although entirely divorced from Christian theology, in designating the world of Ideas or Forms as the true and positive principle of human existence, Plato too expounded an "... ethical concern by adding to the concept of Good a theory of metaphysics, an explanation of the whole structure of reality and the place of morality in it" (Stumpf 61).

The Platonic struggle between realms of light and darkness and the many dialectical variations that these oppositions can express both for him and later thinkers – Appetite vs. Reason, Body vs. Soul – is unified when "reason" restores balance to the opposing entities. The "reason" or mind that brings harmony to the confusion of the cosmos is what Plato termed the *demiurge*, a force which in Christian theology was translated by the term God. In human psychology, or in its societal outward manifestation (i.e., ethical behavior), the harmonious expression of inner well-being was a condition which reflected the effects of virtue. That is, of morality not only related to a cultural expression of socially acceptable standards, but also as it applies to an absolutely essential quality of reason to maintain balance or harmony in the individual, to maintain the soul's health, as it were: Reason has a function, and reason is good only when it is acting as reason should.

As Stumpf observes "... one's reason is not fulfilling its function, if it is overrun by passion. At the same time, spirit has a function, and so do appetites, and the good life is achieved only when every part is fulfilling its function" (71). In his writings, there are several places (especially in the *Timaeus*) where Plato compares the soul's inner balance with the harmony of music, a favorite commonplace in Renaissance expression as well as a direct reflection of this philosophical perspective:

> Quand on cultive avec intelligence le commerce des Muses, l'harmonie, dont les mouvements sont semblables a ceux de notre âme, ne paraît pas desinée à servir, comme elle le fait maintenant, à de frivoles plaisirs; les Muses nous l'ont donnee pour nous aides à régler sur elle et soumettre à ses lois les mouvements désordonnés de notre âme, comme elles nous ont donné le rhythme pour reformer les manières depourvues de mesure et de grâce de la plupart des hommes (Plato *Timée* 149). [2]

With the vogue of Neo-Platonism in the Renaissance (e.g., Cosimo de Medici's Platonic Academy of Florence) this musical metaphor became a powerful vehicle for the expression of the quality so much admired at this time: *virtù* or temperance in moral behavior; that is, the harmony of the soul that only human virtue through the exercise of reason can attain. That this harmony is produced through the tension of opposite forces, as Heraclitus suggested, is observable in a passage of Plato's *Symposium*, where the doctor Eryximachos discusses the earlier philosopher's theory in detail:

> You see one must be able to make loving friends of the greatest enemies in the body. Now the greatest enemies are the most opposite, hot and cold, bitter and sweet, dry and wet, and so forth; our ancestor Asclepios, as our poets here say and I believe, composed our art because he knew how to implant love and concord in these. Then the healing art, as I say, is all guided by this god, and so is gymnastic and agriculture; music too is clearly in the same case with this, as it is plain to anyone who thinks for a moment; and perhaps that is what Heracleitos means, since his words are not very clear. He says, "The One

---

[2] Although there are other Platonic references to the harmony of the eternal spheres and, by association, to the soul (cf. *The Republic*, VII; *Phaedo, Symposium*, etc.), the statement from the *Timaeus* is especially significant due to Chalcidius' early fourth century translation. C. S. Lewis explains that in the Middle Ages "Of Plato himself they had little more than an incomplete Latin version of a single dialogue, the *Timaeus*" (43).

at variance with itself is brought together again, like a harmony of bow and lyre." It is quite illogical to say that a *harmony* is at *variance* with itself or is made up of notes still *at variance*. But perhaps he meant to say that it was made from the high and low notes – first ar variance, then afterwards reconciled together by the art of music. For I suppose there could not be harmony from high and low notes still at variance, for harmony is symphony and symphony is a kind of agreement; but agreement there cannot be of things ar variance so long as they are at variance. But what is at variance, and yet is not unable to be brought into agreement, it is impossible to harmonize. Just so rhythm is made from quick and slow, first differing, then brought into agreement (83).

This harmony of tension is dramatized again and again in humanist renditions of comic drama. In the Hispanic Peninsula the most influential work of the period – the *Celestina* – uses the Platonic metaphor of music to reflect the lover's (Calisto's) state of perplexity: "¿Cómo templará el destemplado? ¿Cómo sentirá el armonia aquel, que consigo está tan discorde? ¿Aquel en quien la voluntad a la razón no obedece?" (Rojas 39-40). Calisto clearly expresses here the concept of "loco amor," the love of pleasure, when he admits that his desire does not obey the moral laws of reason. The distemperance of those who seek love at its lowest level, a Neo-Platonic notion borrowed by Christian moralists, is an attitude that outlines the Christian views on comedy. More specifically, the *comedia*, as genre, is in "tune" not only with the Christian world view of right and wrong, but also with the very important Peninsular concept of "poetic justice," the righting of wrongs that, as we discussed earlier, is an integral part of the Hispanic sense of comedy (cf. A. A. Parker's remark).

That Gil Vicente was aware of the Platonic concept of harmony and its moral and spiritual implications, is well documented in his *Comédia de Rubena* where the "Príncipe" declares that "Mas alta, dize Platon, es la virtude que el estado; . . ." (175). But the harmonious element that the Portuguese dramatist discussed in his *Carta* finds other channels of Platonic expression as well. It is not by coincidence of plot design that Cismena in the *Comédia de Rubena* rejects her frivolous suitors who, like Calisto in the *Celestina,* are examples of this type of unreasoned love. In this *Comédia* the function of the musical metaphor is once again used to emphasize the discord that Felicio feels when Dario Ledo tunes his guitar:

>   (Felicio)   Em tudo a hi temperança
>   por mais que se destempera;
>   mas meu mal não se tempera
>   porque não tem concordança
>   nem comigo não se espera!
>   com razão, quebrar-me fortuna mera
>   as cordas do coração
>   com que nacer não devera! (134-35)

Felicio is here declaring, unknowingly, as a dramatic "anagnorisis", the moral and spiritual consequences that unreasoned love can bring. Like the fictional model, Calisto, in the earlier *Comedia de Calisto e Melibea*, he too will suffer the blows of non-harmonious love.

The moral and metaphysical implications of Plato's ideas about the theory of opposites is preserved in the Neo-Platonists (e.g., Chalcidius, Plotinus, etc.) who in turn were very influential in the writings of the early Christian theologians of the patristic period. Among the most important is, of course, St. Augustine who has already been mentioned as a proponent of this type of ideology. The Platonic ideas about love which Plotinus maintained in his rendition, especially the purifying ascent through knowledge and virtue to the ecstatic union of self with the One (God), is given special significance by St. Augustine who, in Stumpf's words, "... saw in the *Enneads* of Plotinus a strikingly new explanation of evil and of salvation through orderly love" (138). He adds that "Through Augustine, Neo-Platonism became a decisive element in the intellectual expression of the Christian faith during the Middle Ages" (138).

Similar to the dualistic thinkers, but much more theological in intent, St. Augustine too was plagued with the presence of evil and conflict in a world created by a divine will. Perplexed by this enigma he first turned to the Manicheans, who taught that the two basic principles eternally at odds in the universe were light and darkness, symbolic representations of good and evil. This rational theory of opposites intrigued St. Augustine but it did not provide the moralistic channel to salvation that he desired.

In his theological treatise – *The City of God* – he reflects the duality of his earlier models – the Manichean philosophy – in the basic two part, thematic, division of this work: The City of God and the earthly city. Unlike the Manicheans, however, St. Augustine believed in the intrinsic goodness of the created world, for matter had been the product of God's divine nature and could, therefore, not be evil. This idea brings us close once again to the Heraclitean and Boethian concepts, for here we see a view that presupposes some divine purpose or intellectual determination in secular affairs. This, as we will recall, reflects Heraclitus's *logos* as well as Boethius' concept of God's Providence which orders the chaotic, earthly elements according to a predetermined divine plan.

In the realm of moral philosophy St. Augustine postulated, in keeping with the Platonic theory of emanation, that only love can lead man back to God. Faithful also to the principles of duality outlined above, he opposed the love of God to that of pure sensation – lust – which damned man to the fires of hell. This type of love leads to pride for it assumes that man can satisfy for himself an infinite need through finite means. Evil is, therefore, presented to man as a choice, for man is free to choose. Virtue, stated St. Augustine, is the means given to man for reordering the disordered type of love that leads him to damnation.

Like Heraclitus, St. Augustine's theory of natural law – the law that governs the city of the world – reflects the dominion and mechanism of a (Christian) *logos* or supreme entity. That classic entity (i.e., the *logos*), as expressed through reason and will, is God when transferred to the theology of St. Augustine. If justice in man's world was a natural law that reflected God's divine law, then equity in man's affairs was a supreme principle of secular endeavors. It was reflected in man's virtue, the only behavioral trait that was commensurate with the theological concept of justice. In addition to this, this aspect of man's secular ideal, inspired as it was from God's perfect design, was an innate element; it shared its intrinsic nature with eternal law, and reflected, as it were, the primordial law of the "two cities." This standard was also recognized in Plato's moral philosophy, the only evidence of direct Platonic influence in Gil Vicente. All things being governed by this harmonious standard of eternal and natural law, it follows that Love ("caritas"), the point of contact that bridges man with man as well as God with man, is the foundation of justice. It is the harmonizing principle in the conflictive nature of man.

The problem that Gil Vicente encountered in Santarém, however, still remained: how to justify divine equity, governance, in a world split by contradicting elements? St. Augustine's reply anticipates that of the Portuguese dramatist's answer. Peace or unison within the secular domain was to St. Augustine, as it was to Gil Vicente, the "appropriate use" or "value" of "apparent evil." In this harmonizing perspective which Boethius also elaborated in his *Consolation of Philosophy*, St. Augustine fixed the standard not only for a very important theological view (i.e., Providence and Fate in Christian philosophy), but also presented the earliest aesthetic implications of this view, for by insisting on the "beauty" of God's design he elaborated an aesthetic theory:

> Take the case of man's visible appearance. An eyebrow is virtually nothing compared with the whole body; but shave it off and what an immense loss to this beauty! For beauty does not depend on mere size, but on the symmetry and proportion of the component parts (454).

St. Augustine's artistic conception, then, is highly theocentric, and it influenced the writers of the Middle Ages as well as the Christian humanists of the early Renaissance. In the secular notions of Gil Vicente, as witnessed by his own words in the letter of 1531, we observe some conclusions arising from the same motivating principle: the beauty that arises from a providential ordering of conflictive secular materials. The African theologian's metaphysical concern with these aesthetic precepts is more explicitly rendered in chapter eighteen (Book XI) of the *City of God*: "The beauty of the universe, made richer by God's providence, through the opposition of contraries." The importance of this very influential statement on later medieval and humanist theories concerning the structural patterns of literary discourse and, more specifically, comic drama, warrants the inclusion of this short chapter almost in its entirety:

> For God would never have created a man, let alone an angel, in the the foreknowledge of his future evil state, if he had not known at the same time how he would put such creatures to

good use, and thus enrich the course of the world history by the kind of antithesis which gives beauty to a poem. "Antithesis" provides the most attractive figures in literary composition: the Latin equivalent is "opposition," or more accurately, "contra-position". . . . The opposition of such contraries gives an added beauty to speech; and in the same way there is beauty in the composition of the world's history arising from the antithesis of contraries – a kind of eloquence in events, instead of in words. This point is made very clearly in the book Ecclesiasticus, "Good confronts evil, life confronts death: so the sinner confronts the devout." And in this way you should observe all the works of the Most High; two by two; one confronting the other (449).

The Christian perspective of literary discourse, then, was conditioned by this harmonizing theoretical stance toward the tension of opposites. We have already observed the medieval vogue for the "debate," the "disputations" and other forms of underlying binary structures in the literary compositions of the Middle Ages. These structural patterns were not necessarily abandoned at the onset of the Renaissance but rather adapted to new ideological concerns (e.g., as in the morality play). This is especially true in the Iberian Peninsula where, as we have noted elsewhere, the medieval framework was not abandoned but rather transformed into a new reality by evaluating and incorporating the new Humanism within the parameters of its past traditions. Bevington has noted this earlier influence on the humanist drama of England which, like the popular tastes of medieval Spain and Portugal, retained its peculiarly medieval characteristic:

> Although the "new learning" of humanism does represent the sort of change we associate with the term "Renaissance," humanist drama is derived in many important ways from medieval literature and especially from traditions of courtly entertainment (968).

The intricate beauty of the Christian pattern of thought devised by St. Augustine may, of course, be associated with the conflictive duality (and ultimate victory) of the Christian ideal: the *City of God* vs. the earthly city. It is here that his conceptual pattern of binarism has its most eloquent statement:

> My task is to discuss, to the best of my power, the rise, the development and the destined ends of the two cities, the earthly and the heavenly, the cities which we find, as I have said, interwoven, as it were, in this present transitory world, and mingled with one another (430).

All the philosophical views about duality, especially in a specifically Christian context, that have been outline above point out that the binary pattern was seen as particularly well suited to the ideological and even aesthetic needs of the age. This mythic pattern of thought was subliminally reproduced first as an archetypal arrangement – system – of human behaviour through religious ritual and, later, through other less theocentric forms of artistic mimesis (e.g., literary discourse) fostered at the onset of the Renaissance. If, for a moment, one may consider comic drama as a ritualistic process, a mythic projection of man's ideal for harmony and union with his environment and/or that of the gods, then it becomes evident that the historical, theological, ideological, philosophical, context of his endeavor is extremely important in determining the aesthetic characteristics of his art forms. We have observed this process of displacement in the secularization of earlier ritualistic forms of expression (e.g., the *cantigas*), where the humanist dramatist retained the older forms while adapting them to a new contextual reality. At the heart of this procedure lies a binary pattern of opposing tensions which was delimited by the sense of dualism and harmonization of the Christian period.

While we may agree with those critics that see binarism as the universal principle operative in human behavior and, of special interest here, in man's artistic manifestations, it is also true that the ideological and philosophical parameters that condition the relationship of these structural patterns is a matter that will ultimately determine generic distinctions in a given period of time. The concept of unity in drama, for example, as a manifestation of the Aristotelian notion of the organic arrangement of parts, must be understood in relation to these contextual ideas, for only then can unity be correctly defined. Beckerman has already observed this important aspect of Elizabethan drama when he states that "A work of art must be able to be perceived as a totality [!] by the audience. Here, of course, we have the true determinant of unity" (*Shakespeare* 59).

Once again it becomes apparent that the unity of comic action in this age of Christian humanism is qualified by theocentric notions of poetics. Like St. Augustine who saw man's history as a comic drama resolved in the harmonious apprehension of tension and conflict of the two cities, Gil Vicente and his contemporaries dramatized a similar struggle, one which reflected the concerns of their own age while not forgetting the comic formulas of the medieval past.

The medieval version of comedy, as Dante would prescribe, may differ radically from our extremely secularized modern-day renditions, but at the bottom of it all we may observe a basic structural pattern that is determined by the universal elements of the comic vision. In the section that follows we will observe how the same pervasive system of duality can be used to define Gil Vicente's (comic) world: that of God or of religious epiphany, and that of man or of the earthly joys that his communion with God brings.

B) THE VICENTINE FARSAS, COMÉDIAS AND TRAGICOMÉDIAS

The *Copilaçam* of 1562, printed in Lisbon by Luis Vicente, contains the collected works of Gil Vicente, his father. This first edition distributes the Vicentine dramatic and non-dramatic (e.g., the letter of 1531 discussed earlier) achievement in five distinct categories: *Obras de devaçam, Comédias, Tragicomédias, Farsas* and *Obras miudas*.[3] If one considers only the dramatic pieces, the basic division that the *Copilaçam* offers is that of the religious works (*Obras de devaçam*) and the secular dramatic pieces (*Comédias, Farsas* and *Tragicomédias*), a dichotomy which roughly corresponds to the Vicentine concept of the two worlds ("os dous mundos") that has already been discussed. The duality principle and its theological implications appear to be the only valid and exacting criteria that can be used in the classification of these dramatic pieces, especially

---

[3] The *Auto da Festa* recovered by the Conde de Sabugosa in 1906 was omitted from the original (1562) edition. Two other plays, *Auto de Deus Padre, Justiça e Misericórdia* and *Obras da Geração Humana*, are assumed to be the work of Gil Vicente but some critics have denied this hypothesis. The very controversial *Jubileu de Amore* is no longer extant (J. H. Parker 23-24).

if we examine the many ambiguities that are associated with Luis Vicente's generic considerations as well as later categorizations. The *Auto da Visitação*, for example, a plainly secular piece with farcical elements, appears within the category of *Obras de devaçam;* perhaps due to the religious association of the birth of Christ with the birth of the Prince D. João III (1502). The confusion of generic terminology is further evidenced in *Romagem de Agravados* listed as a "tragicomédia" in the *Copilaçam*, where it also appears, according to the instructions, as a "Comédia" (Saraiva *Gil Vicente* 90-91). The equivocal nature of generic nomenclature at this early period of humanistic endeavor in drama appears to be the result of the desintegration of medieval theatrical categories in favor of new "classical" forms of Renaissance drama. Often this was done merely as an external manifestation of classical dramatic influence, for it has already been pointed out that in the development of humanist drama the older, medieval forms of dramatic discourse were only slightly altered to reflect the changing ideology of the age.

Something akin to this happens in the *Celestina* where, as has been previously pointed out, the contributing editor (Proaza), feeling the pressure of a more exacting humanist audience, abandoned the medieval notions of *comedia*, a term which was traditionally more eclectic (cf. Dante's *Commedia*) and more yielding to theological considerations. In the prologue of the Spanish work the editor refers to the work itself as a "comedia" before introducing the notion of "tragicomedia" which critics see as a compromise similar to that observed in Plautus' *Amphytruo*. It is interesting, furthermore, that in discussing the conflict of opposites uncovered by the *Celestina*, the editor observes that no one can be sure of a unique interpretation because of its arbitrary duality: "Assí que quando diez personas se juntaren a oyr esta *comedia* [italics are mine], en quien quepa esta differencia de condiciones, como suele acaescer, ¿quién negará que aya contienda en cosa que de tantas maneras se entienda?" (Rojas 24-25). Further on, Proaza, having used the term *comedia* earlier in his discourse, hesitatingly decides to classify the *comedia* as a *tragicomedia:*

> Otros han litigado sobre el nombre, diziendo que no se auía de llamar comedia, pues acabaua en tristeza, sino que se llamasse

tragedia. El primer auctor quiso darle denominación del principio, que fue plazer, e llamóla comedia. Yo viendo estas discordias, entre estos extremos partí agora por medio la porfía, e llamela tragicomedia" (25).

Why did Proaza make this change, if his convictions were not motivated by structural categories? It seems that the humanist vogue of the new-found Italian conventions of drama (e.g., *Fernandus Servatus*), was strong in determining the new bipartite category. Gil Vicente or, as many believe, his son may have used the same a-critical stance; that is, of following the new Italian theatrical terminology in drama. For his part, Proaza defends his position when he wrote "... miré a donde la mayor parte acostava..." (26).

The new conventions of drama, whatever their criteria may have been, are at the very foundation of Gil Vicente's comic formula. Under the influence of the Renaissance dramatic impetus, and cognizant of the need for change in his theatrical orientation, Gil Vicente embarks in 1521 on a truly significant theatrical undertaking. This new type of comic expression will result in the development of a generic formula which, along with the dramatic activity of Torres Naharro, will help forge the Hispanic concept of *comedia*. Uncertain about the new artistic forms and yet lured by the refined nature of the incoming humanist dramatic impetus, Gil Vicente endeavored to reinvigorate his poetic enterprise within the aesthetic preferences of his learned court audience. These new, elite forces in the artistic expression of the Renaissance dramatists are expressed by Gil Vicente in a dedicatory letter to King D. João III. The letter introduces the "Tragicomédia" of *Dom Duardos* (1522):

> Como quiera, excelente Príncipe y Rey muy poderoso, que las comédias, farças y moralidades que he compuesto en servicio de la Reina vuestra tía, cuanto en casos de amores, fueron figuras baxas, en las cuales no havía conveniente retórica que pudiesse satisfazer al delicado spíritu de V. A., conocí que me cumplía meter más velas a mi pobre fusta. Y assí como desseo de ganar su contentamiento hallé lo que en estremo desseava, que fue Don Duardos y Flérida, que son tan altas figuras como su historia recuenta, con tan dulce retórica y escogido estilo, cuanto se puede alcançar en la humana inteligencia (Teyssier 87).

The new Portuguese court audience, having received influences from abroad through the cultural contact of exploration and through the international dissemination of Renaissance achievements (e.g., the invention of the printing press, economic and political ties with other countries, etc.) demanded a more cultivated kind of poetic skill from their court writers and impresarios:

> A superfície de contacto entre Portugal e a Europa ampliou-se muito e talvez por essa altura se tenha introduzido a idéia de que a *cultura nasce lá fora;* do mesmo modo que ao dinheiro e a todos os produtos manufacturados, é preciso importá-la. Os canais da importação são vários: estudantes portugueses nos centros literários estrangeiros, bolseiros nomeados pelo rei nas universidades de nomeada, professores de outros países contratados para ensinar em Portugal, aos príncipes ou na Universidade. (Saraiva *História* 174)

In the letter to D. João III Gil Vicente underscores the new aesthetic preferences of the cultivated royal court in the first decades of sixteenth century Lisbon. He notes, for example, the lack of literary refinement ("conveniente retórica") in his former plays and emphasizes his need to upgrade his poetic skills: ". . . conocí que me cumplía meter más velas a mi pobre fusta." This humanist spirit of stylistic embellishment is observable in other cultures as well. In England, for example, dramatic trends were echoing the same aesthetic concerns about the emerging Renaissance theater. The prologue to Nicholas Udall's *Ralph Roister Doister* (1550-1553) points to this interest in the new artistic directions of the incoming Renaissance. Udall's comment reiterates that of Gil Vicente (in the *Comédia sobre a Cidade de Coimbra*):

> What creature is in health, either young or old,
> But some mirth with modesty will be glad to use –
> As we in this interlude shall now unfold?
> Wherein all scurrility we utterly refuse,
> Avoiding such mirth wherein is abuse;
> knowing nothing more commendable for a man's recreation
> Than mirth which is used in an honest fashion. (Udall 266)

Years before this statement made by the English scholar and dramatist, Gil Vicente had already expressed the same dramatic concern with the excesses of "abuse" of low forms of comedy. The orientation of drama now, however, was elitist and required the necessary linguistic embellishment to suit the new tastes. In the *Comédia sobre a Divisa da Cidade de Coimbra* (1527), Gil Vicente wrote that the earlier farces were not as elegant as the new *comédia* which he now offered to the King: "Sabey que as farsas todas chocarreiras, nam sam muito finas sem outros primores." This feeling of renewal, then, was a penetrating element which created the foundation of a new dramatic type in Peninsular drama. That form, as we shall observe in more detail, was the *comedia*, a structure that incorporated sound "mirth" and seriousness of intent with excellence of poetic diction. Following Révah's opinion, yet differing somewhat as to generic criteria, Teyssier in a recent book about Gil Vicente has recognized the importance of this new found expression in the dramatic career of Gil Vicente and its subsequent importance in differentiating his concept of *comédia* from other dramatic genres practiced earlier by the Portuguese dramatist:

> As comédias compõem a terceira das categorias mencionadas na carta-prefácio de *Dom Duardos*. E é também o último gênero a aparecer na seqüencia da obra do autor. Havia dezanove anos, com efeito, que Gil Vicente tinha iniciado a sua carreira de escritor teatral quando comecou a elaborar estes autos de novo tipo. Foi em 1521, justamente no final do reinado de D. Manuel, que fez representar *Rubena*, a sua primeira comédia romanesca, e *Cortes de Júpiter*, primeira comédia alegórica. Estas duas obras significam no conjunto da produção vicentina uma fissura fundamental. (82-83)

For his part, Révah had already emphasized this giant leap forward in the development of this type of dramatic composition in the Iberian Peninsula: "... pour les *Comédias de Rubena* et *das Cortes de Júpiter*, nul doute n'est possible: une nouvelle forme théâtrale se dégage nettement et elle va désormais accaparer l'essentiel de l'activité de Gil Vicente" ("La *comédia*" 33).

The concept of "comédia romanesca," which most critics continue to assert as the distinguishing factor of the Vicentine *comédia* is believed to define the specific generic contributions of the *Comédia de Rubena*. With this "romanesca" label the Portuguese critic, António José Saraiva, had already identified the generic attributes of this type of comedy. This foremost critic of Vicentine studies classified the *Tragicomédia de Don Duardos*, the *Tragicomédia do Amadís de Gaula*, the *Comédia do Viúvo*, and the *Comédia de Rubena* as romanesque comedies ("comédias romanescas") in his book *Gil Vicente e o Fim do Teatro Medieval*. According to Saraiva, the romanesque category is related to the narrative categories of medieval chivalric literature from which these four plays derived their basic generic distinctions. Later critics reaffirmed Saraiva's classification without defining the term ('romanesca") more precisely. It is important, therefore, to reconsider first the criteria used in making these affirmations before attempting a new interpretation of the structural units that distinguish the Vicentine *comédia* – *Comédia de Rubena* and *Comédia do Viúvo* – from the other two plays in question: the *Tragicomédia de Dom Duardos* and the *Tragicomédia de Amadis*. Saraiva appears to have based his opinion about the "romanesca" category only on the two "tragicomédias" when he states:

> O teatro romanesco, completamente diferenciado daquele [the medieval miracle play], aparece bem representado. Gil Vicente aproveitou temas romanescos, utilizando por vezes as novelas de cavalaria, em a *Tragicomédia de Dom Duardos*, a *Comédia do Viúvo*, a *Comédia de Rubena* e a *Tragicomédia do Amadís de Gaula* (95-96).

It is true that the chivalric sources for the *Tragicomédias* have been identified (i.e., the *Amadís de Gaula* of 1508 and the *Primaleón* of 1512) but neither Saraiva nor any other critic since his statement has shown the exact narrative sources for the *Comédia de Rubena* nor for the *Comédia do Viúvo*. There is no doubt that these last two plays are strongly influenced by the chivalric and sentimental novel tradition of medieval narratives, but the inventive quality *(inventatio)* that, I believe, differentiates them from the other two plays is a most important element of distinction. We will recall that medieval theatrical traditions used this distinction for the classification of comic drama.

Although later critics echoed similar affirmations, it is obvious that some differences were indeed perceived by them in distinguishing between the two categories above. These distinctions are extremely important in judging the generic attributes of each type of play, for the differences between medieval rhetorical modes of literary discourse (i.e., *inventio* and *imitatio*) are crucial to an understanding of comic development. Whereas Saraiva saw the dramatic poverty of the *Comédia de Rubena* and *Comédia do Viúvo*, Révah, using the same terminology (i.e., "romanesque") appears to have noted the dramatic uniqueness of the *Comédia de Rubena* when he states that along with the *Cortes de Júpiter* these two plays were "l'essentiel de l'activité de Gil Vicente." It is interesting to note that Saraiva has since changed his judgement concerning Gil Vicente's dramatic incapacity, however, and, in fact, has recently restated his position on the matter:

> Não subscrevo hoje todas as teses do meu livrinho de 1942. . . . Em particular, sustentava eu, aí, que a arte cénica de Gil Vicente teria conhecido um pouco a mesma sorte que a arte gótica. . . . Daí o eu ver como única arte cénica possível, a partir do Renascimento, o teatro psicológico cujas obras mais acabadas são o drama Shakespeareano e a tragédia de Racine. . . . E como Gil Vicente me parecia nem sequer suspeitar de uma tal evolução, como ele tinha voltado as costas ao teatro psicológico, dando-nos alegorias, símbolos, tipos e caricaturas, em vez de caracteres, afigurava-se-me que ele tinha cortado a saída a sí próprio, que era pura e simplesmente um fecho, embora um fecho maravilhoso ("Gil Vicente" 465-66).

As it relates to the genre distinctions that we are observing, the importance of these statements might at first appear to be unrelated, but the dramatic significance that Révah and others have noted in the *Comédia de Rubena*, a significance which Saraiva had once denied, is a factor which is crucial to its generic configuration. Unlike his *tragicomédias*, Gil Vicente's *comédias* are an expression of inventive genius, an attempt to bridge the wide gap between the mere dramatization of narrative, poetic as it might be, and dramatic genesis itself. It is understood that these first attempts should be awkward, the work of a "primitivo" (from our modern perspective) who still depends on the symbolic conventions and the motifs of medieval theater. The Hispanic Torres Naharro hailed inventiveness as a fundamental precept in the dramatic elaboration of comedy. It was considered an important innovation when compared to the earlier pastoral influences of the Virgilian models (e.g., Encina, Fernández, etc.) as well as the later adaptations of other literary sources (i.e., the *Amadís* and the *Primaleón*). Saraiva has observed that both the *Farsa de Inês Pereira* and the *Tragicomédia do Amadís* share a narrative construction, but overlooked the essential differences that underlie the dramatic significance of each work. He offers a clue to the issue, however, when he observes that "Quanto ao *Auto de Inês Pereira*. . . . é uma peça narrativa. . . . A história é inspirada por um proverbio *popular* [italics are mine] . . ." ("Gil Vicente" 467).

The difference seems to lie in the key word "popular," an aspect of the *Farsa de Inês Pereira* that widens the gap between it, as an example of popular inspiration and inventive genius (sharing these elements with the *comédia*), and the more linguistically refined, styllistically elaborated, and ideologically elite *tragicomédias*. The *comédia*, then, appears before us as an integration of two dramatic forces that define Peninsular dramaturgy: popular inspiration (i.e., "chocarreiras") as well as the artistic or poetic excellence of the new Renaissance dramatic discourse (i.e., embellished with "primores"). From one type it chose its aristocratic flavor and from the other its national inspiration and popular appeal.

When Révah affirmed that the *Comédia de Rubena* exhibited qualities that were "essential" to the artistic excellence of Gil Vicente it is my opinion that it was this quality of popular inventiveness that he had in mind; that is, the ability to adapt his national and circumstancial reality to "modern" – contemporary – spirit and forms of dramatic expression, preferring the "imago veritatis" approach to his environment while rejecting the scholastic model of authorial wisdom and servile imitation. The dramatic plot construction of the *comédias*, as we shall observe, is affected by this popular inspiration as well as the conventions of dramatic design that Gil Vicente had before him. Inventiveness, originality, and an acute preoccupation with the aesthetic quality of his plays are some of the artistic elements that will distinguish the Vicentine *comédia* from earlier, more "primitive," forms of dramatic discourse.

There are still critics, however, who do not see these differences between the Vicentine *comédia* and *tragicomédia*. Teyssier, for example, basing his opinion on the prefatory letter to the *Dom Duardos* (1522), has decided to follow the tripartite division mentioned in that document:

> Acontece, de facto, que o próprio Gil Vicente se pronunciou sobre a questão. Na carta-prefácio em espanhol em que oferece *Dom Duardos* a D. João III, fala das "comédias, farças y moralidades" que compôs ao serviço da rainha Dona Leonor. Eram essas, conseqüentemente, as três categorias em que classificava os seus autos, pelo menos em 1522, data aproximada da apresentação de *Dom Duardos*. Parece-nos assim melhor deixar-nos orientar por esta divisão tripartida. É o que fazem, na esteira de I. S. Révah, muitos críticos actuais (43).

There are several historical reasons, however, why this classification is not tenable. Although most Vicentine specialists are in agreement as to the apocryphal nature of the term "tragicomédia," a category believed to be unknown as a structural reality to Gil Vicente and misinterpreted in the *Copilaçam* by his son Luis, it should not be assumed that the organizational principles of this "pseudo-genre" has not been considered in some way (e.g., perhaps through the *prólogo* of the *Tragicomedia [!] de Calisto y Melibea*) by the Portuguese dramatist as distinct from his former (i.e., in 1514 and in 1521) *comédias*.

In addition to this, it would appear that Teyssier has overlooked the prefatory statements in reference to the dates he ascribes to the plays in question, especially if the chronological ordering of the four plays is taken into consideration. If we consider that Gil Vicente's *Comédia de Rubena* was represented in 1521 and that the *Dom Duardos* was represented, or read as a closet drama in the royal court, a year later (1522), then it becomes apparent that in the tripartite division (i.e., "comédias, farças, y moralidades"), Gil Vicente was making a generic distinction between the *former* "comédias, farças y moralidades," and this new type of dramatic composition, the *tragicomédia,* now offered to the King (D. João III) as a gift. A changing elitist spirit of the royal court in Lisbon might have provided the basis for this aristocratic swing in dramaturgical practices.

This could certainly be the meaning of the past and present distinctions that Gil Vicente specifies in the structural principles that he outlines in the letter. It is evident from the past tenses of the verbs used to describe the former style – "he compuesto"; "fueron"; "no havía"; "conocí," etc. – that Gil Vicente is here opposing structural categories of the former plays to those of the play he is now offering to the King. More specifically, Gil Vicente, whether he chose to call this new type of dramatic composition *tragicomédia* or not, is differentiating it as to characterization ("figuras baxas" versus "altas figuras"), style ("escogido estilo"), diction ("dulce retórica"), and even source (the popular inspiration of the *comédia* versus the "historia" of the *tragicomédia*).

According to the date given in the *Copilaçam*, the *Comédia do Viúvo* was written in 1514. This would place it before the aesthetic period that has been observed above, the period of the Vicentine *comédia*. Teyssier and Révah, however, have found convincing evidence that would assign the *comédia* to a later date, somewhere between 1521-1524:

> Un dernier problème chronologique retiendra notre attention: celui de la *Comédia do Viúvo*. Il est important, car c'est de lui que dépend l'explication de la genèse de la *comédia* vicentine. La *Compilaçam* déclare que la *Comédia do Viúvo* "foy representada na era do Senhor de M. D. XIII [in reality it reads M. D. XIIII in the facsimile edition]." Notons d'abord que, sans grand souci de la logique, la même édition affirme que la *Comédia de Rubena*, de 1521, est la *première* des comédies vicentines. Il est impossible de concilier les deux affirmations.... L'acceptation de la date de 1514 conduirait à de nombreuses impossibilités. Ayant inventé la *comédia* romanesque peninsulaire en 1514, Gil Vicente aurait attaché si peu de prix à son invention qu'il ne s'en serait souvenu qu'en 1521, sept ans après, avec la *Comédia de Rubena*. Ayant redécouvert la *comédia* a cette date, il lui consacrera la partie essentielle de ses efforts jusqu'à la fin de son activité créatrice. La *Comédia do Viúvo*, avec ses 1.060 vers, serait également la seule pièce dépassant mille vers qu'il ait composée avant 1521.... Ces indications suffisent à dénoncer le caractère apocryphe de l'incise *sendo Príncipe*. Toute porte à croire que la *Comédia do Viúvo* a été representée devant la *Roi Jean III*, trés vraisemblement en 1524. (Révah 28-30)

Teyssier agrees that the *Comédia* is "... posterior a 1521" (90). If this dating is correct – after 1521 – it would mean that, in reference to the prefatory letter, the *Comédia do Viúvo* would not be included among those "comédias" that Gil Vicente had included in the general category of "comédias, farças y moralidades." This in no way invalidates my hypothesis, however, since one of the Vicentine dramatic practices was to include former motifs or modes of dramatic presentation in later theatrical pieces. The vogue of "narrative" dramatizations after 1521, as well as the repetition of previous dramatic structures welcomed by the Portuguese court audience must have aided the development of the *comédia* form. In addition to this, the plays of Gil Vicente exhibit a marked tendency in the later years to incorporate former motifs (e.g., the doting old man) and modes of dramatic presentation (e.g., allegorical) that were developed in the earlier dramatic period.

This dialectical process of dramatic evolution which can best be described as a progression and regression of generic forms, is observed in the *comédias* of Gil Vicente. The *Comédia de Rubena*, for example, employs the same farcical situation that was formerly introduced in the farce, *Velho da Horta*. Likewise, the other so-called *tragicomédias*, with the exception of the romanesque *Amadís* and the *Dom Duardos*, are often little more than a loosely constructed display of allegorical figures in farcical situations.

In addition to the historical reasons given above for abandoning the a-critical tripartite classification, it should be noted that the term *comédia romanesca*, comic drama modeled on narrative medieval literature, is too broad to be acceptable as a generic category in itself. It has been already stated that only the *Amadís* and *Dom Duardos* turn to romance as a source of inspiration for plot construction. Even if we were to elaborate more on the term *romanesca*, adding to its narrative quality the idyllic connotations associated with the world of Romance, only the *Amadís* and the *Dom Duardos* would entirely fit the category. Although we find "romantic" elements in our two *comédias* (i.e., *Rubena* and *Viúvo*), they are, nevertheless quite distinct from the other two plays in question. Both categories are part of the "total mythos of comedy," as Northrop Frye suggests, but the difference lies in the quality of the society that the social forces of the complication transform at the play's end: "With the fourth phase of comedy we begin to move out of the world of experience into the ideal world of innocence and romance" (171, 181-82). This appears to be the generic movement from the Vicentine *comédias* to his two romanesque *tragicomédias*.

It is extremely important to consider the source of the dramatic inspiration, for only then can a true picture of the author's comic vision be ascertained. The difference between a "historical" plot and an "invented" plot was, after all, a discriminating criterion for Renaissance critics of drama:

> Before the middle of the sixteenth century, Horace and Donatus were the principal authorities on dramatic poetry, and the common critical approach at the time was a comparison of the moral purpose and style of comedy and tragedy. Early sixteenth-century critics maintained that comedy, using fictitious plots and characters, presented a familiar image of everyday life, while tragedy, using historical plots and characters, presented an exalted image of noble life (Herrick 36).

In the Vicentine *carta-prefácio* that we are considering here, we may distinguish between the "moral purpose," a term derived from Aristotle's *Poetics*, in this particular case the "figuras baxas" as contrasted with the "altas figuras" of the *tragicomédias*, and the "style" or "conveniente retórica" which was absent or insufficient in the *comédias* ("no havía conveniente retórica") but desired in the *tragicomédias*. In addition to this, one should remember that the concept of history ("história") to the man of the Middle Ages and even the Renaissance did not imply what it does to us today. C. S. Lewis warns that:

> It must be remembered throughout that the texts we should now call historical differed in outlook and narrative texture from those we should call fictions far less than a modern novel.... The elements of epic and romance [N.B.], like those of economic and social history, exist at all times in the real world; and historians, even in dealing with contemporary events, will pick out those elements which the habitual bent of their imagination has conditioned them to notice.... Even the turns of expression may be the same in chronicle and romance. *Or dit le conte* ("now tells the tale") will be found in Froissart (I, iv) (182).

We are reminded that the legendary world of romance that we find in the *Amadís* and the *Dom Duardos* may be likened to historical narrations of the type found in the medieval and Renaissance chronicles.

The Spanish dramatist Bartolomé de Torres Naharro, who was believed to have influenced Gil Vicente in the dramaturgical procedures of his later years as much as Juan del Encina had done earlier, wrote a dramatic treatise (The *Prohemio,* 1517) in which he follows the typology mentioned above by Herrick. In this dramatic treatise, the earliest in the Hispanic Peninsula, Naharro states that the *comedia* is "un artificioso ingenioso." By this statement it is quite evident that the Spanish dramatist is implicitly contrasting the imaginative or ingenious *(ingenio)* plots of some plays with the explicitly imitative ones. In the sixteenth century, before the Aristotelian concept of mimesis – art imitates nature – was re-introduced and accepted, the imitation of former models was an acceptable form of *inventio* or *imitatio*. The artistry of the poet was subordinate to his skill in elaborating upon previous models of literary discourse. This, however, is not the meaning of Naharro's use of the term *ingenioso* which emphasized, instead, the creative "inventiveness" of the Renaissance poet. It was the spirit of individual creativity which the Renaissance fostered, a period in which "The poet exercised his invention, ... he feigned and counterfeited, he made fictions" (Herrick 26).

Joseph Gillet believed that this inventive capacity in Naharro's dramaturgical precepts was particularly influential in the later development of the Peninsular notion of *comedia,* a fact we must consider not only in the generic divisions that are being noted, but also in the relevant importance of the Vicentine *comédia* in the later development of dramatic literature. Gillet observes that Naharro's precept, "un artificio ingenioso," is truly significant in this respect:

> It is a prophetic formula, recognizing a fundamental quality of the Spanish drama: the ingenuity and abundance of invention which a century later was to make of the Spanish *Comedia* a storehouse of plots from which the dramatists of other nations freely borrowed. It carries with it a technical corollary of the first importance, already quite definitely perceptible in the "ingenious" Torres Naharro's own plays: the predominance of plot over character ... (433).

This principle is further complemented by Torres Naharro's division between "Comedia a noticia" and "Comedia a fantasía," a concept that he elaborates by noting that the former category, "de cosa fantástica o fingida, que tenga color de verdad aunque no lo sea," is to be contrasted with the latter of the two comedic types, "de cosa nota y vista en realidad de verdad" (Gillet 441). Gillet adds that "In 1517 the equal recognition of realistic and idealistic literature, although little noticed even now, was a crucial achievement of the first order in the literature of Western Europe" (441). In other words, the "comedias a fantasía" are dramatizations of pure imagination, that is, of invented stories while the "comedias a noticia" are either faithful (or elaborated copies) of pre-existing literary models or, at least, realistic depictions of everyday life.

These dramaturgical rules pronounced by Naharro appear to have influenced Gil Vicente who, in these four "romanesque" plays, follows some of the same typological distinctions prescribed by the "learned" Spanish dramatist. Further evidence of Gil Vicente's debt to the ideology of the *Prohemio* in this respect is found in one of his later *comédia*'s, the *Comédia sobre a Divisa da Cidade de Coimbra* (1527). Although the play itself is not totally representative of the *comédia* genre that we are observing, it is in this work that our dramatist included his definition of comic drama:

> ja sabeis, senhores
> Que toda comedia começa em dolores;
> E inda que toque cousas lastimeiras
> Sabei que as farsas todas chocarreiras
> Não são muito finas sem outros primores
> (Vicente *Copilacão* fol. CVII).

The Pilgrim that introduces the dramatic action of this play also states in an earlier passage that the *comédia* is lowly ("chaa") and moral ("moral"). Although the statement is succinct, there are five elements here that are uncovered about Gil Vicente's concept of the structure and thematic focus of comedy. In a broad sense, it is possible to schematically classify these aspects of comedy within the Aristotelian notions of plot ("começa em dolores"), character delineation ("chaa," where the term is in opposition to, say, "elevada"; that is, as a function of characterization), thought ("moral"), and language (i.e., the stylistic care as evidenced by the words "finas" and "primores" versus "chocarreiras," in the language of the vulgar populace).

If, then, we recall the specific dichotomy that Gil Vicente himself referred to in the letter to the King D. João III, that is, between the earlier *comédias* and the new type of dramatic composition he was now offering the royal house, we arrive at a comprehensive classification of this term as the Portuguese dramatist may have used it.

In light of these thoughts on comedy we observe that Gil Vicente clearly distinguished his *comédias* as to characterization, plot, and language. Stylistic considerations appear to be a reflection of the refined social circumstances of his society, the period known as Renaissance humanism. We observe, furthermore, that the Vicentine secular perspective gathers the past Christian traditions and medieval dramatic conventions and blends them with the ideological concerns and structural patterns informed by the new spirit of classical culture.

In the following two chapters an attempt will be made to ascertain the structural peculiarities of the two Vicentine *comédias* in question: the *Comédia de Rubena* and the *Comédia do Viúvo*. This will allow us to arrive at a more specific and comprehensive definition of the Vicentine comic formula, not only as it relates to its own aesthetic background, but also as a reflection of other, more universal, generic concepts of comedy.

CHAPTER IV

THE *COMÉDIA DE RUBENA*

Before beginning the analysis of Gil Vicente's *Comédia de Rubena* it is first necessary to name the action which the author of the *Comédia* will imitate in his sequential (i.e., diachronic) elaboration of the plot. This action contains, of course, the basic ideas that are here perceived to be the orienting principle of the text. This organizational principle channels all levels of the dramatic discourse into a determined ideological focus, the theme of the work. We must remember that the complicated thematic system of motifs in drama is guided by one single action. This action, as Fergusson suggests, can best be named by the use of an infinitive phrase.[1] The diffuseness of the late medieval and early Renaissance dramaturgical practices (i.e., the sprawling, all encompassing action from which the audience was to abstract a single thematic idea) prevents us from applying Fergusson's formula for dramatic analysis as neatly as he has done with the coherent action of Sophocle's *Oedipus*. It is important to recall, however, that although this play (i.e., the *Rubena*) is admittedly digressive in the presentation of a single comic action, it is this (single) action that we must uncover and define.

In discussing the apparently unrelated incidents which the play presents we must place ourselves, as closely as possible, in the frame of mind of the audience for which Gil Vicente wrote; that

---

[1] "In [Aristotle's] studies of human conduct he speaks of three different forms of *energeia*, which he calls *praxis, poiesis,* and *theoria*. In *praxis* the motive is 'to do' something; we have seen that Oedipus's action, as soon as he sees that he must find the slayer, is a *praxis*" (Aristotle 12).

is, we must abstract, as they must have done, the "spiritual content" (Fergusson 30) of the play from the diverse incidents that were presented. It has already been noted in the discussion of early forms of medieval dramatic practices that the Christian ethical perspectives of liturgical drama remained the predominant motivation for the dramatic presentation of this period which was properly labeled "Christian humanism."

This is important to bear in mind for the *Rubena*, like many plays of its time, seeks to represent, in a final analysis, a higher form of reality than that which might attract the modern theatergoer. Thus we note in these plays an attempt to uncover an allegorical truth (i.e., one conditioned by social reality), one which affects the actantial rhythm of the plot in such a way that it appears digressive in its dramatic movement. Yet the rich texture of medieval dramaturgical skills (i.e., the allegorical approach to dramatic presentation, the symbolic mode of conveying human truth, the narrative models often used, the anachronistic practices), when taken into consideration, provides the key to the unity of these early Renaissance attempts at dramatic representation.

This is especially true of the *Rubena* in which Gil Vicente apparently fails to unite the many incidents of his bipartite "narrative" – Rubena's part and Cismena's part – into a single dramatic action. The external division of three acts or "scenas" appears to have been an attempt by the author himself or by his later editor to provide the unifying construct of the play but, in fact, it proves to be an entirely artificial division which in no way reflects the internal, a-dramatic organization of the play's system of causally related incidents. Not unlike many medieval and Renaissance playwrights, Gil Vicente here overlooks the *presentation* of an organic dramatic action in favor of a narrative, sequential outline which focuses the overwhelmingly more important *thematic* concern of the author. The all-important thematic perspective in Peninsular dramaturgy is an issue that has been already been discussed by A. A. Parker in his poignant discussion of Golden Age Drama:

> What the dramatist offers us, then, is not a series of complete characters, but a complete action. By a complete action I do not only mean one that hangs together, that ties up at the end all the loose strands, I mean an action that is a significant whole, one

that discloses a theme that has a significant bearing on experience, a theme that can be taken out of the particular action and universalized in the form of an important judgment on some aspect of human life (41-42).

Because we are confronted with a dramatic text which does not respond to the aesthetic organization of the Sophocles play studied by Fergusson, and because Gil Vicente's *Rubena* is, in fact, a play that is divided into two distinct actantial movements, I have decided to name the action of these two parts of the drama separately. The final analysis will show, however, that the two parts are thematically related.

The first act of the *Rubena* presents a dramatic sequence that is best stated thus: to restore Rubena's lost moral standing. Further analysis will quickly show that the action concerns Rubena's lost moral virtue of honor, which must, in some way, be restored if the play is to have any semblance of a comic resolution. This atonement for lost moral virtue appears, at first, to be totally frustrated since Rubena never re-appears as agent of the comic action after the first of the two parts, corresponding to the first of the three acts. We will see, however, that the ideological perspectives of Gil Vicente, still guided as they were by a medieval frame of reference, directed him to see the action of the *Rubena* on a higher plane of human understanding – the collective level of accepted and/or transgressed societal norms – not as a psychological or individualized form of dramatic action. This will be the function of the birth of Cismena at the end of act I: to transmit the action of the plot from mother (Rubena) to daughter (Cismena). When this transmission of the comic action is accomplished, the action defined above will be re-stated in such a way that it will include not only the particular dramatic situation of Rubena but also of her daughter, who fulfills the demands of the precipitating circumstances: Rubena's plight. That is to say, the first act will be entirely dependent upon the second and third acts; or in other words, the first act sets the problem that is solved in the second and third acts.

The dramatic action identified above is stated at the onset of the first "cena" or act in the words of the Scholar, who relates the story or background of that action and introduces Rubena to the spectators:

> Un clérigo moço, que era su [Rubena's father] criado,
> enamoróse de aquella donzella:
> la conversación acabó con ella
> lo que no deviera aver começado (43).

The erotic nature of the dramatic agent's moral transgression recalls St. Isidore's thematic formula for the dramatic action of the earlier comedians: "atque stupra virginum et amores meretricum in suis fabulis exprimebant." The illicit quality of the character's moral mistake is further made clear and reinforced in Rubena's monologue that immediately follows the Scholar's introduction. Gil Vicente has Rubena begin the representation of the action at its most crucial moment, the inevitable, unescapable moment of the consequence of Rubena's foolishness, the time when parturition is near. Necessarily, then, in her first words Rubena recognizes her illicit transgression and its societal consequence to her father and to herself.

In keeping with the medieval formula for comic action, we note that the plot begins in turmoil and, in this respect, one can detect in Rubena's predicament elements that would, if further elaborated, prefigure the plot construction of a tragic incident as stipulated by Aristotle in his *Poetics*. Yet, to be sure, these elements are not manifested in a tragic organization. We are, thus, in the presence of a "reversal of a situation," and we, furthermore, observe the "recognition" and ensuing "pathos," where the protagonist, Rubena, is represented in the middle of her suffering. These organic elements characteristic of tragic plots are not all actualized or represented organically, but simply narrated or expressed in Rubena's poetic lament. The recognition of the unhappy situation – Rubena's awareness of her foolishness – and the pathos are tragic elements that are prompted by the reversal of the happy situation in which she found herself before the unfortunate consequences (i.e., her unsanctioned pregnancy), resulting from her once happy relationship with the young cleric who fled. Unlike the tragic movement, however, the actualization of the dramatic action is given over to Rubena's suffering or "pathos," which overcomes the spectator with its lyrical tension.

In terms of dramatic effect, we must take into consideration that Gil Vicente is representing in the beginning of his *Comédia* the climax of a pathetic, almost tragic, situation. This selection of organic parts reflects not only the medieval formula for comic action but, more specifically, the author's own remarks, in the prologue of the *Comédia sobre a Divisa da Cidade de Coimbra*, about the structure and thematic contents of comic form. In her painful monologue Rubena expresses the recognition of her flaw (reminiscent but not reflective of the true tragic "harmatia") and suffers the potential, societal, ridicule that comes as a result of the unethical behavior. This beginning, then, fits well within the structural divisions of the comic action as guided by author's comic vision.

In the first scene of suffering Rubena fits rather well within the Aristotelian concept of character that is termed "habitual action," for all she says and does is oriented to the main pathetic problem which defines her as well as triggers the subsequent actualized dramatic action. That is, Rubena's speech focuses the moral dilemma that results from the misguided choice of what turns out to be a false love. Rubena here is in a terrible quandary, one so terrible that there is no way out, at least none that her pride or her fear allow her to take. In this situation, alone ("sin más compañía"), helpless ("no puedo"), and afraid ("no oso"), all she can do is lament her plight. The Scholar tells us that she is "sufriendo sus penas con mucha cordura." This suffering is voiced as lyrical lament, thus reflecting the pathos of the situation as it elicits from the reader a sense of pity and sorrow.

It is lyricism that constantly echoes the sad beauty of those feminine voices of the early *kharjahs* and the later *cantigas* of the Galaico-Portuguese school of poetry. Rubena's situation is parallel to that outlined in an earlier lyric song, written by Mendinho, about a young girl abandoned by love to a sad fate:

> I sat in the chapel of Saint Simeon
> and great waves crept around me, came on and on,
>   waiting for my love,
>   waiting for my love!
> I stood in the chapel, at the altar-side,
> and the waves crept around me, the great sea tide,
>   waiting for my love,
>   waiting for my love!
> And the waves crept around me, waves so great –
> I have no boatman to row my boat,

> waiting for my love,
> waiting for my love!
>
> And the waves crept around from the sea below;
> I have no boatman, I cannot row,
> waiting for my love,
> waiting for my love!
>
> I have no boatman to row for me –
> my beauty will die in the boundless sea,
> waiting for my love,
> waiting for my love!
>
> I have no boatman I cannot row –
> my beauty will die in the deep sea's flow,
> waiting for my love,
> waiting for my love! (Dronke 102)[2]

One observes the intensity of this dilemma when Rubena states that the pain caused by this problem is far more damaging than the physical pain caused by her pregnancy:

> Ay, que me ciercan puntadas!
> Mis angustias son llegadas
> y accidentes!
> Yo misma quiero el morir!
> Porque m'apertais, dolores?
> Que más duele arrepentir
> dos mil vezes que el parir. (47-48)

Rubena's plight is worsened by her knowledge that she is entirely responsible for her present state, that she took a voluntary part in a past situation that defines her predicament:

---

[2] Dronke considers this "cantiga de amigo" to be one of the best examples of medieval songs that lead to dramatic elaboration: "The song that seems to come nearest to a truly dramatic inspiration is one by Mendinho, a *jogral* perhaps from Vigo of whom we know nothing beyond this single lyric that survives under his name.... At the same time, the intensity and inexorable movement are gathered into a single image, an image larger than life, within which the dramatic possibilities – has her lover abandoned her? has he died at sea? will the little chapel be washed away in the flood? – are held in tension but deliberately not unfolded. But it is the inward symbolic associations rather than the narrative ones that predominate: the sight of the nearing tide makes the girl feel engulfed in the greatness of possible disappointment; the sea is time, is waiting with no way out; the sea is separation" (102-3).

> Ay de mí! de mi robada
> y no de otros robadores!
> Ay de mí, desventurada! (45)

She recognizes the deception of this "falso amor," of the deceptive love of the young cleric, in damaging her honor. In this respect, she is also aware of herself as a victim, expressed through the use of such words as "robada," "desventurada," "mocedad desdichada," "engañada sin sentido," "desamparada," etc. Her agony is further aggravated when she compares herself with other young virgins who save themselves for the right partner:

> Oo, quanto benditas son
> muchas donzellas que ví
> que para su proprio barón
> guardaron su perfección,
> y no la triste de mí! (47)

Rubena's grief is intensified when she pictures her past, as an overly pampered child, at peace, respected, and free from wrong-doing:

> En pensar quanto preciada
> desde niña fuy criada,
> ....
> Siempre de mi padre amada,
> siempre de todos querida,
> siempre vestida arrayada,
> siempre señora llamada,
> siempre adorada y servida,
> siempre horra y muy isienta,
> siempre en puerto sin tormenta,
> maas mirada que la luna,
> siempre leda, muy contenta.
> Mas aora me toma cuenta
> la fortuna! (48-49)

Happiness and social acceptability are here associated with chastity, the wise guarding of one's "perfección" until its loss is sanctioned by the holy sacrament of matrimony: "Benditas y bien libradas, / desposadas y casadas, / corona de sus parientes!" (47), a loss she regrets in the frenzy of her passion: "Qué haré, triste preñada / sin marido?" (45).

Rubena's only way out of her dilemma is through death, which she invokes in the hope of achieving peace:

> Quién tuviera, o quién hallara
> una preciosa vara
> que tuviera tal condón
> que emproviso me llevara
> a alguno que me sacara
> el coraçon!   (46)

In this part of Rubena's soliloquy, where she states "If only I had, If only I could find a wonderful wand that might have such a power that it would suddenly carry me off to a place where my heart would be removed!" we witness her quest for self annihilation. In doing so, Rubena shows her willingness to pay for her foolish mistake.

Rubena is totally defenseless and, while she is interiorizing the lamentable events that have overcome her, she exhibits at the same time a fear of being found out by others, a fear of social condemnation and, of course, fear of what her *fuerte, cruel, celoso,* and *bravo* father would do to her:

> Oo! triste de mí, Rubena!
> A quién me descubriré?
> A quién contaré mi pena?
> Cómo porné en mano agena
> mi vida, mi honrra y fee?   (45)

In her state of utter despair she considers the alternatives for action, disclosing the chaotic effects of the present circumstance of misery:

> Yo si me descubriere
> a Benita, dezir-lo-há;
> si solo en mi cabo pariere
> y pariendo me muriere
> muy más claro se veraa!
> Sin-ventura, que haré?   (49-50)

In her dilemma, Rubena vacilates, she again faces the problem of choice: disclose her pain to Benita, her maid, or die giving birth to the child. This latter choice grieves her, for it will nonetheless stain her reputation and thus not remedy the problem. It is in this dramatic impasse of the "pathos" that the end of the first act takes place.

The last scene of the first act, in which the devils are summoned to carry Rubena away, can be dramatically compared to a "deus ex machina." It is the answer to Rubena's prayers: the clouds, however, have now been replaced by the devils and the dark valley by the dense forest (i.e., the "montaña"). The dramatic function of this precipitous exit must here be considered as a reversal of the comic, Christian ending, for it is the devils who provide the means of overcoming the tragic chain of events that would lead to an acceptable type of salvation. In any case, the problem derived from Rubena's "pathos" is harmonized in the sense that it ends, rather hurriedly, her state of misery.

Rubena disappears to bear the child which, as was suggested previously, is the instrument of the subsequent organization of the plot. This generational, mother-daughter, concept of plot construction is more explicitly suggested by the Scholar who terminates all the action of the first act by announcing that these disastrous problems of Rubena are "too profound" and "too lengthy" for further investigation. His words, if we may surmise some authorial point of view here, would necessarily restrain the virtual "tragic" chain of events, for the classic notion of tragedy was not theologically possible within this period of Christian humanism. The following two acts or "cenas," as they are called in the *Copilaçam*, further the harmonizing principle which is closely associated with Gil Vicente's dramatic intention of creating a new theatrical form – the *comédia* – through the formal and stylistic revision of former models.

The action assigned to Cismena, the dramatic agent of the second and third acts is, at first sight, not seemingly connected to the first act. At least, this seems to be the case when compared to the Aristotelian concept of "organic parts," of the linear-causal arrangement of dramatic segments that dictate its structural coherence. This total absence of the Aristotelian notions is extremely important in the comic vision that orients the dramatic design of Gil Vicente, especially as it relates to the harmonizing principle that guided this dramatist's comic vision. This will be a topic for more extensive elaboration, for it explains not only Gil Vicente's own philosophy which conditions his literary construct, but also points to the Peninsular interpretation and elaboration of former theories on comedy. Once again we may observe in Peninsular dramatic activity the medieval vision taking precedence over the categorical precepts of the Renaissance theorists.

Thus it becomes apparent that the dramatic arrangement of these elements discloses an "organic" ordering of dramatic segments that is first and foremost a subordination to thematic concerns. The interest in the theme orients the Vicentine perspective to the extent that it subordinates the structural logic of the dramatic action, as dictated by the canons of circumstantial reality. In this sense the "allegorical" process – the reliance on an ulterior truth – is not totally lacking in this work, although allegory as a process of characterization is not an aspect of the Vicentine comic formula.

We will remember with Bevington, however, that humanist drama made use of the allegorizing principles found in the changing medieval morality plays:

> The morality play was also beginning to show an awareness of social and economic issues during the early Tudor period. Even in the early *Mankind*, the tempters are not simple allegorical abstractions but rowdies, highwaymen, and tavern-frequenters who pose a threat to order (967).

To this process of secularization, whereby the morality play bridges the gap between the Christian allegories and the secular issues of the Renaissance, Gil Vicente's debt is quite clear. In the *Comédia* which is here being considered, let it suffice to say that the names "Rubena" and "Cismena" present an ideological opposition of moral and theological ideas that are clearly noted in the morphological-semantic: "Rubena" = (< rubi), red, passion, and "Cismena" = (< cismar), to think, to reason. The affinities of the two terms in the dramatic representation of these two opposing camps of action ("loco amor" vs. "buen amor") is made evident by the coincidence of the suffix "-ena" in both names. This process clearly equates these two "allegorical" figures. The fact that the two feminine characters are far more individualized than some of Gil

Vicente's former characters – with the exception of *Inês Pereira* – is an indication of the extent to which secularization had entered the comic formula of Gil Vicente by this period.

Counterbalancing Rubena's error, her lost honor, which would logically be resolved through individual punishment of some sort, is the ideological subject of the ensuing two acts. Cismena, then, is not only the actantial expedient of that mission (i.e. to restore family honor) but also the ideological instrument of that societal quest: the loss of virtue is evil, its preservation is good. However secularized or worldly the society in which these two women are depicted, the interaction of "Good" and "Evil" reflects the moral and theological context of the medieval Christian background which influenced Gil Vicente.

This background is reflected in the element of magic (devils) that encloses an ambiguity of motifs which can be seen as theologically paradoxical. They do not entirely represent in this *Comédia* the conventional association of demonic figures with the forces of evil; on the contrary, they are responsible for the well-being of an ethically desirable type of Christian virtue: charity or the protection of innocence; in this case, the innocence of Rubena's daughter: Cismena. Gil Vicente has very interestingly presented in Rubena's wish:

> Quién tuviera, o quién hallara
> una preciosa vara
> que tuviera tal condón
> que emproviso me llevara
> a alguno que me sacara
> el coraçón! (46)

and in her prayer:

> Oo, tristes nuves escuras
> que tan rezias caminais,
> sacadme d'estas tristuras
> y llevadme a las honduras
> de la mar, adonde vais!
> Duélanvos mis tristes hadas
> y llevadme apressuradas
> a aquel valle de tristura
> donde están las malhadadas,

>   donde están las sin-ventura
>   sepultadas.   (46-47)

the possibility of non-demonic forces acting as savior. In the lyric passivity of the "sad clouds," we observe a positive force at work, this same lyricism neutralizes whatever negativity they may possess in terms of Rubena's end; they are not intrinsically, dynamically evil as are the devils. The playwright has, however, chosen to have Rubena's wish and prayer not be fulfilled by a magic wand or by clouds or by some lyric convention but rather, given his interest in "pacíficas concordanças," he uses demonic beings and a witch to bring about a positive, virtuous outcome. Moreover, he forces this positive accomplishment beyond the witch's original purpose of bringing Rubena back free of the newly born child by having the devils fail in their task and bring back the child instead.

This reversal of motifs – good resulting from evil – is from the outset very significant by the fact that it is cooperating with the ideological parameters of Christian humanism and its particular Peninsular focus. In a number of instances Cismena considers herself to be the ill-fated child of her mother's sin and this feeling becomes one of her major psychological obstacles.[3]

The secular and moral salvation that will come to Cismena, unlike that of her mother, is that which she herself seeks, that which consists of her free choice: original sin exists for her as it did for her mother (or for anyone else) but she will superimpose her morally directed will upon the forces which deter her as they once did her mother. There are other instances in which Gil Vicente presents the hand of providence undoing the forces of evil. This is the playwright's ideological use of dramatic irony; reflecting, once again, the "harmonizing perspective" in which conflicting elements are resolved in a harmonious context.

---

[3] The idea of inherited sin was particularly important within the context of the Iberian social reality, especially as a metaphor for the struggle between the "New Christian" and the "Old Christian." Friar Domingo de Valtanás would insist in 1556 (*Apología sobre ciertas materias morales en que hay opinión*) that "No castiga Dios con penas espirituales a los hijos por la culpa de los padres, como lo dize Jeremías. Y no obstante el pecado de los judíos, dellos escogió Dios a Sant Pedro y a Sant Juan y a los otros apostólos y discípulos que los más principales fueron judíos" (Castro 96).

Such comments, however, take us much too far in our ideologial investigation of the meaning of the play at this point. It would be better, and perhaps more objective, to continue our look at the immanence or structural reality of the piece in view of the action that it will represent: the thematic unity of Rubena's moral transgression (with the idea of self-condemnation due to loss of honor, which here is related to evil and unhappiness) as it is structurally encased and transferred to its felicitous resolution in her daughter – Cismena. This character, through her moral tenacity, restores the family name that her mother had forsaken through her unethical behavior, and thus brings to the *Comédia* the collective idea of virtue restored (honor), an ultimate good that brings the comic action to a felicitous conclusion.

If we may once again return to the last scene with Rubena, the moment of her miraculous exit, we will note that the conflictive situation is realized through a tense juxtaposition of realities – the recognition of her moral error versus accepted societal norms – and not through a dramatically acceptable resolution of conflict. Rubena's character is *dramatically* passive because she lacks the dynamic interraction (i.e., a determined stance) with her potentially tragic environment. Representationally, the devils determine the actualization of her end.

In the process toward resolution, after Rubena's opening monologue, new characters are introduced which polarize the dramatic action into two distinct camps of interaction: on one side the hostile Benita, Rubena's maid, who resents her mistress' duplicity and lack of confidence in her, and on the other side those characters or agents of the dramatic action which aid Rubena in her dilemma: The midwife, the witch and the four devils (i.e., Plutão, Legião, Caroto, Draguinho). Thus, the "subject" or the dramatic action (Rubena) desires the "object" of this same action (to preserve her social standing by restoring her lost virtue), having on one side those who oppose her and on the other those who will help her in her quest.

The antagonist to that moral search is, as mentioned previously, Benita who represents the morally acceptable side of Rubena's dilemma. Her function as antagonist, however, needs some explanation, for it is not an open obstacle that she places in Rubena's way, but rather a mild censure which is reflected in her social status, that of maid to the household. Nonetheless, Benita is a "father-ally" who opposes her mistress' wrongdoing. Although her lack of sympathy is not consciously aimed against any determined moral stance, she is the spokesperson of the ethical, accepted code of behavior that is opposed to Rubena's foolish conduct. Her burlesque commentaries on the situation – the possibility of Rubena's peaked complexion being a result of a cold she had *nine months earlier!* – is more characteristically the function of the *alazon* who ridicules those who transgress society's laws. In this situation Benita functions, on an artistic level, as the castigator of moral evil, purveyor of the "ridendo castigat mores" mentality.

In keeping with the oppositional principles set out by A.J. Greimas in his *Structural Semantics* one could graphically represent the "Rubena" segment of the *Comédia* as shown in Figure 1. The diagram that is used here has been slightly altered to fit the needs of our analysis, reflecting the particular focus of the *Comédia*. Greimas, for example, uses the word "sender" where I have chosen "donors," preferring instead a plural concept that would encompass and accomodate the magical, non-realistic, forces operative in the play. Also, the Greimasian actantial model uses "receiver" where I have preferred "beneficiary." This is due to the fact that in the *Comédia*, as we have already stated, Rubena – the "subject" in the first segment only – is not a direct "receiver" of the whole dramatic action, given the fact that the "object" of that complete action (to restore lost virtue) vis-à-vis the help of the devils is not represented actantially by this dramatic agent but rather by another, her daughter; that is, this segment of the dramatic action is not represented according to the concept of the logical arrangement of "organic parts" in the Aristotelian notion of plot construction. This allows us to observe, once again, that the principle that guides the imitation of the action in the *Comédia*, with the subsequent exchange of dramatic agents between the first and second acts: Rubena > Cismena, resides in its impersonal thematic relationship, which would be best described by the term "beneficiary."

Let us see now in what way Greimas' diagram throws light on the dramatic sequence that we are observing by noting its ordering of the plot as it is related to the level of characterization ("character delineation") and that of style ("language and thought"). Soon after Rubena's appearance in the initial dramatic segment (this character's function in the plot has already been studied) the

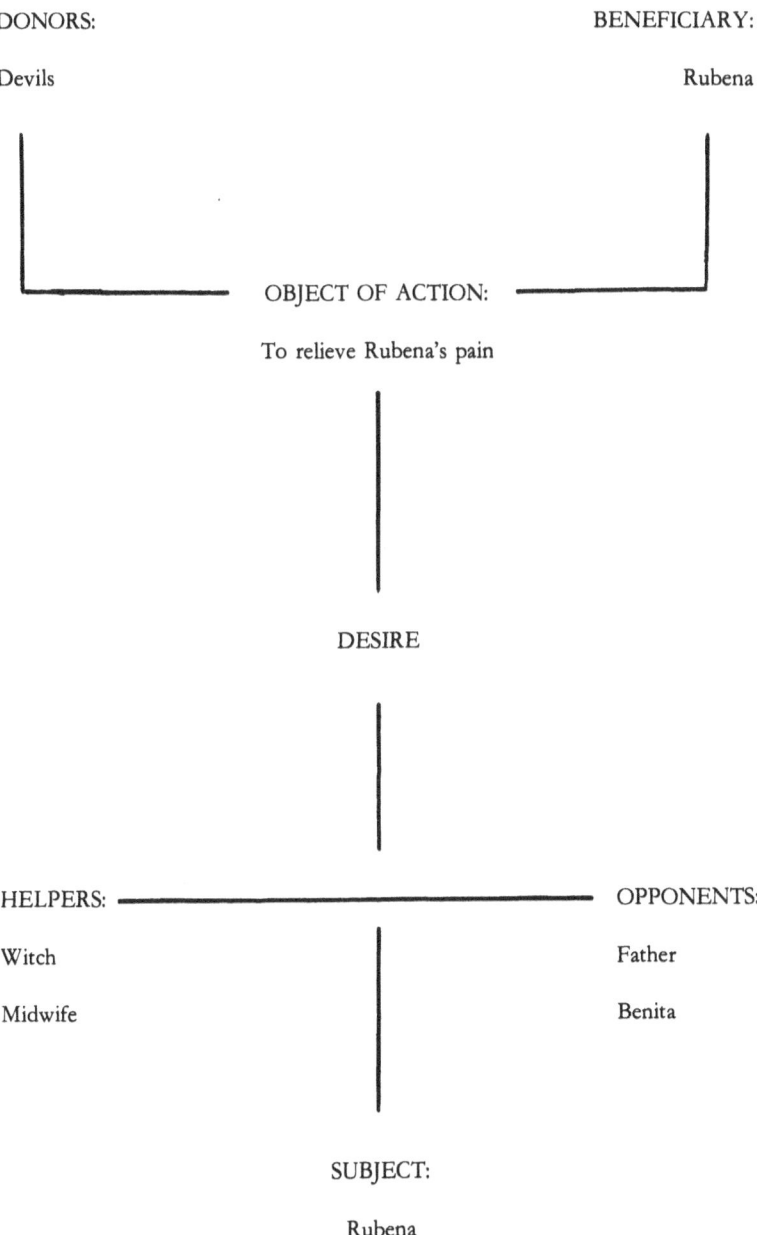

Figure 1. The Comédia de Rubena (Act I)

first character that begins a dialogic situation is Benita, the maid. We notice that she arrives just as soon as the main character reaches her most heated state of passion (*pathos*). Her function as "opponent" is not to present a conflict, but rather to aggravate the possible resolution of that conflict by frustratingly retarding its final outcome. For this very reason the dialogic interchange that ensues between these two women does not intensify the dramatic action (i.e., does not dramatize Rubena's monologic lament), for it is based on the subduing process of the comic *quid pro quo* or comicality of language which denies the type of actantial movement that defines dramatic action.

The dramatic segments of this type of encounter between Rubena and her maid is best exemplified in the following passages:

>   (RUBENA) Ay! dolores de pesar!
>   (BENITA) Bien entiendo a mi señora
>   y ella quéreme cegar.   [mumbled aside]
>   (RUBENA) Quée?
>   (BENITA) Digo que no sé pensar
>   qué remedio os busque aora . . .   (51-52)

And further on:

>   (RUBENA) Llámame Genebra acá,
>   que te haden buenas hadas!
>   Que me venga
>   a bendezir
>   del quebranto, mucho presto!
>   Presto, que quiero morir!
>   (BENITA) Paréceme esto parir!   [mumbled aside]
>   (RUBENA) Que?
>   (BENITA)   Digo que me pesa d'esto
>   en gran manera.   (53-54)

Gil Vicente could have learned this technique of the *quid-pro-quo* aside or antagonistic mumble followed by lying explanations from *La Celestina* where it is used as a means of realizing the servant-versus-master motif. The comic effect produced by the backbiting, spiteful asides of Benita juxtaposes comicality to Rubena's suffering. The Portuguese playwright is using it to intensify the isolation of Rubena. Her aloneness in her plight is now confirmed. Her distrust of her maid is shown to be justified by the lack of sympathy that Benita slyly tries to hide from her. Like the dialogues between Calixto and Sempronio as well as between Celestina and Melibea, Benita and her mistress reflect a lack of confidence and trust. The criticism of a high character by a low one, muttered or spoken under the breath, and then lying to hide the true feelings are part of a breakdown of the channels of communication (mirroring social, extra-literary facts) that within the play reflect the fear ("no oso") and isolation which Rubena has brought upon herself because of the foolish love practiced by some – in this case, a priest! – in her permissive society. Notice that Rubena had been a pampered darling and that Benita (for reasons not made entirely clear but that are reminiscent of those shared by Sempronio, Celestina and, later, Parmeno in the *Celestina*) is happy to see her brought low.

Besides the ridiculing asides of Rubena's maid, there is another recourse she uses in delaying the dramatic action: the absurdity of her anecdotes and songs which apparently have no bearing on the dramatic situation before us. More specifically, Benita's delaying tactics include an interrupted tale about a squire. Rubena, meanwhile, had already ordered her maid to go fetch the midwife to cure her (moral and) physical suffering, "quebranto," which was, in fact, a way of dissimulating her pregnancy in front of Benita, and possibly finding some hope of escape from her misery.

The narration concerning the squire (without apparent logic in this dramatic segment) acquires significance within the general symbolic texture of the *Comédia*, at a highly metaphorical level which will be considered elsewhere. Later, Benita interrupts the logical sequence of the dialogue with her mistress to sing a "cantiga," making it difficult for Rubena to hide her physical suffering and her frustration. These functional units of meaning (the "absurd" story and the "silly" song) operate, according to the critical aparatus of Roland Barthes, as "integrative functions" of the text. That is, they present themselves as "índices" of the literary discourse. Carlos Reis explains these concepts when he observes that:

> É efectivamente esta perspectiva funcional que inspira a determinação de unidades narrativas em que se concentram dois tipos disintos [sic] de *funções:* as designadas como *distribucionais,* cuja funcionalidade se exerce sempre ao mesmo nível, e as

> denominadas *integrativas*, cuja característica primeira reside no facto de só saturarem a sua funcionalidade num nível superior. No nível distribucional inserem-se dois tipos de funções: as *cardinais* (ou *núcleos*) e as *catálises*. As primeiras são concebidas como acontecimentos fulcrais em que se concretizam os avanços da acção; as segundas constituem momentos de pausa dessa mesma acção ou, como diz Barthes, "des notations subsidiaires, que s'agglomèrent autour d'un noyau ou d'un autre sans en modifier la nature alternative." O segundo tipo de funções comprende: os *indícios* (cuja apreensão exige, como se verá, uma certa subtileza de detecção), destinados a sugerir, por vezes de modo extremadamente *dissimulado* [underlining is mine], significados implícitos ou dissimulados; os *informantes* que, referenciado a acção em termos espácio-temporais explícitos, servem "à authentifier la réalité du référent, à enraciner la fiction dans le réel." (278-79)

In the space designated by the term "helper," to return once again to our diagram, the characters are grouped according to the function of the actions which they perform; a natural level, when the action of these dramatic agents are equivalent to our actions (i.e., human actions) and a supernatural level, when the same actions are above our own possibilities, being, therefore, superior to the level of natural phenomena. At this stage, according to the archetypal classifications of Northrop Frye, the text enters the world of the demonic.

The figures associated directly or indirectly with this demonic world are: the witch, the medium between the natural and supernatural worlds, and the devils, prototypes of this sinister world. These characters are woven into the dramatic action through the midwife, the healer who Rubena calls to cure her pregnant condition or, as she refers to it, "quebranto."

Figure 2 demonstrates the two extremities of these worlds — natural and supernatural — as well as the chain of events initiated by Rubena's prayer to the Virgin Mary. The passage from the natural plane of the dramatic action to that of the supernatural is not done *ex-abrupto*, but rather gradually, through the interaction and transference of increasingly higher powers of control. The midwife enters first and, incapable of resolving Rubena's plaint, she summons the transcendent powers of the devils. All the transference, however, seems to be directly under the control of divine

THE *COMÉDIA DE RUBENA* 129

SUPERNATURAL

Devils

Witch

Midwife

NATURAL

Figure 2. Rubena's prayer to the Virgin Mary

will for it is all motivated and set in motion by Rubena's prayer to the Virgin Mary (Act I, scene 3). It is interesting to note, especially in reference to Gil Vicente's secular perspective, that these conventional representatives of the forces of evil are dominated by a higher authority which delimits their sphere of influence. This is made apparent in Legião's remark: "O que há de ser, há de ser, / Porque seraa o que for!" (67-68). This idea has been studied by Paul Teyssier who observes that order and harmony are at the core of Gil Vicente's Christian vision (141-73). We have already observed the importance of the concept of providence vis-à-vis fate in the secular perspectives of the Portuguese dramatist.

This supernatural world represents the "donors" of circumstances which will "favor" the securing of the "object" of the action, and it possesses significant importance for the cosmological conception that we observe in Vicentine ideology as related to the general significance (*dianoia*) of the work. There appears to be an intrinsic logic, on the level of the "actualization of possibilities" (i.e., the formal logic of motivation and unfolding of the dramatic action), reflected in the necessity of the demonic intervention – a formal logic of motifs that reflects the ideological, thematic motivation of the action disclosed.

The engagement of the supernatural is already implicit at its lowest level in the fact that the midwife (whom Rubena sends Benita for) comes under the guise, or disguise, of a *bendicideira,* a woman who has, or claims to have, contact with the higher-world powers for the purpose of healing. She enters (Act I, scene 4) uttering holy names with at least the pretense of enlisting divine aid. But even before she has entered, Rubena has herself attempted to attract a most powerful higher-world ally; immediately after she sends Benita for the *bendicideira,* she prays to the Virgin Mary:

> Oo dulce virgen gloriosa,
> a ti pido, sospirando,
> que te passes d'este bando
> de Rubena desdichosa.
> Tu que tuviste encubierto
> aquel divino secreto,
> encubre mi triste suerte!
> No mires mi desconcierto,

>   que sin ti hago concierto
>   con la muerte!   (57)

This prayer, as the cover speech for the entrance of the midwife, effectively (i.e., dramatically) places the scenes that follow under the protection of a transcendental power. That is, Rubena, in seeking the interference of the supernatural apparently manages to set into motion the forces that will bring about the answer to her own problem as well as the final comic resolution of the entire action of the play. This is clear in the fact that Rubena's problem is solved by non-natural means. Gil Vicente has thus used a device that would have been obvious to an audience of his time: how could the Virgin Mary possibly ignore the prayer of a young girl who is so clearly in desperate need and who is so filled with regret over her mistake? To be sure, the comic force cannot condone Rubena's foolish act; not only has she lost her virginity but has advertised the loss by getting pregnant. She must unavoidably fare badly. But that force can operate in such a happy way that Cismena is born and brought back, so that out of foolishness is born wisdom. Unlike Berceo in *Los Milagros de Nuestra Señora*, Gil Vicente prefers to see the change from bad to good fortune that the Virgin Mary brings about from a generational (i.e., societal) point of view, not that of the individual.

Rubena's prayer to the Virgin, then, is the device that Gil Vicente uses to activate and unfold the required supernatural intervention. To be sure, this intervention is never brought out onto the verbal surface, as is the case of the *Comédia do Viúvo*, and there is no direct, simple solution of problems, but his indirect working out of the problem accords well with the basic Vicentine precept that the divine moves in mysterious ways.

What is apparent is the way in which the more-or-less natural-world efforts of the midwife fail. After examining Rubena, she realizes that the birthing will be extremely difficult and will require more time:

>   (Parteira)   Mostrade cá, filha amiga,
>   verey em que pontos estais.
>   Muy alta estaa a criancinha!
>   Nam parireis tan asinha:
>   asinha vos voos agastais. (63)

And further on, while she squats to urinate in a corner (or as the instructions state: "Faz que se assenta a mijar a hum canto"), as if to relieve the nervousness brought on by her failure to bring about the delivery, she reaches a decision about what must be done:

> Olhade cá, filha amiga,
> feyticeyra aveis mister,
> porque (quereis que vos diga?)
> ver-vos-edes em fadiga
> si vosso pay cá vier! (66)

That is, the frustration and failure of the natural level requires recourse to the supernatural. It might seem that the failure of the midwife to deliver the baby represents a failure of the higher-world forces, since she was brought on stage under their aegis. And, indeed, at this point the play seems to turn away from the higher world to the lower world. Just as the midwife's entrance was preceded by Rubena's prayer to the Virgin, the entrance of the witch is introduced by Rubena's self-resignation to hell (scene 7):

> Venga ya todo el infierno
> por esta triste Rubena:
> que ya bien sé y discierno
> que el infiernal fuego eterno
> no se yguala a esta pena!
> Y pues mi suerte lo quiso,
> no espero paraiso
> ni acá sino tristura;
> venga el infierno improviso
> que lleve a quien, sin aviso,
> escogió mala ventura! (67)

But there is not just this parallelism. Gil Vicente has, furthermore, insisted on this transition device. After the entrance of the witch and the conjuring scene (scene 8, which is only described in the instructions and has no spoken lines), and the appearance of the devils (Legião in scene 9 and Draguinho, Caroto, and Plutão in scene 10), the playwright has Rubena in scene 11 continue her acceptance-of-death speech begun in scene 7. This scene 11 speech serves as a preparation for the witch and the devils to approach Rubena in scene 12. The technique of presentation here is curious for several reasons. It requires a multiple stage representation, since the witch and the devils do not enter Rubena's room until scene 12.

Moreover, the place of the conjuring scene (scene 8) is not the same as the place where first Legião (scene 9) and then the other devils (scene 10) appear, since at the end of their scene the instructions indicate the four devils are to exit to go answer the witch's summons. But of more importance for our present purpose is the fact that Gil Vicente has interrupted Rubena's anguished capitulation to death and hell with the comic antics of the devils, devils who have been summoned to help her, not to drag her off to hell as she might imagine. By encapsulating comicality within pathos (scenes 7 and 11), Gil Vicente has allowed the comic (i.e., ameliorating), invisible presence of the Virgin (prayer in scene 3) to assert itself. The presence of devils rather than angels recognizes the seriousness of Rubena's transgression (the foolish loss of virginity), but the fact that these are country-bumpkin devils, not serious, fire-and-brimstone, vengeful ogres, signals that a more benign force is at work in the play.

The benignity of the witch's characterization is also made manifest. She is presented as being concerned for the welfare of her client. Her purpose is to transport Rubena to a secret place where she can give birth to the child without anyone knowing and then to get rid of the evidence, so that afterwards Rubena can return to society with her honor intact. The witch is, then, a lower-world fairy godmother. The fact that her plans are outdone is not due to any lack of concern or professional competence on her part; it is due, rather, to the transcendental (genre-structural and societal) forces at work, not only the demands of poetic justice, the fact that wrong should be punished, but more importantly the need to fulfill the comic vision, bringing light out of darkness, hope out of despair, joy out of dismay, wisdom out of foolishness, and, in terms of the play, Cismena, literally, out of Rubena.

In response to these demands and this need Rubena must be sacrificed, and Gil Vicente has clearly decided to let bungling agents of darkness be responsible for the frustration of the witch's good-hearted but wrong-headed plans. It is, moreover, entirely appropriate that Rubena lend herself to this outcome, since it proves that she is truly contrite. She thus shows herself to be wiser than the witch, whose solution to the problem avoids questions of responsibility for one's actions. Rubena's guilt-laden conscience thus stands as the possibility for, and a justification of, her daughter's wisdom. The calm acceptance of her fate, the regret that she has for her father's sadness, her greater concern for him than for herself, all these measure the shift from desperation to resignation that demonstrate the growth from foolishness to recognition. Gil Vicente has carefully orchestrated that development from Rubena's first lines:

> Ay de mi!, de mi robada
> y no de otros robadores! (45)

to her last speech:

> Señora, pues consenti
> contra mi tan mala suerte,
> voyme del todo d'aquí. (73)

by way of that still hopeful plea to the Virgin (scene 3):

> que sin ti hago concierto
> con la muerte! (57)

and the irony that, not without her but mysteriously, hiddenly, with her, Rubena comes to her self-exiled end.

Returning again to the prayer to the Virgin (scene 3) we see that on the level of stylistic elaboration of language (i.e., metaphorically) Rubena's situation is compared to that of the Virgin Mary. We must remember that the "humanization" of divine Christian entities was not considered irreverent at this time as witnessed by the very earthly endeavors of the Mother of God in the medieval miracle stories (e.g., *Los milagros de Nuestra Señora, Cantigas de Santa María,* etc.).

This comparison, by contrast to the Immaculate Conception of the Virgin Mary, would lead us to believe that Cismena's birth is equated, by indirect association, to the category of original sin. Symbolically, the juxtaposition of two worlds in this segment – the demonic and the apocalyptic – is semantically responsible for the thematic development of the dramatic discourse. That is to say, the obvious reversal of the order — apocalyptic and demonic — imparts signification through the non-dramatic technique of suggestive oppositions: the demonic world into which Cismena is born reflects that world which our first parents (Adam and Eve) inherited after the Fall; like Rubena, Eve too was condemned by God for her sins: "I will multiply your pains in childbearing, you shall give birth to your children in pain" (Genesis 3:17-18). One cannot help recalling, in this respect, the moralistic delight that medieval man took in contrasting these two worlds:

> ....
> *entre Ave Eva*
> *gran departiment'a.*
>   Eva nos enserrou
>   os ceos sen chave,
>   e María britou
>   as portas per Ave.
> *Entre Ave Eva*
> *gran departiment'a.*
>   (Alfonso el Sabio 51)

The implicit contrast of Rubena's painful childbirth with that of the Virgin Mary is more explicitly stated in scene 5 by the midwife who renders the Christian apocryphal account (cf. the *Protoevangelium of James*) of the Virgin's immaculate birth: "... Vay Joachim apos o carneyro / e n'aquella hora que, Deos verdadeyro, / concebeo Ana em limpo celeyro / a Sancta Maria..." (61). The divine help of God ("Deos verdadeyro") is juxtaposed here with the demonic help that will bring Cismena to the existential world.

It is that same character, the midwife, who repeats a motif (the anecdote-riddle of the squire) which will emancipate, by comparison and contrast, the "indícios" (i.e., the non-actantial semantic units of signification) in Benita's tales and songs. It is important, therefore, to include the textual references of those two segments:

> (BENITA)   Quiéroos dezir un cuento.
>   Diz que era un escudero,
>   tenía la muger tiñosa
>   y subiendo en un otero

> encontró con un vaquero
> desollando una raposa.
> El escudero, cuytado,
> andava desarrapado,
> las nalgas todas de fuera
> y el has desemparado,
> y el cogote trasquilado,
> sin osar dezir quien era. (54-55)

On a symbolic level of analysis (assuming that individual segments of the dramatic discourse — words as well as narrative units — are *not* gratuitous and that, in fact, they contribute to the semantic whole) these enigmatic and non-sensical details, in which is inserted the word-metaphor "escudeiro," should be compared to those made by the Parteira when she imparts courage to Rubena in her difficult task of giving birth:

> (Parteira) Ora sus, minha santinha,
> que se chega a vossa hora!
> Empuxay, minha pombinha,
> e veredes can asinha
> sae o cordeyrinho fora!
> Day de mão ao pousadeyro,
> leyxay yr o escudeyro. (65)

If one accepts the "escudeiro"-motif as a functional part of the whole discourse, one would have to note that in the first passage the image of the squire is directly related to the (sacrificial) motif of the skinning of a fox while in the statements made by the midwife, the same motif is associated with Rubena's child. This suggests that the explicit motif of the squire ("escudeiro") is a symbol related in the first passage to social disruption, and, in the second passage, to an obstacle in Rubena's difficult parturition. The association of the same motifs in different contexts is significant. Further analysis of these segments prove to be a bit more intricate than what has been suggested above.

The squire, as we noted above, appears in isotopic (i.e., coherence of repeated units of textual signification) relationship with the destruction of the fox. He too is presented as social degradation and waste: "El escudero, cuytado, / andava desarrapado, / las nalgas todas de fuera / y el has desemparado, / el cogote trasquilado..." (55). By an analogy of images, one notes the symbolic proximity of the image of the squire with that of the fox which, as literary convention has it, is traditionally synonymous with astuteness and ruse in its unbridled attempt to overcome the accepted norms of society. These symbols combine to give the idea of deception and loss of social status. The skinning of the wily fox as well as the social decadence of the squire, a motif often satirized in Iberian literature (cf. *Lazarillo de Tormes*, etc.), are, then, "indícios" which focus and reflect Rubena's problem: the loss of moral standing through the trickery of the cleric. In addition to this, the ritualistic destruction of the fox is an additional sign of the *Comédia's* resolution, for it signifies the end of trickery; at least for the fortunate Cismena.

It is not by accident that, contrary to accepted codes of ethical behavior, the midwife has more liberal ideas concerning the immoral situation in which Rubena finds herself:

    (RUBEIRA)   Estoy mucho afatigada.
    (PARTEIRA)   Nam ajades vós aquella!
                       Bem vejo que estaes pejada
                       Isto hé cousa natural
                       e muyto acontecedeyra:
                       se nunca fora outra tal
                       disséramos que era mal
                       por serdes vós a primeyra! (58)

When she encourages Rubena not to worry, "leyxay ir o escudeyro," there is a desire to set Rubena at ease. The reference to the squire, then, is the loss of honor that Rubena must redeem as she brings to light her daughter, Cismena. The Parteira, then, attempts to relieve Rubena's suffering, to make her more comfortable with her moral position, so that she will finally unmask herself and accept the true consequences of her encounter with the young cleric: "... e nam vos há-de lembrar / vergonha nem cortesia" (65).

Still another reference, now much more explicit, to the idea of nativity is expressed when the midwife welcomes Rubena's child with textual references to the Biblical tradition. The liturgical citations are, of course, greatly altered to fit the present (tragicomic) situation and are given in macarronic latin interspersed with religious motifs of the folk Church tradition:

> Kyrieleysam, Christeleysam.
> Dizey tres vezes passinho
> "o verbo caro fato hé!": (64)

As the second act commences, this same procedure appears in the witch's monologue. She, as the very important medium between the natural and supernatural worlds, gives a more elaborate rendition of these liturgical prayers. These litanies are direct parodies of the Bible; more specifically, of the *Book of John*. The words reflect the Church rituals for salvation and the Catholic dogma of God as the *primum mobile* of the Universe, of the creator of all things, of life and light, of the world:

> *Quequinque vulto salmus es*
> *ante monia opus es.*
> Huy! tem a gayola *fidém*
> *cam nisi que* antre o gram
> e tudo per hi alem.
> No principio o verbo era
> era do verbïo cheo:
> o verbio era *apodeo*
> e n'essa mita m'era.
> Esta voz era *lux vera*
> que vay la no nenïente.
> Nam era elle luz luzente
> como este lume de cera.
> E o mundo, mundo x'era,
> mundo x'era e mundo x'é.
> E si n'isso fato nichee
> e elle n'isso mita era.
> E mundos nam convinarão
> junto com *missus a Deo,*
> *testimonio, testimonio meo,*
> cujo nome era João. (76-78)[4]

---

[4] Giuseppe Tavani has given the correct latin version of this macarronic rendition given by the witch. Although the text of his footnote is rather long, it uncovers some very interesting philological and literary notions that are directly related to the stylistic embellishment of the text (i.e., "thought and language"): "Inizio del cosiddetto 'Simbolo Atanasiano' o, dalle parole iniziali, *Quicumque vult:*

The most important part of these semi-religious litanies pronounced by the midwife and the witch is the idea of God as the generator of light and life on earth, a notion that directs our attention on the contention of the two worlds that has been discussed previously: the *City of God* and the earthly city. This concept, discussed in a letter which Gil Vicente sent to the King, D. João III, in 1531, reflects the ideological framework of the basic Vicentine notion of the *comédia* form (i.e., the harmonious resolution of conflictive elements), and which is likewise noticeable in the *Comédia de Rubena*.

This idea is verbalized more explicitly when the witch pronounces "E mundos não combinarão," a statement which reflects the ideology of the two worlds through a contrastive juxtaposition in which those two worlds are placed. The interactive process of those two worlds is metaphorically inserted into the dramatic text in more than one instance of textual signification, the semantic aspects of this interaction will be studied when we consider the binary structure of the *Comédia* in detail.

'Quicumque vult salvus esse ante omnia opus est ut teneat catholicam fidem, quam nisi quisque integram inviolatamque servaverit absque dubio in aeternum peribit.' Del testo, cit. in *Buen Amor* 378 d, esiste una parafrasi poetica di Juan del Encina: *Canc.* 1496, ff. 26 v.-27 r., 'Qualquiera que quiere ser'. La parodia gilvicentina in parte altera il testo latino, in parte lo riduce in portoghese con parole in assonanza con quelle originali (*ut teneat catholicam* > *Huy! tem a gayola; integram* > *antre o gram; dubio... peribit* > *tudo per hi*). Cf. Michaëlis, *NV*, pp. 294-95. Sulla parafrasi in Gil Vicente cf. inoltre Teyssier, pp. 447-51 e L. Stegagno Picchio, *Il Pater Noster dell'*Auto do Velho da Horta, in 'Annali dell'Istituto Univ. Orient. - Sezione Romanza', III, 1961, pp. 191-98 [192, n. 1; 196-98]. Al v. 465 *vulto* può essere ridotto a *vult*, perché il v. è ipermetro: ma la correzione no è indispensabile, eseguendola si rischierebbe di eliminare uno degli elementi deformanti della parodia ripristinando una forma corretta in un testo tutto scorretto. Al v. 467 *fidem*, in rima con *alem*, è ossitono, come altrove *amém* in rima con *bem, ninguém, também* (cf. Teyssier, pp. 93-94). 'In principio erat Verbum, et Verbum erat apud Deum, et Deus erat Verbum. Hoc erat in principio apud Deum. Omnia per ipsum facta sunt, et sine ipso factum est nihil, quod factum est. In ipso vita erat et vita erat lux hominum' (Ioan. 1, 1-4). *mita m'era: mitam era* per *vita(m) era[t]*. Il v. è ipometro. Cf. Michaëlis, *NV*, p. 276. '*Erat lux vera*, quae illuminat omnem hominem *venientem* in hunc mundum' (Ioan. 1, 9). 'Non erat ille lux sed ut testimonium perhiberet de lumine' (Ioan. 1, 8). Contaminazione tra Ioan. 1, 10 e 1, 3-4: 'In mundo erat, et mundus per ipsum factus est, et mundus cum non cognovit' (vv. 478-479 e 482) e '... et sine ipso factum est nihil... In ipso vita erat...' (vv. 480-481). 'Fuit homo missus a Deo, cui nomen erat Ioanes' (Ioan. 1, 6); cf. Michaëlis, *NV*, p. 276. 'Hic venit in testimonium, ut testimonium perhiberet de lumine, ut omnes crederent per illum' (Ioan. 1, 7). Cf. Michaëlis, *NV*, p. 309 (76-78)."

Before Rubena's departure *deus ex machina,* the action-filled first act continues with the invocation of four devils ("per esconjurações e feytiços"), as the instructions affirm, who will finally remove Rubena from the scene, on a litter ("hum andor"). It is not known where they came from although it is stated that they came "d'arrancada," all of a sudden, to do the witches bidding. Legião, the leader of this comically nefarious group, is not happy about the mission and manifests his anger in the typical anti-feminist tirade:

> (Legião) O que há-de ser há-de ser
> porque seraa o que for!
> Porém, forçar hua molher
> tod'o infernal poder!
> Ja nam pode ser pior!
> Hé hũa torta defumada,
> tapadeyro de privada
> que faz tanta rapazia
> na metá de hua encruzilhada,
> que nos trouxe d'arrancada
> a fazer-lhe cortesia. (67-68)

This interesting passage, as related to the duality concept which shapes the dramatic piece, shows that the witch, acting from the natural world of everyday phenomena, has supernatural powers to command the demonic world. This allows for a closer relationship between the natural and supernatural spheres of influence, allowing us to observe a certain degree of correspondence between them. This confrontation of two distinct and opposing levels (natural and supernatural, good and evil, etc.) leads us to suppose that there are, indeed, conflictive forces which dynamically. The play becomes saturated with this pervasive dualistic ideology to the extent that it conditions the dramatic action, reflected now in character portrayal, the linguistic pattern, and the imagery of the dramatic discourse. The dialectics of interaction between opposing forces (here, the power of interaction with the forces of evil) is manifested also on the level of "character delineation" through the dialectical (thought/action) portrayal of the two characters (Rubena and Cismena) who best exemplify the basic idea of contrast; that is, between passivity and action, where the former represents actantial passivity and a static dialogic situation – the inertia of lyricism — and the latter represents dynamic interaction, especially in spatial (i.e., actantial) terms.

It would appear, then, that the action of the *Comédia* finds its potential structural pattern, on the level of plot-making, in a binary opposition of dramatic agents whose function it is to divide the ensuing allegorical struggle among them, creating dramatic situations and a verbal pattern of corresponding images that are akin to the less realistic morality plays of the Middle Ages.

The function of "donors," which the devils represent in the actantial diagram above, through the expressed demands of the witch, aims at the direct harmonization of the desired "object" in the dramatic action of Act I. Ideally this interaction would restore Rubena to her prior state of innocence but this, of course, would be quite impossible and the witch, in the typical "Celestina" stance, tries the second best thing: trickery. In the dialogue between the four devils and the witch this intention is made manifest:

> (Caroto) Que demandas? em que andas?
> (Feiticeira) Que sirvaes esta senhora.
> Ora sus! remedeá-la,
> levay-a muyto escondida
> e trazede-m'a parida!
> A criancinha engeytá-la
> onde seja recolhida. (72-73)

That is, they are specifically ordered to bring back Rubena after she has given birth and to abandon the child somewhere where it can be found. The contrary, however, takes place: Cismeninha, Rubena's daughter, is the one whom the devils bring back from their secret undertakings. Rubena flees after giving birth to her daughter. The quoted speech of the witch offers us an insight into the deliberate structuring of the work. Semiologically, it opens up an obvious and easy resolution to the conflict through the *deus ex machina* technique, which Gil Vicente had already used in other plays. But this resolution is rejected by the devils' failure to carry out the witch's orders. The work, then, does not end after the first act but is forced to continue on for two more acts so that the Cismena situation (closely related to the thematic material of the first act) can be dealt with. This comic design appears verbalized at the very end of the first act where the Scholar once again comes on stage, this time in an epiloguist role to report tersely on Rubena's withdrawal from society ("sin otra compaña sino soledad") but then shifting briefly to a prologuist role to point ahead to the ensuing dramatic action of acts two and three. In this narrative segment attention is focussed on the thematic content of the ensuing story rather than on the causal-consequential unity of action or organic parts which a truly dramatic text demands.

The plot in the second part of the *Comédia*, that corresponding to the "Segunda Cena" and "Terceira Cena," will develop the story of Cismena. We know that Rubena's dilemma was resolved *only* through a symbolic interpretation of textual images (i.e., not actantially), while the action that is now to ensue (to withstand the moral test) will be achieved only thematically, by an extension of the family line (mother-daughter); that is, through the unfolding drama of Cismena's virtuous struggle with the temptations that brought her mother to her sad end. This realignment of purpose, therefore, is reproduced structurally through a syntagmatic or sequential ordering of the plot in such a way that one dramatic agent is substituted for another (Cismena for Rubena). This "primitive" technique, if we must label as such the literary conventions of the past, is amply indicative of Gil Vicente's desired end – the creation of a Christian vision of comic drama not unlike that which guided the intention of Dante in his *Commedia*. This idea is clearly expressed by the Scholar who reinforces Gil Vicente's definition of comedy (as opposed to tragedy) when he notes that Rubena's final situation (potentially "tragic") "es cosa profunda," a subject relegated to the mysterious by the playwright in order to lend it an air of importance while, at the same time, he disposes of the no longer needed character.

A paradigmatic reading – an inventory and appraisal of the vertical coherence of images – shows, however, that the association of these two characters (Rubena and her daughter) goes beyond a mere substitution of dramatic agents that uncover an allegorical message. Cismena is given over by the devils, instead of the expected Rubena, and ends up in the hands of the witch who takes over the task of the child's guidance. That character (the witch), furthermore, invokes once again her privileged supernatural powers to call upon the fairies who will prophesy Cismena's arduous struggle in life and her ultimate happiness. They promise to help her in her difficult situation.

At this point we enter a pagan world, a world populated by fanciful entities of magical powers:

> (Feiticeyra) Diabos! Por meu amor,
> filhos meus e meus senhores,
> yde-me aa deosa mayor:
> dizey que, por seu louvor,
> me mande as fadas mayores,
> as suas duas fermosas,
> com melodia serena,
> que me fadem a Cismena
> sobre todas as ditosas. (90)

Further on we observe that the path which Cismena will follow, according to the desire of the witch, who has now become even more of a fairy godmother to Cismena than she was to Rubena (because she makes a petition to the *deosa mayor* who rules over the fairies), will be a flowery way, a most pleasurable road that is reminiscent of the medieval *locus amoenus* here associated, of course, with Rubena's state of virginity before the unfortunate loss of that virtue (i.e., virginity = honor).

This Edenic way, however, is soon proscribed by Ledera (one of the melodious fairies) who, in the usual a-dramatic, narrative technique of Gil Vicente, warns that Cismena will encounter many unfortunate perils:

> Esta naceo em tal hora
> que ha-de correr gram tormenta
> dolorosa.
> Depois seraa gram senhora
> de toda fortuna isenta,
> muy ditosa.
> Mas primeyro muy chorosa,
> sem emparo, aqui em Creta
> se veraa,
> e a poder de fermosa
> e de casta e de discreta
> tornaraa. (92-93)

This is a specific realization of Gil Vicente's comic formula: "prymeyro ... chorosa" and "Depois ... muy ditosa." This fortune-telling of the fairies seems to suggest that acts two and three (the Cismena story) is a complete comedy (unhappy beginning shifting to happy ending) according to a straight-forward reading of Gil Vicente's own definition of the *comédia* form. Since this seems so strongly to be the case, it becomes even more imperative to look beyond that definition to a more comprehensive understanding of what this comedy form meant to him; that is, it forces us to look for an explanation of the existense of the first act. It becomes clear that the trajectory of unhappiness-to-happiness had to also include the fundamental notion of "pacíficas concordanças" (the harmonizing perspective). That is, without the Rubena-segment the Cismena-segment is incomplete, a fragment rather than a full work. And this fact is what makes his vision of the comedy form unique. Another artist could very easily have made one play out of the first act and another play out of the second and third acts. Gil Vicente, however, finds unity in what could easily have been two separate unities. The Vicentine concept of unity is, then, a very special thing and must be understood on its own terms to be properly appreciated, especially since that concept is manifested in both of his works that embody the comedy-form.

In order to make the correct thematic associations required by the Vicentine concept of the *comédia* form, let us compare this prophesied idyllic future of Cismena with that of her mother (Rubena) before the fall:

> Siempre de mi padre amada,
> siempre de todos querida,
> siempre vestida arrayada,
> siempre señora llamada,
> siempre adorada y servida,
> siempre horra y muy isienta. (48-49)

In addition to portraying Rubena as having been pampered into foolishness, the temporal references in these two passages points to a very different perspective on the part of the dramatist; especially as they relate to the two dramatic agents put into focus (Rubena and Cismena). There is a marked contrast between the verbal patterns in question. Whereas Rubena is (temporally) portrayed by the anaphoric use of the word "siempre" which restricts her sphere of activity to the past (as connoted by the past participles: "amada," "querida," etc.), Cismena, quite on the contrary, is the "subject" of a transitive and dynamic action which seems to temporally and spatially represent an act of volition, of her own free will to overcome the arduous turmoil of her future life. This observation, meanwhile, throws metaphorical light on the comic action through an emphasis on the semantic properties of the verbal proposition "to restore" or, as is now the case, to maintain virtue in a cynical world.

This perspective, if considered within the conventional literary traditions of medieval discourse, places Cismena in a heroic position similar to that of the chilvalric hero whose prowess must be displayed through the overcoming of a set number of almost impossible ordeals and whose virtuous victory over the forces of evil is rewarded with a prize. Also associated with the traditional romance *mythos* is the obscure past of the heroe or, in this case, of the heroine. This allows us to consider the story of Cismena as displaying some of the characteristics of the chivalric tradition. Northrop Frye has noted that:

> Romance, like comedy, has six isolatable phases, and as it moves from the tragic to the comic area, the first three are parallel to the first three phases of tragedy and the second three to the second three phases of comedy . . . (199)

The last three phases, as Frye describes, are by far the most important phases that Gil Vicente dramatizes, not only spatially (i.e., only the first act of this *Comédia* is partly representative of the first three phases belonging to the tragic rhythm), but also in the acute focus on societal renewal which defines the comic action (163-206). The movement towards a new society that abolishes the absurd conventions of the old (that is, from *pistis* to *gnosis*) is the comic perspective that, by far, operates as the motivating principle in the *Comédia de Rubena*. It is difficult for us to detect that change within a highly theological context of societal renewal, but it nevertheless exists as a transformation expressing secular concerns. In this particular comic vision that we are observing, the conversion process that must operate in the comedy may be summed up in the authoritative words of the prince who says:

> Más alta, dice Platon,
> es la virtud que el estado;
> y a esta es obligado
> el mundo de dalhe el don
> y el cetro mas honrado. (157)

It is here that theological concepts are secularized by Gil Vicente in an attempt to provide a framework for societal renovation; still a monarquical concept to be sure, but humanistic in its vision of the common man's ability to overcome the obstacles of his past.

Cismena, as we shall see, is the incarnation of this humanist concept of inborn, not inherited, virtue which reflects the Renaissance, Christian re-interpretation of Platonic philosophy:

> The Florentine [Neo-Platonic] philosopher Pico della Mirandola (1463-1494) wrote an *Oration on the Dignity of Man* (1498) in which he located human dignity in man's freedom from any fixed or static place in the chain of being that links him to the angels and to God above him and to the animals, plants, and inert matter below him. Man is an autonomous moral agent, containing in his own nature the possibility of the most varied development, who can by free choice become akin to any being, become like a rock or plant or beast [cf. Rubena = sirena] if he should turn toward evil, like the angels or like a mortal god [cf. Cismena = Diana] if he turn toward good. . . . Freedom is the harmonious union of knowledge, capacity, and will, and this freedom is a human conquest, the result of the gradual development, through education and a long series of appropriate choices, of the habit of virtue (Rice 78).

It is in this capacity, as J. R. Andrews has noted, that the *Comédia de Rubena* approaches what would best be described as a *bildengsdrama*, a drama "of the gradual development" and ultimate "human conquest" of virtue through rational understanding.

In this respect, we observe in the *Comédia* Cismena's struggle to overcome her obscure descent. We note that this character, considering Frye's archetypal notions once again, is given tasks that she must overcome if virtue is to win out; but unlike the world of romance, these feats are placed within the realistic categories of everyday life, thus placing her dilemma within the context of the comic vision, one which the audience, any audience, can find plausible. The pastoral elements, for example, if compared with the highly idealized versions of the world of romance, are here related entirely within the confines of realistic and at times almost satirical literature. In this we note a similarity to the earlier farces; especially in the burlesque elaboration of the shepherd(ess) "Cismeninha" in terms of a country bumpkin.

In the Vicentine *comédia*, there is an attraction for the medieval (chilvalric and pastoral) literary motifs. They are often placed, however, in the context of a changing society in which there is an alarming concern with "legitimizing bourgeois pretensions":

> A popular genre of humanist ethical literature in the Renaissance was the treatise *De vera nobilitate* ("of true nobility") which put true nobility in virtue and personal merit rather than in birth and taught that virtue is acquired, not inherited.... The idea of virtue, moreover, was itself given a positive middleclass content.... Fundamentally, to live nobly meant to fight and not to work. Above all, the noble was thought to derogate from his nobility ... if he engaged in trade. In contrast, beourgeois morality attributed positive value to productive work. The great sin became idleness rather than dishonor (Rice 56).[5]

Cismena, having been adopted by peasants, is later about to be auctioned off as a moorish slave when the fairies, once again through fortuitous means, save her from this end. She flees to "Arrouchelas," a wooded area. In this thicket she is nourished by a savage beast, a mythological and legendary motif of folkloric tradition. In this we see the function of these motifs to underscore the heroine's association with the world of Romance: Cismena's (mythological) relationship with the natural world which she "domesticates," as it were, proving her superior category, as well as the motif of the hero (nurtured by an animal) whose unknown

---

[5] Note Clita's remark to the indolent Felicio: "Que fazeis ca tod'o dia? / Vós nam tendes que fazer? / ... / Hide buscar de comer!" (130). This would not explain the ritualistic comic ending of Gil Vicente, where the non-aristocratic citizen is integrated into a traditionally noble lineage, were it not for the fact that "in practice ... bourgeois virtue rarely resisted the attraction of aristocratic status; and the ambition of most merchants was to exchange the social ambiguities of trade for the universally recognized prestige of nobility" (Rice 57).

origin is no obstacle in forging a new historical reality (cf. the legend of Romulus and Remus). Cismena thus proves her excellence not only in relationship to nature but also to other individuals less fortunate than she. This, of course, outlines her characterization in such a way that her felicitous wedding at the end of the *Comédia* appears as the just recompense of an exceptional individual.

One other element that should be mentioned in relationship to Cismena's heroic depiction concerns the spatial category. It is characteristic of the romance to relate the *mythos* in terms of a sequential ordering of the heroe's life: "The essential element of plot in romance is adventure, which means that romance is naturally a sequential and processional form . . ." (Frye 186).

In the *Comédia,* however, the shape of the romantic quest is neutralized by the total disregard for spatial realism (i.e., the unity of place is omitted in the dramatist's concept of comic action): Cismena is in Crete when her obnoxious Portuguese flatterers court her and when she and the court seamstresses sew their fineries for the "Bispo do Funchal" and other dignitaries of Portugal. This lack of spatial authenticity has caused many a critic to ponder over this technique of "sovrapposizione di piani geografici" which Tavani as well as Michaëlis have observed. But we have seen that the causally elaborated plot construction in Gil Vicente is subordinated to thematic interests. The neglect of geographical and even temporal coherence serves to universalize the central idea, a poetic conception that parallels the poet's non-realistic (i.e., non-heroic) depiction of the comic character. The sometimes realistic portrayal of character, however, helps divorce the comic action from the world of romance and reverts the audience to their own reality, a major issue in comic design. Robert Scholes reminds us, noting Frye's notions of generic categorization, that "Romance offers us superhuman types in an ideal world" (133).

We have seen some of these elements and their functional purpose in the *comédia* structure: the supernatural motifs (intervention of types such as the devils and the fairies), Cismena's perils (her foster parent's intention of selling her as a Moorish slave and her narrow escape into the forest), and finally the mythological nourishment by the beast, all serve to idealize the heroine's character and endear her to her audience while, at the same time, remaining close to everyday reality. Yet, it must be restated,

Cismena's idealization functions in the *Comédia* as a conventional demonstration, or proof, of her superior virtues. These are presented in practical, not romantic terms, for, by contrast to the world of heroic values, she is highly ironic and satirical when it comes to censuring the false gallantry of her chivalric suitors.

Cismena, unlike Rubena, is endowed, from her very beginning, with a strong sense of chastity and discretion, virtues that are of utmost importance in the preservation of honor. We observe this in her conscious agony over her mother's mysterious and unfortunate disappearance and her own hapless illegitimacy (i.e., she is conscious of being a bastard child) both of which make her feel a true "estrangeira" of life. And yet, Cismena's extraordinary virtue allows her to find the honor which her mother was unable to retain and which she must "win" as she struggles through life's way.

Cismena's misery seems to be duplicated when, at the death of her adopted mother, the noble woman of Crete, she is once again left an orphan, alone but this time not without a sizeable fortune. Once again, Cismena is fortuitously singled out in the comic action.[6] Still, Cismena laments her state of solitude:

> Choraraa meu coração!
> Vós, olhos, olhay por mim
> porque veja posto em fim
> meu proposito muy sam,
> casto como seraphim!
> E assi, como marfim,
> seja clara minha vida
> e minha honrra luzida,

---

[6] Could these fortuitous happenings (symbolic manifestations of God's grace?) be an implicit reference to Cismena's preordained state, as the radical church reformers of the sixteenth century would have it? Is the dialectical ("bad/good" fortune) process in plot design a deliberate attempt to see fate as the temporal manifestation of God's divine providence? These considerations are questions that we may consider for further speculation in reference to the *dianoia* of the *comédia*. In terms of plot construction, the casual (i.e., coincidental) organization of occurrences has always been deemed proper to the comic action, while the causal (i.e., organic) syntax in drama has been traditionally reserved for tragic or "more serious" actions. For his part, Frye notes in *Anatomy of Criticism* that "Unlikely conversions, miraculous transformations, and providential assistance are inseparable from comedy" (170).

e como fino robim
assí seja esclarecida! (110)

Cismena's lament provides an occasion to re-state her very serious proposal of counteracting her inherited misfortune which, although it does not define her as an individual, is nonetheless an obstacle. This is apparent in her continuous lament, her feelings of estrangement which reminds the audience of Rubena's sin. This is important to mention because we must not forget that it is the opposition of good (Cismena's virtuous behavior) to evil (the constant focus on her mother's dim past) that is at the very core of the ideological (allegorical) struggle in the text.

The images of "seraphim" and "marfim" emphasize the purity of her intentions, while the adjective "fino" in association with "robim" is a direct reference to Cismena's affliction: the counterbalancing of her mother's sin through a kind of generational transformation in which she, through the dramatic (and at times contrived) miracle of poetic justice, overcomes her dark origin. By juxtaposing "fino" and "robim" the playwright is skillfully comparing Cismena's refinement (i.e., "fino") through virtuous behavior (i.e., reason and chastity) with the deceptive love (unbridled passion or "falso amor") that damned her mother (Rubena = "robim").

As the first test to her chaste resolve, now that she is of a nubile age and alone and unprotected, Cismena meets a formidable threat to her virginity, one with a long Peninsular tradition: the old go-between. The deceptive panderess becomes the self-appointed "protector" of Cismena's virtue. The comic yet dangerous endeavor of this old woman shows her in a role opposite to that of the two characters in the play modeled after Celestina, the midwife and the witch. While the latter women try to help Rubena out of trouble, the panderess tries to entice Cismena into it. These opposing dimensions of the Celestina characters – the dissembling of virginity lost (one of Celestina's skills was resewing hymens) and the attack against virginity retained – were both carried out by means of guile and trickery, one against society, the other against an individual. Cismena, of course, refuses the old woman's indecent proposals. This dramatic segment offers an opportunity to present the conventional appearance-versus-reality motif (i.e., "ser" versus "parecer") so popular and particularly reflective of Peninsular social realities at this time. It complements the squire/fox image (also representative of trickery and dissimulation), formerly discussed, in its attempt to reverse the conventional societal norms:

> (Beata) Como teverdes terceyra
> podeis vos aproveytar
> e a fama estar inteyra
> com gentil dissimular
> S'eu, mana, nam fora freyra,
> porque isto nam me hé dado . . .
> hum senhor muy estimado
> me rogou que vos requeyra
> e me deu d'isso cuydado. (119)

It is important to highlight the contrast that the cluster of images associated with Cismena ("seraphim," "marfim," etc.) makes with those of the panderess involving the idea of "dissimular," of falsified honor. These symbols of purity, reason, and chastity are elaborated when Cismena is presented in close approximation to the classical Apollo and Diana, mythological figures representing the attributes that Cismena avidly desires to protect (reason and chastity):

> Ao deus claro, convertida
> encomendo minha vida
> sem amparo;
> pois nascer me custou caro
> favorece-me, Dïana,
> que atee 'qui
> o ceo me foy sempre avaro
> e a ventura tirana
> pera mi. (121-22)

Tavani prefers the first line of this verse ("Ao deus claro, convertida") from the *Compilaçam* of 1586 to the one that appears in the *Compilaçam* of 1562 ("Ao d's Apolo Claro") because the latter is not an eight syllable verse as it should be: "il v. ["Ao d's Apolo Claro . . ."] è ipermetro, senza alcuna giustificazione, e non è riducible all'isosillabismo . . ." (121). The two lines, however, are identical in idea, that is, Apolo = deus Claro. J. E. Cirlot in *A Dictionary of Symbols* gives us a complete version of the attributes that these mythological characters possess. Its importance in the complex of images of the *Comédia* is essential:

> Apollo: In mythology and alchemy, his spiritual and symbolic significance is identical with that of the sun.... (14) In theogony... [Apollo] represents the moment (surpassing all others in the succession of celestial dynasties) when the heroic principle shines at its brightest.... On occasion, the Sun appears as the direct son and heir of the god of heaven, and Krappe notes that he inherits one of the most notable and moral of the attributes of this deity: he sees all and, in consequence, knows all. In India, as Sûrya, it is the eye of Varuna; in Persia, it is the eye of Ahuramazda; in Greece, as Helios, the eye of Zeus (or of Uranus); in Egypt it is the eye of Ra, and Islam, of Allah (302).

We will remember that, in her defensive stance, Cismena resorts to the image of the "eye" ("Vos, olhos, olhay por mim") which we must necessarily equate to human understanding or reason, so clearly associated with the mythological definition of Apollo. The idea is further elaborated by the "light" images of the former passage which are indicative of Cismena's chastity (i.e., "*clara* vida," "honra *luzida*,", and "*esclarecida*" [italics are mine]). Likewise, Cirlot explains the archetypal meaning of Diana when he observes that she is:

> The goddess of woods, related to nature in general and to fertility and wild animals. She bears the Greek name of *Hecate,* meaning "she who succeeds from afar," and she is therefore linked with the "Accursed Hunter" (such as Wotan).... It has been pointed out that her characteristics vary with the phases of the moon: Diana, Jana, Janus. This is why some mythological and emblematic designs show her as Hecate with three heads, a famous, triform symbol which – like the trident of the three heads of Cerberus – is the infernal inversion or the trinitarian form of the upper world. According to Diel, these threefold symbolic forms of the underworld allude also to the perversion of the three essential "urges" of man: conservation, reproduction and spiritual evolution. If this is so, then Diana emphasizes the terrible aspect of Woman's nature. Nevertheless, because of her vows of virginity, she was endowed with a morally good

character as opposed to that of Venus, as can be seen in the *Hippolytus* of Euripides (77-78).

It becomes clear, then, that the references to Apollo and Diana are metaphorically componential in the text of the *Comédia*. One might think, in fact, that Gil Vicente's repertoire of classical symbols would be more weighty, if not more abundant, than some critics have previously considered. Within the binary system that structures the text these elements mirror its theme: the search for moral integrity which is dialectically polarized between reason, ordered human understanding – the Sun (Apollo) as the "eye" of discernment – and the ambiguous status of Diana (moon), potentially lascivious yet chaste. Furthermore, the motifs of lust and chastity reflect the binary opposition of two protagonists that, as previously stated, are morphologically represented in their names: (Rubena = Rubi = passion) versus (Cisma = cismar = to reason). Exactly how Cismena interacts "actantially" in this symbolic context is the subject of the comic resolution that will be discussed in depth later. For now let it suffice to say that Cismena uses this "solar" impetus (reason and life) vis-à-vis the dubious image of chastity (Diana, the accursed huntress) to underscore the comic *mythos* of Spring: the saturation of vital impulse at a level commensurate with acceptable societal norms, or, more specifically, the restoration of morally approved behavior through the institution of marriage, which, in the *Comédia*, was perverted by the unrestrained passion of Rubena. In addition to this, the final epiphany of matrimony is representative of social escalation through personal merits identified here with a Christian concept of virtue.

When Clita, Cismena's maid, refers to the panderess as a tricky fox, "Cheyrais-me vós a raposa / que nam acha que caçar" (121), the audience (or reader) is reverted to the same imagery of social deception formerly used in act I by Benita, Rubena's maid. The semantic attributes unleashed by the repetition of that image when juxtaposed to the idea associated with the mythological figures of Apollo and Diana, connote Cismena's moral struggle: her contention with deceit in her search for light and truth, archetypically represented by the two cyclical forces. This leads us to another observation concerning Gil Vicente's world view: dissimulation (appearance = disorder) is opposed to moral integrity (reality =

natural order), as the two opposing channels of social behavior that must be harmonized in the end. Frye notes that in:

> the action of comedy... moving from one social center to another is not unlike the action of a lawsuit, in which the plaintiff and defendant construct different version of the same situation, one finally judged as real and the other as illusory (166).

These mythological motifs, like that of Cismena being favored by Diana, are not only used as illustrative references. Cismena vis-à-vis Diana brings to the plot design of the *Comédia,* a prefiguration of the moral attributes that will bring about the "coincidental" ending; that in which the prince serves as the instrument of harmonization. Therefore, Cismena, through the process of metaphorization, comes to possess all the ambivalent traits of the Roman divinity: the woman of nature with her instinctual bend toward passion, but at the same time keeping her virginity in check through constant exertion of her will to do what is morally best.

We see Cismena in her natural state when she laments her sordid fortune and fears that her luck will be that of her mother's:

> Oo mãy da filha perdida!
> Oo filha da mãy prenhada
> sem ventura!
> Alma sem vida nacida,
> filha da morte acordada
> sempre escura!
> Oo minha mãy! Onde estais?
> Minha mãy, onde me vou?
> Minha mãy, nam me buscais?
> Vós, bem sey que sospiraes,
> porque os sospiros que eu dou
> sam os mesmos que vós daes! (108)

Leaving aside the obvious symbolic signification of such words as "escura" in the contextual situation of comparison with Rubena, Cismena is here equated in a much more fundamental and significant manner: "os sospiros que eu dou" = "os mesmos que vós daes!" This makes the generational association between Rubena, the symbol of passion ("mãy prenhada sem ventura"), and Cismena, the restraint of that instinct, unmistakably clear.

We have already observed Cismena's response to the forces within her in her Apollonian cry for help, her desire to discern the truth with the light of reason that her mother was not able to perceive. Thus we note that in the substitution of dramatic agents (Cismena for Rubena) the theme is dramatically furthered, from Act I to Acts II and III, through the complex system of images that elaborate, expand, and complete the symbolism introduced in Act I. The idea of maintaining honor, then, becomes all the more meaningful through this character Cismena, through her means of perceiving and motivating herself to act in keeping with the desired fulfillment of that action. Cismena will prove her moral integrity by refusing the unreasoned proposals of her chivalrous suitors. Her prize will be the comic resolution of the play.

In addition to those meanings observed above, there remains another association between Cismena and the goddess Diana that adds weight to the metaphorical development of these ideas. The analogy Diana = moon alludes to the paradoxical characteristics of Diana that would define her as pure yet sensually coveted (cf. Federico García Lorca's "En el aire conmovido / mueve la luna sus brazos / y enseña, *lúbrica e pura,* / sus senos de duro estaño [italics mine])," from his *Romance de la luna, luna*). Symbolically, the image of the moon is laden with ancient archetypal notions of instability; of cyclical change. This idea of instability and cyclical mutation (appearance, waning and final disappearance before reappearance) closely resembles the rhythm of life: birth, growth, and death (Cirlot 205).

For the purposes of our observations, considering the action of the *Comédia* diachronically vis-à-vis the symbolism of the lunar cycles, it should be noticed that these phases reflect the archetypal motion from the *mythos* of Autumn (Rubena and the tragic effect) to that of Spring (Cismena and the comic resolution), with the corresponding ideas of destruction-death and renewal-life. This cyclical movement underscores the basic notion of the Myth of Spring which aims, as its final goal, at the epiphany or celebration of life's instinctual impulse in the creation of a new and better social order. Cismena is that rebirth of a new society through the socially acceptable sacrament of marriage. James George Frazer reminds us in *The Golden Bough* that Diana was above all a symbol of fertility. His description explains clearly the appropriateness of the classic myth in Gil Vicente's representation:

> Diana was not merely a patroness of wild beasts, a mistress of woods and hills, of lonely glades and sounding rivers; conceived as the moon, and especially, it would seem, as the yellow harvest moon, she filled the farmer's grange with goodly fruits, and heard prayers of women in travail. In her sacred grove at Nemi, as we have seen, she was especially worshipped as a goddess of childbirth, who bestowed offspring on men and women (163).

The fact that Cismena is associated with the images of Apollo (sun) and of Diana (moon), further suggests, in reference to the metaphor of difficult renewal (Cismena herself states that "nascer me custa caro"), the mythological connotation of "*hieros gamos*, generally understood as the marriage of heaven and earth." As Frazer explains, "the sun arises again after the gloom of night" (204). The harmonization suggested by this association of images, once again, emphasizes the idea of finality in the *Comédia*, a representation of the ritualistic function of the *mythos* of Spring.

The image of the *sun* (advocated by the use of Apollo – god of the sun) is clearly observed in the heroine's powers of discerning between right and wrong. Here we must note that Cismena, in spite of the marvelous resolution of the *Comédia* in which everything "ends happily ever after" like the magic world of the fairytale, does not appear as a true heroine of the world of romance. She is entirely depicted in realistic terms and even the obnoxious, irrational suitors are not representatives of that fanciful world of magic: there are no indications of their chivalric virtues, they are passively and despondently lost in the illusive world of their "falso amor" for the young Cismena. In fact, they are portrayed as satirically as possible; they are caricatures of a decadent society. Even the prince, we might add, a possible source for the introduction of the genuinely romanesque theme, does not dynamically "prove" himself worthy.

This dramatic agent – the prince – may further help us distinguish between the elements of dramatic comedy on one hand and the romanesque aspects of the *Comédia* on the other. Harold C. Knutson makes a clear distinction between dramatic comedy and romance when, in considering the function of the heroe of those two types of narratives *(mythoi)*, he points out their archetypal importance. His views may throw some light on the important distinctions that we are making about the Vicentine notion of comedy. That is, to demonstrate that the romanesque elements of the *Comédia* do not function as an element of that particular mythic configuration; serving, instead, as a *displaced* element within the (comic) ideological context of the *Comédia de Rubena*.

Knutson's words lead us to assume that the essential elements of the world of romance are missing from this Vicentine *Comédia:*

> Romance appears most forcefully in drama when the sequence enacted happens to be the major adventure, an *agon* which results in the apotheosis of the hero. . . . The hero must have an antagonist worthy of his struggle; the more arduous the combat, the more glorious the victory (120).

We should note here that the heroe (i.e., heroine) of our story is Cismena and not the prince. He is considered a statically "noble" character, that is, of nobility as social state with the corresponding and conventional qualities of regal honor: bravura, integrity of character, etc. These supreme qualities, however, (as he announces himself) must give way to the eminence of moral character that Cismena, a member of the lower class, displays. This interaction between persons of diverse social standing and the final victory of the inferior class (Cismena is not only given precedence for her superior moral qualities, but she is also incorporated – elevated – to a higher social position) over the superior class serves to support the ideological stance of Gil Vicente which reflects what would be the *ideal* of the Portuguese monarch: incorporating, from his people, the best qualities.

Here are combined in the *Comédia* the integrative functions of both generic plots, of the romance and of the comic mythos:

> We find, then, in romance a polarity strongly suggestive of the comic *mythos*. Indeed, comedy can be easily viewed as a down-to-earth, more socialized form of romance (120).

We can discern this socialized form of romance in the *Comédia* when the motif of the disguised prince is introduced as a method of establishing contact with a member of the lower class. In doing so, the prince is de-categorizing himself as a personage of the typical romance:

> The hero of romance is far more exalted in rank and in character than the usual bland comic hero. He is a prince with a sense of decorum suitable to this station, not a "fils de maison" from the upper middle class. Impetuous though the romantic hero may be, his behaviour as a lover is marked by restraint, articulateness, and magnificence. For these reasons, the dialectic of romance is more pronounced and more clearly moral than social; since kings and princes touch on the divine, their antagonists must be presented in a demonic light. The struggle between the ardent young man of comedy and his *barbon* deals with only one question: whose norms should dictate society? The laws of probability are suspended but not the laws of nature. The hero in comedy is one of us and subject to our limitations; the miracle which allows him to triumph is not of his making. In romance, however, magic, both black and white, plays havoc with the natural order; superhuman virtue combats superhuman malevolence. Not only is the moral polarity of romance on an epic scale, but the dramatic weight given to the two conflicting forces is the reverse of comedy. The latter depicts the movement from one society to another, a development fully realized only at the dénouement. The old régime of bondage holds the reins of power until the newly-formed, free society finally wrests them away.... In romance, the idealized society is before our eyes from the outset.... In romance, finally, the hero is not the central figure and the sole concern of his beloved, as he tends to be in comedy.... On the other hand, the hero of chivalric romance tends to be but one competitor among many for a lady who makes a special point of showing no preference (Knutson 120-21).

These ideas are sufficient to prove that the Vicentine *comédia* possesses qualities that are indicative of both types of *mythoi:* the romance and the comedy; yet it appears that both *comédias* (*Rubena* and *Viúvo*) are significantly closer to the genre of comedy in that they reflect the realistic side of society, the social and contemporary reality that rejects the chivalric narrative models and seeks instead the inventive capacity of the playwright. It is here that the plots of those *comédias* become a product of the dramatist's own observation. The social aspect (and, of course, its mortal implications) is far more important in these *comédias* than the ideal, romanesque stylizations that point to a different vision of reality.

The distinctions pointed to above are further underscored by the changing attitude of this noble character in contrast to the other suitors. At first, we note that instead of the usual romanesque qualities of the hero, the characterization of the prince is closely allied to the aspects of the suitors that Cismena rejects; that is, to the lovelorn behavior found in the *cancioneiro* love tradition of "cuidar e sospirar," proper to the courtly-love conventions of a static, medieval society, without the dynamic bourgeois virtues of work and thrift that define the new spirit of the Renaissance. Clita's remark to Felicio, "Que fazeis cá tod'o dia? / Vós nam tendes que fazer? / ... / Pera que he tanta perfia? / Hide buscar de comer!" (130), vehemently opposes the suitors passive concept of love. The only merit that one finds in the prince is his social status. The fact that he later recognizes Cismena's moral superiority not only marks an important attitudinal change in this dramatic agent, announcing the integrative end of the play's thematic constant, but also points to the harmonizing perspective (natural order = harmony = political stability) that the playwright defines as the monarchical stance.

Cismena, in her conscientious refusal of her suitors, is presented as an agent that functions as a true judge of the prevailing social code: the courtly tradition of chivalric love. Irony and sarcasm are her arms of defense in the bitter criticisms she raises against the absurd conventions of her society, thus leveling this would-be romance to the "low mimetic satire" stage that Frye has explained: "The chief difference between the high and low mimetic comedy, however, is that the resolution of the latter more frequently involves a social promotion" (44-45).

In this respect, the typology of the characters Felicio, Dario Ledo and Crasto Liberal is entirely a caricature of the types in Gil Vicente's society; they are indeed "flat characters" which are identified through a specific trait elaborated to exaggeration. That characteristic element of each will be the point of attack that Cismena will exploit with bitter sarcasm and irony.

Felicio is the prototype of the discrete and pining nobleman, victim of the poison-of-love (i.e., "Cárcel de amor") mentality of the contemporary sentimental novels. Although this figure is by far the most sympathetic and honest in his expression of love, he still represents the "falso amor" (i.e., "loco amor") that brought Cismena's mother to her ruin, for it is these same "novels" of ill-begotten love that the deceitful panderess would have Cismena read in the convent if she were to become a nun ("freyra"[!]): "ler-vos-ey *Cárcel d'amor* / e *Peregrino amador*" (114).

Crasto Liberal represents the ridiculed "senex," a man who has lost moral integrity and represents the absurd law of traditional norms, while Dario Ledo, another "blocking character," depicts the happy-go-lucky troubadour, another usurper of moral values. Such characters represent the conventional codes of love, of exploitation and seduction without moral consequence, that must be eliminated from a prosperous society.

The functional model that was earlier applied to the agents of the dramatic action would place these figures in the category of "opponents" vis-à-vis the desired thematic "object" of the action. They are in direct opposition to Cismena, the "subject" of the action: to maintain honor through the preservation and defense of the same virtue that her mother lost (i.e., chastity). In the category of "donor" one would place the fairies (Minea and Ledera), and in that of "helper," Clita and, to some extent (almost statically), the court seamstresses.

While the structural model used for a synchronic vision of the functional units of the *Comédia*'s action may be helpful, let us now consider, diachronically, the same segmental units in motion (the *mythos*), remembering Bremond's "logic of narrative possibilities" vis-à-vis the unity of thematic parts that structures the action of the dramatic piece.[7]

Figure 3 shows that although the Greimasian model was conceived initially with narrative discourse in mind, its applicability is,

---

[7] Claude Bremond observes that: "A narrative consists of a discourse which integrates a sequence of events of human interest into the unity of a single plot. Without succession there is no narrative, but rather description (if the objects of the discourse are associated through spatial contiguity), deduction (if these objects imply one another), lyrical effusion (if they evoke one another through metaphor of metonymy). Neither does narrative exist without integration into the unity of a plot, but only chronology, an enunciation of a succession of uncoordinated facts. Finally, where there is no implied human interest (narrated events neither being produced by agents nor experienced by anthropomorphic beings), there can be no narrative, for it is only in relation to a plan conceived by man that events gain meaning and can be organized into a structured temporal sequence" (390).

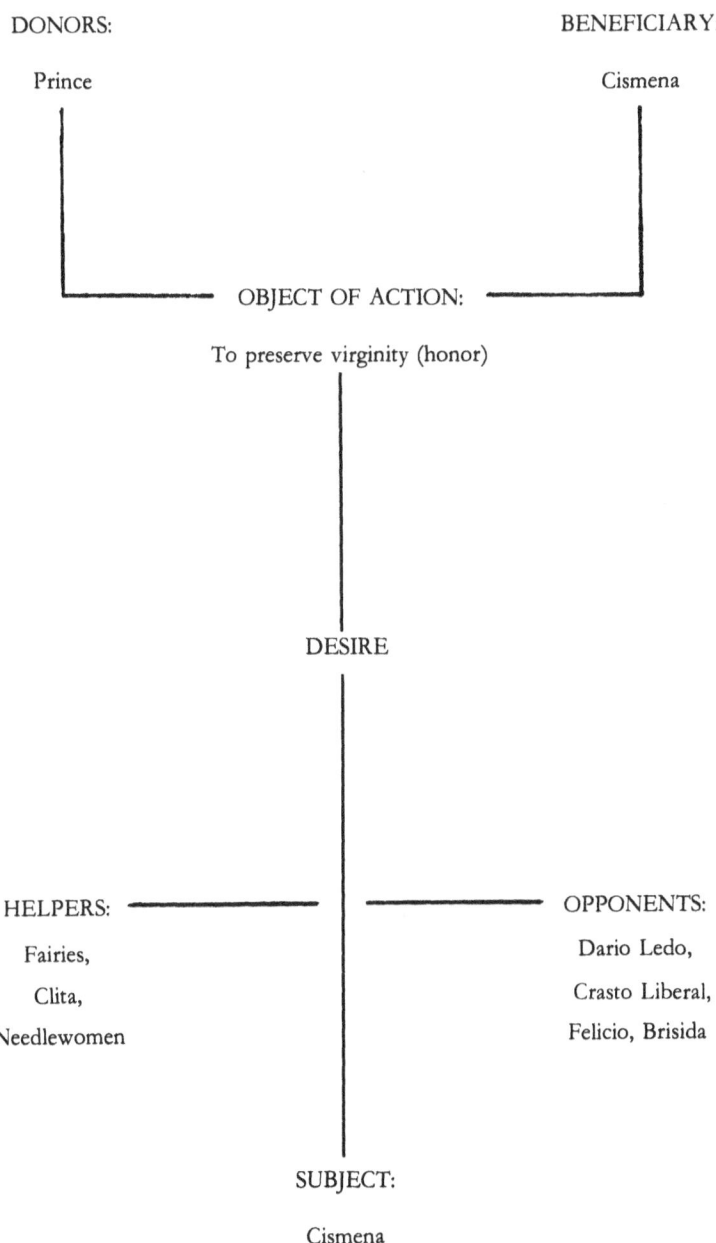

Figure 3. The *Comédia de Rubena* (Acts II and III)

nonetheless, valuable in this dramatic text because of its narrative scaffolding. In this respect it is interesting to note that the narrative aspect of the work reflects its source of inspiration (i.e., the novel of chivalry and the sentimental novel). There are several instances in which Gil Vicente depends on narrative exposition for the development of the plot. Without the Licenceado, for example, how would the audience know that Cismena is fifteen years old? or how were they to know that the *parvo's* name is Afonso? But the most narrative segment not theatricalized is that which starts "Hum príncipe de Síria veyo desconhecido. . . ." Here there is more than just incidental description and information. The actual motivational elaboration of the dramatic plot is abandoned to the narrative mode, thus eliminating any possible dramatic tension or suspense. More important to Gil Vicente, as we have observed, is the lyrical effusion of the (virtually) dramatic moment.

The process of actantial mimesis of the *Comédia*, as viewed from the preferred thematic perspective of Gil Vicente, would represent schematically the sequential segmentation of "degradation" and "amelioration" as follows:

> 1. "degradation" of Rubena: the process of degradation (error and consequential moral suffering) → degradation actualized (symbolic death)
> 2. "amelioration" as actualized by Cismena (projected attempt to maintain honor through the avoidance of her mother's error): the process of amelioration through moral tests → amelioration actualized (honor maintained and rewarded through the socio-spiritual sanctioning of virtue in the sacrament of marriage)

Up to this point we have been considering the action of the comic *mythos* in its process of development, of sequential syntax: the *mythos* or structure in movement, as Frye calls it. Let us now look at the structure in "stasis" or *dianoia:* ". . . the secondary imitation of thought, a *mimesis logou,* concerned with typical thought, with images, metaphors, diagrams, and verbal ambiguities out of which specific ideas develop" (83).

The *dianoia*, in this respect, outlines the pattern of images of the *Comédia de Rubena* in two distinct camps of signification which, as we have noted, obeys the binary principle. The basic idea of that binarism is found in the sequential elaboration of the two main segments (Rubena versus Cismena) which, as we observed above, is neatly divided between the two terms borrowed from Bremond: "degradation" and "amelioration," corresponding to the "tragic" dramatic agent (Rubena) and the comic dramatic agent (Cismena). In archetypal criticism, this progressive movement reflects the cyclical passage from the Myth of Autumn to that of Spring with its corresponding ideas of death (degradation) and life (amelioration) that underscore this type of anagogic analysis.

In the realm of textual images, these two ideas are metaphorically depicted in such a way that we may uncover the central ideological focus *(mimesis logou)* of the dramatic text. In order to do this, however, it is important that we always refer to the main action defined as the comic *mythos* of this *Comédia*. The concept of *mimesis* is a dynamic notion that depends on the apprehension of the total verbal structure of literary discourse: plot, characters (as functional agents of the plot) and thought and language (as symbolic reflections which organize the final meaning, the theme, of the plot).

In the *Comédia*, this organic notion of action defined as "to maintain honor through virtue" is reflected in moral terms and could easily be equated, by moral judgement, in the following manner:

> RUBENA: Loss of honor = degradation = death
> CISMENA: Preservation of honor = amelioration = life

Life and death are here the punishment and reward. Cismena's reward is connoted by the marriage that, in archetypal terms, functions as the guarantee and preservation of life, reproduction as a social factor, a renewal of society. The punishment of Rubena, on the other hand, is observed in the images alluding to a veritable *locus horrendus* in which that figure is totally aware of her moral transgression (*anagnorisis* → *pathos*): "Oo, tristes nuves escuras," etc. (46).

The supernatural world that comes in support of Rubena, through the intervention of the four devils (the existential demonic world), reiterates the idea of chaos and natural disorder that Rubena undergoes in her suffering. Here the images of "escuridão" and "mar profundo" connote the personal disorder and fearful state of that dramatic character. These ideas are, in turn, associated with the sinister symbols related to Rubena's final *dénouement:* the dense forest where the devils will take her in flight. The symbolic importance of this *topos* is not only complicated but also indispensable to the complex system of signs which exposes the *dianoia* of the text.

The forest and the images of height ("cume," "serra," and "outeiro"), symbolically considered in keeping with the mystical conceptions of the Judeo-Christian tradition (so very popular in the *early* Renaissance), have always been deemed the place *par excellence* of meditation and spiritual asceticism, given its distance from the secular turmoil of the city (civilization) and given its proximity to the ethereal realms. The symbol, furthermore, functions as an *axis mundi,* the center of the universe, the primeval force of creation touching upon that mythic *illo tempore* when man was in tune with the eternal realm of the divine (cf. Moses). In the *Comédia,* lest we forget, the devils have an engagement to meet in an elevated place, the same place where they were all to congregate before descending to do the witches bidding. It is also to this deserted place that, ultimately, Rubena will be taken to be relieved of her physical and moral suffering, although, on the contrary, it was her explicit desire to be taken to the depths of existence: "Y llevadme a las honduras," ". . . a aquel valle de tristuras" (46-47). Once again the playwright has harmonized "as avessas" or by the contrary, for the geographical location of the dramatic moment is reversed: "valle" ⟶ "serra." The archetype ("serra"), then, would appear to be of great significance to the text. In the process of "displacement" within its symbolic-mythological context, it is interesting to note that the apocalyptic motif of that symbol, its spirituality, is inverted in order to reproduce the world of demonic materialism.

Inversion, then, will be the key word in this displacement of a conventional archetype. Legião, the leader of the devils, is the first to direct our attention to the motif of density and elevation. He flies to its height like a "peixe-voador" ("Pollo ar yrey milhor / como peyxe voador"). This metaphorical paradox places the devil, perhaps Satan himself, in a position of reversal of the natural order, connoted by the idea of a "flying fish." The idea here, in reference to the demonic agents, is the exchange of one location for another, for although "flying fish" are a part of the natural order, they are, nonetheless, displaced unless found in water, their natural habitat. Legião is thus representative of the existential world seen as an upside down, adulterated reflection of the ordered world that Gil Vicente had discussed in his letter (1531). We immediately associate these demonic images (the reversal of the natural order) with the Stygian images uttered in Rubena's moment of pathos.

We have already observed that the witch had proposed using the world of the demonic to cover Rubena's error and therefore, restore the situation to its former state by inverting the normative moral concepts of society through trickery (appearance versus reality). This would be the category of reversal that corresponds to that character, that is, virtue as a condition of what is only apparent to others.

The inversion of the ethical codes of society are closely related to the symbol of elevation and dense vegetation, for it is there, the elevated forest region, that a myriad of symbols are fused metaphorically to the idea of inversion. This becomes clear through Legião's physical description of Plutão who is placed in the context of the conventional *locus horrendus*, a deformed entity of the tenebrous realms of hell: "Plutam faz rasto de cam / com as unhas ao través." The demonic action of that figure is extremely significant in that his bestial tracks are back to front ("ao través"). Spatially, this connotes the idea of advancement as a reversal, or as a descending progression instead of an ascending motion. All of the devils are characterized as the reversal of man, that is, as the bestial counterparts of the apocalyptic world: "God said, 'Let us make man in our own image, in the likeness of ourselves, and let them be masters of the fish of the sea, the birds of heaven, the cattle, all the wild beasts and all the reptiles that crawl upon earth' " (Genesis I:1).

Finally, the devils find themselves "ao longo desta ribeira," a reference which completes the symbolic association of reversals. The height and density of the region where Rubena will meet her end, at this point in the development of the linguistic pattern of verbal images, is metaphorically upside down, and thus negates the transcendental values that are sometimes associated with this motif. Its spiritual side, however, is brought about by the birth of Cismena at which time the perversion of the demonic world of the devils (and of Rubena before her ascent) gives way to the natural ordering of the apocalyptic vision. It is in this way that Rubena's purifying ascent up the "serra" may be likened to Cismena's moral "ascent" through life. We have observed that this symbolism often "blends" the two elements, the two worlds. This allows us to make the following antagonistic associations with respect to the *Comédia:* Rubena = tragedy-shadows-death versus Cismena = comedy-clarity-life; all of which is a reflection of the symbols of light and darkness, of Apollonian clarity and the tenebrous realms of the underworld.

The metaphorical meaning of "ribeira" in relation to the symbols of elevation is mentioned three times in the text: in the midwife's prayer to cure Rubena's "quebranto," in Legião's expressed wish to wait for the other devils by the streamlet, and in the Scholar's closing speech concerning Rubena's end:

> Como se vido ya fuera de pena
> hechó sus vestidos en una ribera,
> ceñió su camisa las carnes de fuera,
> hermosa en cabello como una serena. (74)

All of the three images of the "ribeira" (brook) are presented with a strong moral connotation that the motif assumes in its context: they are associated with Rubena's transgression. The image "ribeira" (as a water symbol) is saturated with this idea in the last of the three references in which it is associated with the term "sirena." The symbol unleashes the sematic reality of the earlier development: Rubena, as she undresses, is symbolically transformed into a siren ("ceñió su camisa las carnes de fuera"). This metamorphosis relegates her to the level of the subhuman creatures of the lower world, a punishment well-deserved for unreasoned surrender. The image is further detailed by the fact that the siren is the symbol of temptation, of the lubricity of man's instinct and of his perdition. We may recall, in this respect, that in Act VIII of the *Celestina,* the old go-between induces her "daughter," Areusa, to enjoy herself with Parmeno. In this sensuous scene of carnal delights, Celestina refers to Areusa as a siren ("pareces serena") because she appears half covered with the bed sheets. Rojas was shrewd in chosing this felicitous image (248).

The fact that the siren (water symbols) are associated to womanhood (i.e., fertility, generating instinct, and, often, promiscuity) allows us to observe the final meaning of the metaphor:

Rubena is passion, libidinous instinct, destruction to her society in terms of moral and religious standards; Cismena, on the other hand, is the total control of these pernicious qualities in man. Her Apollonian balance represents, in Freudian terms, the manifestation in the individual of the socially grounded superego which directs the ego (conscience) away from the transgression of communal laws and towards the acceptable channels of moral and spiritual values.

It is interesting to notice, meanwhile, that Rubena continues her ascent up the mountain after she has cast off her only wordly possessions (her clothing). This leads us to believe that Rubena was at least seeking moral direction at the end, a spiritual purging represented in the plot by the ascending movement.

If we observe the idea of degradation, formerly presented in Bremond's scheme, we will note that, in relationship to Rubena, it may be explained in terms of Freudian psychoanalytic nomenclature which may clarify the theme further. In this respect we can relate Rubena's action to the activity of the id or the realm of primordial, instinctive images. The id is the sphere of the human psyche that is directly involved with vitality; this impulse, in turn, can bring new life or its destruction.

Rubena is the symbol of unbridled passion which brought her moral decay. Her superego acted *a posteriori*, only as a mechanism of self-condemnation after the immoral act had been committed. In this respect we may note that this character is not without knowledge of the strict norms of conduct that her society imposes as a rule to be followed religiously. Within that moral consciousness, Rubena is quite aware that only matrimony serves as a channel for these vital impulses. Therefore, her dilemma lies not in the natural act of love, but in the transgression of the moral code of her society, a motif that becomes the staple of Peninsular comedic form. We observe that, in some instances, Rubena is far more concerned with hiding her error from her society's view. That is, we cannot assume that she is entirely without fault in the witches attempt to solve the problem through trickery. But, "poetic justice" inverts the expected turn of events and Cismena is introduced to a dramatic sequence in which we can observe the symbolic idea of original sin: Cismena may save herself (maintain her honor) if she learns to discriminate between right and wrong, if she chooses good over evil.

The binary principle that has been discussed previously informs the structure of the *Comédia* when we observe the passages of unconscious reality (Rubena's instinctive surrender to passion) to a state of consciousness (the rational discernment of Cismena). On the level of linguistic elaboration, of metaphorical elaboration, this is represented by the "primordial images" of darkness and light. Associated with the first of these images we have Rubena with the respective ideas of "escuridão," "seréia," and "demônios." Cismena, of course, belongs to the second of the two symbolic complexes of images, connoted now by clarity and chastity (Apollo, Diana and the luminous world of the fairies – in the sense that they open the way and guide Cismena in the rationalizing process of discernment).

The passage from irresponsible behavior to that of conscientious reasoning demands proofs of valor, of merit and victory over evil through virtuous behavior. Here we observe Cismena once again in terms of the romance hero(ine) who must prove that his or her conduct and superior qualities are indeed more meritorious than that of the natural world. This character overcomes deceitful corruption (e.g., the Beata) and the trickery of inconsequential flattery proposed in favor of carnal pleasures (the parasitic suitors with their chivalric and courtly love code of ethics). Cismena completes the cycle opened by her mother when she establishes all of her well-deserved virtues by the marriage to the prince, which, as we noted earlier, consecrates the marriage in secular terms – to replenish societal needs – and in theological terms: to fulfill God's natural laws. Only in this socio-religious sacrament can the qualities of purity, beauty and discretion be valid.

The Freudian comparison made earlier elucidates the structural model proposed by Greimas. Cismena's suitors function as "opponents" and they are the actantial representatives of the libidinous instinct (id) that motivates their actions, an obstacle to Cismena's resolved purpose. The concept of struggle – superego versus id – that outlines the attitudes of the ego or conscience of this character is expressed by the following complex of images: Cismena is compared not only to the mythological huntress, but also to the belligerent heron ("garça"), a commonplace medieval metaphor. The seamstresses catalyze the significance of this last metaphor in the manner of the Greek chorus whose purpose, according to Aristotle, is to orient the perception of truth embryonically contained in the dramatic action:

> The chorus cannot *do* anything to advance the quest, but as it suffers its passions of fear and pity it can grope through associated images of light and darkness, healing and disease, life and death, toward the perception of truth (Aristotle 29).

The perception of truth that the chorus of seamstresses patronize is that which orients the conscience of Cismena in her attempt to preserve herself against the instinctual attacks of seduction that had victimized her mother and even one of her suitors (Felicio). These destructive and uncontrolled appetites of love destroy Felicio and topple Dario Ledo and Crasto Liberal who, like Felicio, are alienated from their conscious behavior:

> (FELICIO) Que direy a mi de mi?
> porque quanto a mi digo
> falo com o mor imigo
> que eu nunca conheci,
> tanto mal tenho comigo!
> A ninguem nam me descubro
> e a mi nam sey que diga;
> descobre-me minha fadiga
> quantos secretos encubro
> e nam sey que via siga! (127)

Felicio's estrangement echoes that of Rubena in the first act. Dario Ledo finds himself in a similar state of (Petrarquistic) alienation:

> Minhas lagrymas ausentes,
> meus sospiros sem ventura,
> oo, minhas dores ardentes!
> Agora que estaes presentes
> alegray vossa tristura!
> Saudades, porque calaes?
> Angustias, que nam dizeis?
> Gemidos, que nam falaes
> os tormentos que me daes,
> os males que fazeis? (133)

No marked difference is noticeable in the *senex* figure of the lecherous old man, Crasto Liberal, when he says to Cismena:

> Com esse ar, com esse geyto,
> minha vida e meu espelho,
> me tendes todo desfeyto! (137)

Metaphorically, the *pathos* of these characters is very closely related to that of Rubena in Act I, with the difference that she suffers the conscientious knowledge of having committed the foolish error. The lovelorn suitors, however, suffer not being able to give vent to their libidinous desires.

The metaphorical analogy of love as passion continues to the very moment when the prince enters as the new admirer. At first he too reveals himself as the symbol of unbridled love, of the passion-of-love victim:

> Piedad, señora, espero,
> preso de vuestra beldad!
> Oo, señora! Pïedad,
> que soes el mi amor primero,
> amor en gran cantidad!
> Castigad vuestra beldad
> regurosa
> y mirad mi magestad
> y mi pena dolorosa,
> y que muero en tierna edad! (156)

Cismena, however, resists the insane advances of his passion:

> Señor, eu n'isto me fundo:
> dou-lhe que sejaes alteza!
> Nam darey minha limpeza
> ao mayor rey do mundo,
> nem por nenhũa riqueza! (156)

The prince continues this nonsensical tone of solicitation until at last, by opposition to the courtly lovers, he decides to offer a more consequential type of union: the legalization of love through marriage. The triumph of virtue is justified in Platonic terms when the prince states:

> Mas alta, dize Platon,
> Es la virtud que el estado;
> y esta es obligado
> el mundo de dalhe el don
> y el cetro mas honrado.
> Dadme la mano, señora,
> por mi esposa y laureola,
> pues que sois merecedora
> pera ser emperadora!
> Quant'a más, princesa sola! (157-58)

The idea of a binary structure which pervades the entire texture of images studied, resides in the philosophic (Platonic) meaning of the universe's ethical division: the world of Supreme Virtue (Beauty as reflection of the Absolute Idea) and the secular world in which only degrees of Virtue are possible to attain. Let us see how this idea has significant implications for the binary principle that focuses the central ideology of the *Comédia* (i.e., *dianoia*). We know that the protagonists of this work (Rubena and Cismena) are characters that belong to a lower class as compared with that of the prince. We know too that the mimesis of the action at the level of character delineation elevates or enhances the ethical aspects of Cismena. This character represents the highest gradation of virtue (Cismena = emperadora) which allows us to conclude that the divine values are a reflection of those that organize the moral world of man. These worlds interact at various levels:

1. *Philosophical dimension:* The mythological level that motivates the structuring of the piece in terms of the demonic world of chaos (Rubena) versus the apocalyptic natural order (Apollo-Cismena).
2. *Psychological dimension:* The archetypal symbols used revert the audience to primeval symbols of light and darkness; of rational behavior (Cismena) versus passionate obsession (Rubena).
3. *Moral dimension:* Dishonor (Rubena) versus honor (Cismena) with the corresponding implications.
4. *Social dimension:* Virtue (honor) as the reward for social recognition and ascension (Cismena).

5. *Political dimension:* The virtuosity of the future monarch (prince) versus the popular codes of ethical behavior which are further subdivided between models of national excellence (Cismena) and national decay (Rubena, Beata, Dario Ledo, et. al.).

Thus we observe that all of the levels of existential reality mentioned above find a mirror (at times distorted) in the upper spheres of the divine realm. The sacrament of marriage is the instrument by which all of the secular elements are harmoniously gathered and perpetuated in what seems to be an ascending (Platonic) movement. The metaphorical (final) relationship to the monarch, is an expression of the divine will by proxy, for the king was considered to be at this time the foremost secular representative of divine law on earth (the role of the Pope as mediator between God and secular government had been severely restricted). This Thomist view of moral Christian philosophy is at the very core of the dualistic movement of plot and the contrastive pattern of imagery.

The Vicentine concept of comedy, therefore, is not simply the archetypical promotion of instinctual satisfaction (vital energy) through seasonal renewal of pagan life impulses (the Myth of Spring). Nor can we reduce it to the highly theological notions of comic epiphany that we observe in the *Divina Commedia* of Dante. More than all this, as an expression of the *early* Renaissance, the comic *mythos* represented by Gil Vicente seeks the harmony of vital and instinctual impulses at a level commensurate with the moral and social necessities of his turbulent society.

The binary principle that structures the *Comédia* (i.e., the system of contrastive elements) outlines the action on all levels of the representational mimesis, as the passage from the state of disorder to that of order (Rubena : disorder → Cismena : order). In the *Comédia de Rubena* the focus of the action presents an interaction of antagonistic forces of human nature: passion versus reason. Such an interaction does not forget to distribute agents of the supernatural world accordingly: the world of the demonic (contingent with our existential world through actantial interaction) versus the magical forces of the fairytale, associated with the luminosity of Cismena's purpose.

These ideas bring us face to face with the letter of 1531 in which the constant convulsion of the demonic world (the existential world being a *displacement* of that sinister archetype) confronts the naturally ordered world, harmonious through the reasoned approximation with the divine. This theomorphic concept, the harmonious union of opposites, is explained through the relativistic condition of salvation that is represented in the *Comédia*, that is, as an expression of free choice in forging one's way through life. In this respect, as an expression of freedom of choice, Rubena succumbs to and Cismena overcomes the troublesome obstacles that society places before her. This would appear to be yet another level of the contrastive "pacíficas concordanças" that Gil Vicente refers to in the letter. The idea of an invented plot, a category that defines the *comédia*, is an artistic reflection of the humanistic ideas as Gil Vicente envisioned them: the elaboration of plot as an expression of individual concern, of ingenuity of thought and of refined artistry that, in Gil Vicente's own words, could satisfy the highest aspirations of aesthetic communication: "cuanto se puede alcançar en la humana inteligencia."

It is interesting to note in retrospect that the "generational" concept of plot design – the mother to daughter transfer – becomes an "organic whole" only when the two distinct (but associated) parts are compared, a good example of the contrastive yet harmonious binary pattern of plot design used by Gil Vicente. We may thus arrive at the following thematic statement (i.e., *dianoia*): Honor lies in integrity not inherited status. The implications of this maxim within the social context of Gil Vicente's society is of prime importance to the definition of the Vicentine notion of comedy, and will be considered in the conclusion of this study.

A final glance at the plot design, if we further elaborate the structural model proposed by Greimas, would represent the relationship of the two parts of the *Comédia de Rubena* as shown in Figure 4.

174   GIL VICENTE

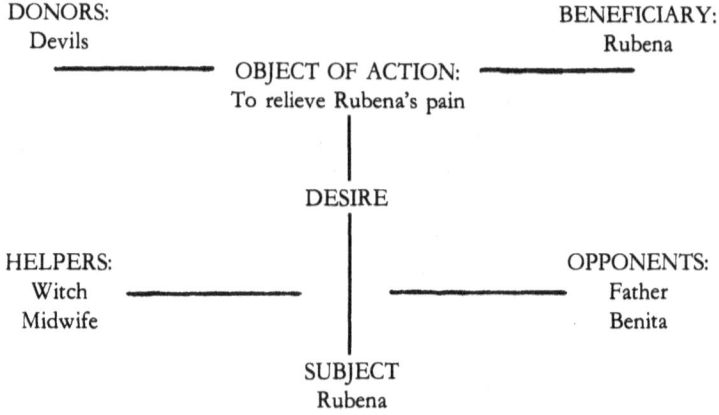

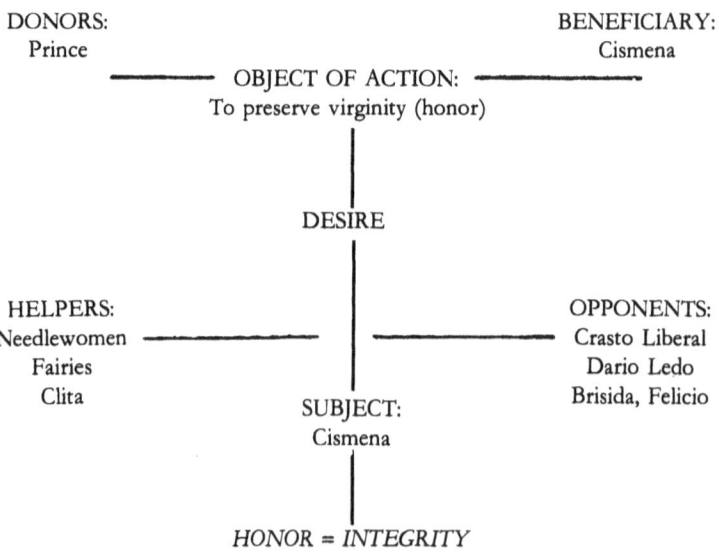

Figure 4. The *Comédia de Rubena*

CHAPTER V

THE *COMÉDIA DO VIÚVO*

Gil Vicente's *Comédia do Viúvo* has received the most varied aesthetic opinions from Vicentine scholars. Most of these opinions censure the dramatic piece, but none, to my knowledge, has dealt in any significant depth with the structure of the *Comédia* itself. This, of course, would be the first logical step in assessing its aesthetic value, both historically (as a genre) and as an artistic example of the Portuguese dramatist's genius.

Among those that believe in the artistic merit of the *Comédia do Viúvo* stands Thomas Hart who notes that ". . . .a la mayor parte de los lectores, la *Comedia del viudo* les parece dos acciones distintas, muy torpemente ligadas entre sí. Tal interpretación, sin embargo, no me parece muy acertada" (xxxvii).

This critic begins his explication of the *Comédia's* significance with a very brief outline of the plot and, in so doing, renders an interesting interpretation of its meaning, marred only by the paucity of details that the scope of his study demanded. In his observations we note that, once again, the secularizing tendency of Gil Vicente's humanist *comédia* will focus its attention on the monarch as the sovereign prince whose command is a reflection of Divine governance; that is, as *"vicarius Dei supra terram"* (xl).

This repeats the thematic concern – already observed in the *Comédia de Rubena* – with the harmonious ordering of conflicting secular phemomena as a reflection of God's plan for man. In the *Comédia*, this idea is given structural reality through the dramatic technique of incorporating the audience into its denouement: Prince D. João (later D. João III), who must be present in the audience (fictionally, that is) in modern renditions of that play, decided *ex cathedra* the fate of the fictional characters (Melicia and Paula). This blending of both realities, the fictional and the circumstantial, leads us to believe that play performing was more than just entertainment at this time, it was also a serious ideological tool of the monarchy.

The earliest detailed account of the *Comédia do Viúvo's* artistic excellence belongs to the unpublished study of Andrews who very clearly points out that [the *Comédia*] ... responds to an involved and intricate exposition of the theme of matrimony" (*Artistry* 138). Complementing the opinion of Hart, Andrews adds that:

> Upon the cloth of this simple theme, Gil Vicente has woven an intricate and complicated tapestry whose main dialectical design of love gains depth and perspective with the interplay of light and shadows, of life and death. The entire *Comédia* is a veritable tour de force of coalescing synthesis (138).

I have already noted the special interest of comedy with the subject of marriage, not only as a social necessity reflecting the moral ordering of divine justice, but also as a symbol of political stability through national strength. Andrews is careful to point out that the structure of the work – the basic interplay of "antipodal pairs" that underlies its composition – is deliberately intended to communicate a coherent vision of reality through the use of contrastive symbols: "Gil Vicente's main interest in the interaction and opposition of contrasts lies in their reconciliation and unification" (140). The idea of "reconciliation" of opposite entities reflects Gil Vicente's notions of comedic form as related to his preocupation with "pacíficas concordanças," a constant and essential premise for understanding his work.

One of the more recent interpretations of the *Comédia* is that of Edward A. Riggio who, in opposition to T. P. Waldron's aesthetic evaluation ("[a] primitive specimen of the genre"), and in agreement with the judgement of Andrews, has observed that "Such skillfully placed and carefully timed, modes of contrasts seem to indicate that Vicente has created in the *Comédia do Viúvo* a play of greater artistry than has been generally appreciated" (103).[1]

---

[1] Riggio was here referring, more specifically, to the skillful balance of a symbolic motif: the first friar that appears in the plot counseled the widower to

Although the critical perspective toward this Vicentine play would appear to be gaining more and more grounds for analytical evaluation, there are still those who would think that the *Comédia* is aesthetically obtuse. Stephen Reckert, for example, has reserved one brief comment about the *Comédia* in which he compares it with the *Tragicomédia de Don Duardos*, "... para la que la *Comedia del Viudo* puede considerarse un delicioso borrador en miniatura" (38).

Although the category of "delicioso borrador" does not do sufficient justice to the dramatic piece, which merits much more historical and aesthetic consideration than that given by Reckert, it must still be considered a valuable opinion as compared to the more stern views of Humberto López Morales:

> Las comedias adolecen de una desproporción, ya notada por Dámaso Alonso en su estudio de *Don Duardos*, y de la cual la *Comedia del viudo* es, sin duda, el ejemplo más representativo. No se trata sólo de un conglomerado de escenas de arbitraria duración, sino de la mezcla inarmónica [!] e inhábil de dos argumentos diferentes. El resultado es tan pobre, que, a pesar de su buena voluntad, Thomas Hart no logra convencer a nadie de que la comedia sea algo más que unas pesadas consideraciones morales sobre el comportamiento de la mujer en el matrimonio, seguidas de una intriga con príncipe disfrazado de rústico (209).

It is unfortunate that the opinions of the censuring critic were not more extensively explained, for they might have proven the austerity of his critical perspective. The same may be said concerning a more recent study of Paul Teyssier (1982), whose first contribution to Vicentine studies – a linguistic analysis of Gil Vicentine's works – is still the most completely critical evaluation of its kind. His opinion about the *Comédia do Viúvo*, however, like that of López Morales, is too severe in its conclusive remarks concerning the play and its importance; and, once again, the critical stance is not detailed enough to sustain his critical stance:

---

substitute his black garments for *red* ones; later, D. Rosvel invents a story about his past which involves his mother's illicit relationship with a friar who gave her a *red sash* as a gift.

"Tal é a peça, um tanto incoerente e, para falar com clareza, medíocre" (91).

These objections echo those of António J. Saraiva for whom the *Comédia* was an "irregular" dramatic piece which paradoxically was an example of a genre – the "comédia romanesca" – "... por onde o drama entrou no teatro" (129). In his investigation, Saraiva questioned the coherence of the *Comédia's* structural pattern: "Mas qual a relação das duas partes? Qual o papel do viúvo? Parece que o viúvo desempenha duas funções diferentes, uma na qualidade de viúvo, outra na de pai de duas filhas, e que é esta a única ligação entre os dois episódios" (130-31). We know, however, that the opinions of the Portuguese critic were admittedly conditioned by a false historical perspective which he later rectified; namely, the application of modern dramaturgical conventions to the work of a Peninsular humanist playwright. To what extent his influential remarks about the *Comédia* influenced subsequent opinions, is a matter of serious concern.

These disapprovals of the *Comédia*, however, are totally misleading (as Saraiva later admitted), and, furthermore, they fail to objectify the reasons for the rebuttal. They contribute little to an understanding of the work's intrinsic design – actantial plot movement – as well as to the immanent and complex configuration of symbolic associations ("thought and language"). In addition to this, these censuring views overlook the privileged position of the *Comédia* within the *corpus* of Vicentine dramaturgy, for the *Comédia* is a prime example not only of the *comédia* genre, but also of a transitional piece between that particular genre (*comédia*) and the more novelesque tragicomedies that were developed from this very important dramatic form.

Furthermore, if in this *Comédia* we accept the biographical account of many "Vicentistas," we may discern in its structure a deeply felt reflection of, and personal commitment to, those notions of the harmonious assimilation of discord that Gil Vicente had discussed in his letter to the king, D. João III, in 1531. That biographical theory, expounded especially by Brito Rebelo, Queirós Veloso and Braamcamp Freire, identifies the author with the "viúvo" of the dramatic piece. The biographical account does not, in any way, prove or disprove that the structural design of the *Comédia* is reflective of that personal perspective, yet it does cast some interesting and revealing light onto the author's artistic projection as related to his pervasive concern and personal involvement with these notions (Oscar de Pratt 179-84). Although the idea is interesting, the facts seem to disprove the identification of the fictional "viúvo" with Gil Vicente. Pratt convincingly traces the biographical theory and finally rejects it:

> Eu não quero negar a possibilidade da viuvez e segundo casamento de Gil Vicente, se isso importa às conclusões da genealogia vicentina. O que pretendo é apenas pôr em evidência o nulo valor documental do chamado epitáfio de Branca Becerra, reputando também extremamente fantasiosa a suposição de que a *Comédia do Viúvo* expresse sentimentos subjectivos e descreve situações da vida íntima do poeta, sem estabelecer, entre os supostos factos da vida do autor e a idealização dramática, nenhuma conexão ou concordância" (184).

Whatever theory is accepted, biographical or not, the *Comédia do Viúvo* will be studied here as an expression of the author's aesthetic and social concerns conditioned, as they must always be, by literary convention and philosophical world view; none of which necessarily needs authorial identification with the fictional account (cf. Juan Ruiz, *El Arcipreste de Hita*). Like the procedure that was chosen in the discussion of the *Comédia de Rubena*, the analysis that follows is an attempt to re-define more critically those views which delve into the structure of the dramatic piece so as to uncover its semiological system of communication. As in the *Rubena*, the only historical interest that concerns this study will be that which will help define the concept of genre (*comedia*) as it applies to the investigation of the work's structural design. The logic of its design, of its structural system, will necessarily reflect the ideological context, the semantic world it mirrors.

The action that Gil Vicente imitated in this *Comédia* is best defined if we turn to the *Comédia de Rubena*. There too, we will recall, the main action represented a thematic concern with honor (*honra*), a concept extremely important to the Peninsular codes of ethical standards and, consequently, to the development of the *comedia* form. Unlike the *Comédia de Rubena*, however, we are closer in the *Comédia do Viúvo* to a causally related plot design. Whether this is a natural, evolutionary, consequence of Gil Vicente's dramaturgical skills or not, is a matter that is debated by critics who would have the *Comédia* represented in 1514 (cf. *Copilação*) as opposed to those who assign it to a later date (e.g., Révah and Teyssier). Pratt suggests that it was written earlier but "retouched" at a later date:

> A *Comédia do Viúvo*, representada a D. Manuel em 1514, foi retocada depois de 1521, isto é, depois da aclamação de D. João III. Prova-o claramente uma das rubricas finais, a qual só poderia ter sido redigida depois deste facto: "Tirou dom Rosvel o chapeyrão & ficou vestido como quem era, & forão se as moças *a el Rey dom João III, sendo principe,* que no seram estava, & lhe perguntarao ... (179).

This would explain the insertion of the biographical materials that reflect an earlier date of composition.

In the *Comédia do Viúvo* we observe a tighter concept of dramaturgical design which, nonetheless, remains far from the Aristotelian notions of organic unity; at least as it was interpreted by Renaissance (neo-classic) playwrights and theorists. Still, the unity is much more coherent than previous Vicentine attempts not only in terms of unity of time but also of place. The spatial dislocation and superimposition of different planes of reality which was observed in the *Rubena* is now reduced to a minimum in this *Comédia:* a remark about D. Rosvel's whereabouts as related to his parents by witches. It is also important to observe the conspicuous lack of introductory explanation, of prologic or interlogic material by a character that does not participate in the stage action. In this sense, and from a modern perspective of dramaturgical skills, Vicente's artistry excels that of Naharro who invariably used such a procedure to introduce his dramatic action. Only in the end does this concept of unity become distorted by the *deus ex machina* finale in which D. Rosvel, as himself, interrupts the stage fiction to ask the prince (who later became King D. João III), present in the audience, to decide which of the two girls (Paula or Melicia) should wed first. It is also important to note that this ending, more than just an ingenious technical device, allies the theme of the play's action with the court reality (i.e., D. João), which is very significant to the thematic constant (the king as *vicarius Dei supra terram*) already noted in the *Comédia de Rubena*.

This kingly vision of authority, where the supreme secular leader brings Christian ethics to an unruly world, is the ideological foundation not only for the Vicentine *comédia* but also for that which later became the prime example of the Spanish Golden Age of drama: "En el espíritu, o más bien en la concepción de la vida, el teatro español de entonces [The Golden Age] se centra en tres ideas, o quizá sea mejor decir sentimientos, inmutables: honor, monarquía y fe católica" (Angel and Amelia Del Río). This concept of *comedia* distinguishes also that type of comic drama that we have been observing in the Vicentine *comédia* forms. Del Río observes the following notions of the *comedia* that reflect the Vicentine design:

> El honor se presenta en el teatro – dejando aparte las exageraciones en que frecuentemente caen muchas comedias – como el patrimonio esencial de la vida, síntesis de la dignidad humana, de la propia estimación, y sujeto a una ley inflexible según la cual toda ofensa a la honra de la mujer requiere reparación inmediata o venganza sangrienta. La idea monárquica, combinada con un sentimiento democrático de carácter muy especial, se traduce en la lealtad al rey, símbolo y ejecutor de la justicia, ante quien todos – el noble y el villano – son iguales. El fondo católico se ve claro en la multitud de asuntos religiosos que el teatro trata, siempre dentro de los límites de la ortodoxia (355).

Although relatively little attention has been given to these two plays (i.e., *Rubena* and *Viúvo*), especially as they relate to their specific ideological context and as precursors of the Golden Age *comedia*, it seems most appropriate to consider the importance of these motifs of faith, honor, and the monarch in these two Vicentine dramatic works. Margaret Wilson observes that "The three great motifs of Golden Age drama are undoubtedly religion, love and honour" (42). Love, of course, is the traditional harmonizing principle (rarely divorced in the Iberian Peninsula from theological orthodoxy) that orients the *basic* motif of honor. Wilson is quick to point out that the all encompassing concept of honor, which according to her was first used by Torres Naharro (43), was a code which:

> ... regulated all social relationships: those between king and subject, between superior and inferior, between friend and friend, and beteween members of the same family.... Its basis

is the paramount importance of the right ordering of social relationships (43).

These same concepts are dramatized, however "primitive" the dramatic skills of the author, in the two Vicentine plays in question.

In the *Comédia do Viúvo* there is an expressed intention to place in the hands of the future prince of Oxford, D. Rosvel, the elevation of moral virtues when he explains to his brother, Gilberto, that he should marry the younger Melicia:

> Amparemos e honremos
> huérfanas tan preciosas,
> que en las cosas virtuosas
> los estremos.
> Villas y tierras tenemos;
> hagamos esta hazaña
> que quede exemplo en España,
> y no tardemos.
>   Toma ésta por muger
> y a mí darás la vida
> y ternás muger nacida
> a tu plazer.
> Quien casa por solo haver,
> casamiento es temporal. (156-57)

The central unifying motif of marriage, as we noted in *Rubena*, serves here, once again, to sanction, before God and his secular social representative (the Prince, D. Rosvel), the union of two distinct social castes. Unlike the farces (e.g., *Inês Pereira*), where marriage is satirically depicted, here the holy sacrament performed by the (*deus ex machina*) "clérigo" is a serious statement about God and society, one which must be contrasted with the opposing views of the "compadre" at the beginning of the play.

The thematic blending of upper and lower or middle class individuals in the final wedding vows points to a very significant aspect of the Vicentine *comédia*. It reflects a preocupation with two economic levels that Gil Vicente, as he insinuated in his letter (1531), wanted to harmonize. Whereas in the Spanish Golden Age *comedia* the "democratizing" characteristics of the plays uncover a need to exalt the Old Christian ("cristiano viejo"), the "labriego," in the face of a corrupted, perhaps impure aristocracy, these *comédias* delight in harmonizing two levels that, at the time, needed mutual support: the aristocracy and the new nobility or the merchant (perhaps "converso") class that promoted the type of dynamic, economic activity that was needed in the early Renaissance. It is known that Gil Vicente promoted economic support for the king (D. Manuel) in the *Exhortação da Guerra:* "Foi na ocasião da partida de D. Jaime de Bragança (1513) para a conquista dessa praça africana, que Gil Vicente escreveu a *Exhortação da Guerra*" (Michaelis 379). And Pratt observes that:

> há alusão clara [in the *Exhortação da Guerra*] às pretensões diplomáticas de D. Manuel na corte pontifícia. Entre estas o rei solicitava a concessão das terças e dízimas dos rendimentos do clero para as despesas a fazer com a guerra de Fez e Marrocos (176).

We also know that this attempt was utterly frustrated. Could the *Comédia* be an instrument for this type of much needed incorporation of economic support? On another level of analysis, could it be a call for Peninsular unity (i.e., Spain and Portugal)? This may be one of the many reasons for the linguistic "harmony" (bilingualism) of some of the plays and also of their setting: in Spain, Burgos, for the *Viúvo* and partially in Spain for *Rubena*. These interesting questions will appear again when we consider the *dianoia* of the *Comédia* and its ideological ramifications. For now, further comment will be reserved until the structure of the play is examined and its semantic properties appraised.

The action that Gil Vicente imitates in this *comédia* is, very succinctly stated: to preserve honor. We must here, once again refer to the all-encompassing notions of honor that have already been observed above, especially that of Margaret Wilson who makes of the Peninsular social code of honor one that "regulated all social relationships: [including] those between members of the same family..." (43).

In the context of the play's dramatic design Wilson's observations allow us to incorporate into the stated action above the addition of the word "family," for it is this type of relationship which is here clearly expressed. This allows us to consider adding the following statement to the play's action: to preserve family honor. We know that the harmonizing perspective of Gil Vicente, as noted in the *Rubena*, is one of total, cosmic unison and, that like *Rubena*, this type of total coherence (i.e., secular and metaphysical unity) is accomplished through only one acceptible channel: the holy bonds of matrimony. It is thus that the "clérigo" interprets the ceremonial marriage which concludes the dramatic piece.

>   Este sancto sacramiento,
>   magníficos desposados,
>   es precioso ayuntamiento.
>   Dios mismo fue el instrumento
>   de los primeros casados:
>   por su boca son sagrados.
>   Serán dos en carne una,
>   benditos del sol y luna,
>   en un amor conservados.   (159)

Matrimony, then, is the structural vehicle by which Gil Vicente (and his contemporaries) resolved the many levels of antagonistic elements – binary oppositions – presented in the sequential dramatic ordering of the plot. To be sure, not all of these binary pairs are necessarily contrastive; at times they seem, instead, to complement each other depending on the contextual relationship of the linguistic sign. An inventory of these different types of binarisms or "antipodal pairs" will be uncovered and outlined in the investigation concerning the *Comédia*'s plot design. We must remember, however, that in defining these oppositions – "the internal arrangement of the terms in an associative or paradigmatic field" (Barthes 73) – a *significant* distinction must be made, for as Barthes notes: "to deal with the opposition can only mean to observe the relations of similarity or difference which may exist betweeen the terms of the oppositions, that is, quite precisely, to classify them" (74). As Andrews has observed, the point where dualities coalesce is the *Comédia*'s "veritable tour de force" (138).

This being the case, we may add one further comment which more clearly reflects the action which the *Comédia do Viúvo* imitates: "to preserve family honor (through marriage)." Of course, the action is not defined as such from its very beginning; and it is for this very reason that I have place "through marriage" within parenthesis, for matrimony is only the instrument of the comic resolution and not of the complete mimesis in syntagmatic movement. At the play's beginning we simply have the classic medieval comedic situation of bringing felicity to a potentially tragic moment. If we apply the same structural model that proved operative in analyzing the *Comédia de Rubena* to the action defined above, we would observe the schema as shown in Figure 5.

We must remember, however, that Greimas' model was particularly well suited to the *Comédia de Rubena* because of its essentially narrative aspect. Nevertheless, Figure 5 proves that the same actantial interaction – the opposition of forces – may also apply to dramatic discourse. The applicability of the model here reflects Greimas' debt not only to Vladimir Propp's *Morphology of the Folktale*, but most importantly to Etienne Souriau's *Les 200.000 situations dramatiques*.

In this *Comédia*, Gil Vicente proves his skill of dramatic technique, for he does not introduce by means of an enacted prologue the story of the plot as found in the *Rubena*, a procedure utilized in other plays as well. This, of course, places the action to be imitated in a totally dramatic plane. There is, however, a problem here for the instructions deal with narrative material that is not necessarily manifested on the dramatic level. Such information (e.g., the fact that the widower is a merchant living in Burgos), while available to a reader, could very well be omitted in the play as performed. As in the case of *Rubena* Gil Vicente appears to have ignored the complete dramatization of the narrative information he was working with. Still, one must assume that the narrative information given in the instructions designed primarily for a reader, if not apocryphal, are indicative of the semiological presence on stage of that information; that is, one can only assume that the widower is visually depicted before an audience in keeping with the characterization assigned (e.g., the correct attire for a merchant of Burgos). This is not to say that Gil Vicente's other plays are not "dramatic," but rather that in this particular *Play of the Widower* the concept of drama, especially as we know it in contemporary terms, is better delineated. Susanne Langer has aptly explained this notion of dramatic skill:

> An act, whether instinctive or deliberate, is normally oriented toward the future. Drama, though it implies past actions (the "situation"), moves not toward the present, as narrative does, but toward something beyond; it deals essentially with commit-

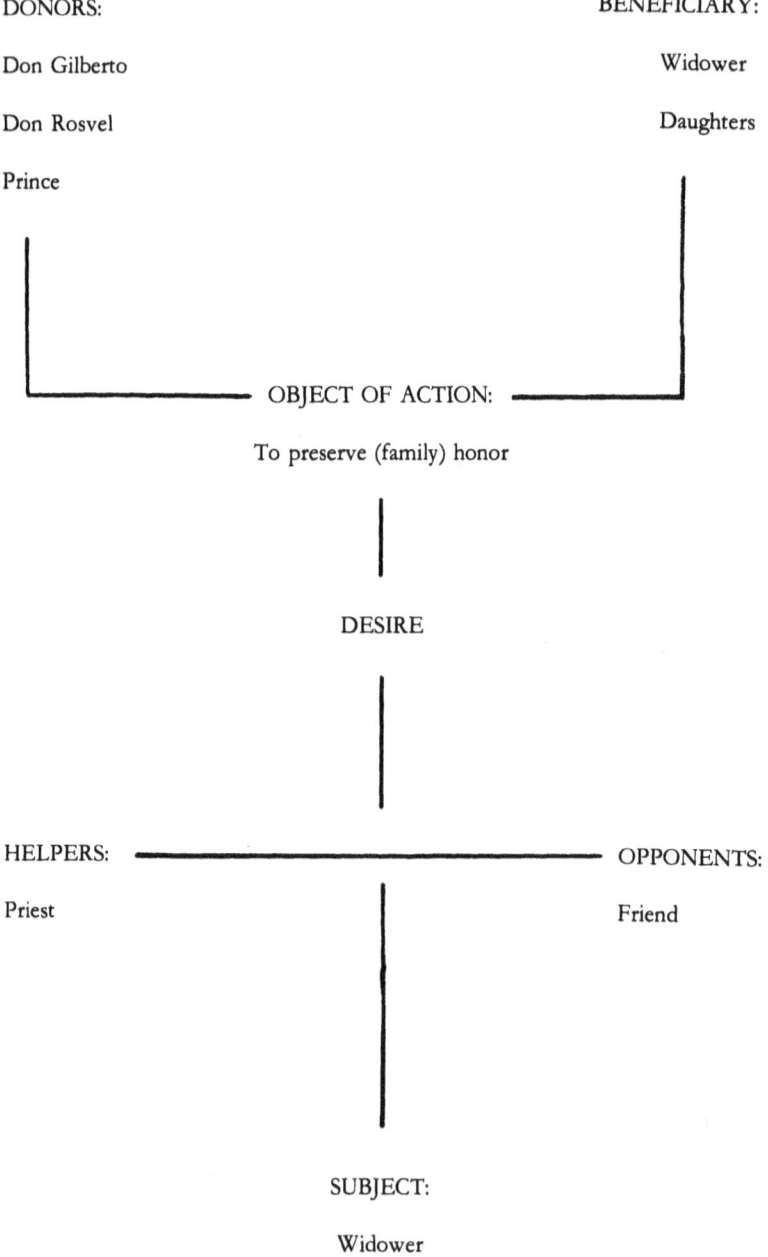

Figure 5. The *Comédia do Viúvo*

ments and consequences. Persons, too, in drama are purely agents – whether consciously or blindly, makers of the future. This future, which is made before our eyes, gives importance to the very beginnings of dramatic acts, i.e., to the motives from which the acts arise, and the situations in which they develop; the making of it is the principle that unifies and organizes the continuum of stage action. It has been said repeatedly that the theater creates a perpetual present moment [cf. R. E. Jones, *The Dramatic Imagination*, 40]; but is is only a present filled with its own future that is really dramatic. A sheer immediacy, an imperishable direct experience without the ominous forward movement of consequential action, would not be so. As literature creates a virtual past, drama creates a virtual future. The literary mode is the mode of memory; the dramatic is the mode of Destiny (307).

It is precisely this mode of fictional representation, i.e., drama, that is arrested when the dramatist allows the "Destiny" to be foretold in the literary mode (i.e., "Memory"). This is not the case in the *Comédia do Viúvo*.

The initial statement of the *Comédia*, the "virtual future" to be dramatically structured, is essentially a tragic moment which needs reparation. Like that of the *Rubena*, the beginning symbolically produces an instinctual desire to reverse the dramatic situation. This idea is conveyed by lyrical effusion, Gil Vicente's preferred mode of fictional course. That is, we are aware from the very beginning that the widower is in need of recovering his past happiness when he resorts to such phrases as "desastrada vida," "amara y dolorida." It is almost immediately, however, that the motif of marriage is brought into play, thus lending support to the actantial mimesis that was stated above:

> Esta desastrada vida
> ¿qué perdiera yo en perdella
> quando al mundo fue venida?
> Pues amara y dolorida
> es toda mi parte de ella,
> que perdí muger tan bella
> como estrella.
> Y pues triste me dexó
> muriera mezquino yo
> y no ella. (127)

It is at this point of potential suicide that we are cast into the very core of a truly dramatic situation. How Gil Vicente structurally defines that situation actantially (i.e., *mythos*) and thematically (i.e., *dianoia*) will be the subject of the following analysis.

It is soon after the initial lament that the action to be imitated is translated in terms of the protection that the widower's two daughters, Paula and Melicia, must have after their mother's death. The widower's tragic situation is philosophically delineated in terms of his own loss until a "fraile" enters and gives counsel to the entire family:

> Vuestras hijas consolad
> con gracia muy amorosa.
> Vos, hermanas, descansad:
> a Dios os encomendad
> y a la Virgen gloriosa.
> Inclinaos a toda cosa
> virtuosa:
> ternéis vida descansada,
> que sin esto es la passada
> peligrosa. (132)

The friar turns the widower's lament of death into a joyous event by equating the two contrasting terms (death = life):

> Y los que mueren honrados
> como acá vuestra muger,
> contritos y confessados,
> ¿qué haze luto menester?
> Lo que, hermano, havéis de hazer
> ha de ser
> a aquel dador de las vidas
> dalde gracias infinitas
> con plazer. (131-32)

This initial unity of opposites (death = life) is, of course, conditioned by an orthodox church view; here described as the philosophy of *memento mori* so popular in the Middle Ages and the early Renaissance (e.g., *La danza de la muerte*). It is not coincidental that the first mention of the two "huérfanas," Paula and Melicia, is in the form of an exaltation of virtue, for the widower's initial lament was a panegyric extolling the virtues of his lost wife. This constant reminder throughout the play of the importance of virtue, i.e., honor, is the main link (the "movement of spirit") between the initial expository lament and the intrigue that ensues. All obstacles to this dramatic action (the preservation of family honor) must be overcome if the play is to end happily.

Meanwhile, let us return to the widower's lament which gives momentum to the action defined above. There is a tripartite movement to this beginning exposition which is further subdivided into two repeated segments: (1) the lament (2) the extolling of his dead wife's virtues (3) return to the lament. In the two segments of the lament the widower, like the friar, also equates life and death; but this time the metaphor is completely secularized and conveyed by natural phenomena:

> En el punto que partiste
> no deviera quedar yo,
> porque la vida que es triste,
> más muere quien la resiste
> que el muerto que la dexó.
> A aquel Dios que la llevó
> pido yo
> muerte luego por vitoria,
> pues la vida de mi gloria
> ya passó. (129)

In this last section of the three part movement stated above one can observe several instances of binary elements that complement each other: "partiste" = "no deviera quedar yo," a return to the initial situation, and a further development of the idea of the second movement (the extolling of his wife's virtues) which the widower equates in the following manner: "muerte" = "vitoria." The "tristeza" that somehow pervades this lament, however, is later conditioned by the friar's addition of the healing powers of divine love (i.e., *caritas*). We may observe that the friar also uses "vitoria" in his speech: "Los que mueren por la ley / mueren con dulce vitoria"; but this time it is equated with divine justice (i.e., "ley"), thus rendering the following binary concepts:

1. Widower = "vitoria" > negation of life's vital instinct.

2. Friar = "vitoria" > affirmation of life's "sweet" reward: "ley" = natural law governed by God's divine providence.

The widower's tragic loss is, therefore, an illusion when considered in light of the "harmonizing perspective" that the friar's speech brings to the initial situation:

> Tomad un consejo, hermano,
> de este amigo singular:
> pensad cómo lo humano,
> unos tarde, otros templano,
> nacimos para acabar;
> y todo nuestro tardar,
> a buen juzgar,
> por más trabajo se cuenta,
> pues no se escusa tormenta
> 'n este mar.   (130)

With these lines, which bring to mind Jorge Manrique's philosophy of the waning Middle Ages ("nuestras vidas son los ríos que van a dar a la mar, que es el morir"), the priest explains to the widower the falsity of his former lament, for the widower selfishly pined over his loss of help, "amparo," and protection, "abrigo," forgetting his wife's just reward in heaven for the same virtues that he claimed for her. The priest continues this line of reasoning, the deception of those who place all faith on human existence, when he tells the widower to caste off the visible "paños negrosos" in favor of the intimate feelings of sorrow: "Tristeza, fuerça es tenella, / y lo al son desvaríos." The widower recognizes the revered words of this "amigo singular" and exclaims that he understand: "Padre, quedo consolado."

It is important to note, however, the emphasis that the friar placed on the quality of human existence, for this element is essential to a just reward for the dead as well as to consolation for the living. The thematic interaction of the two parts, the widower's soliloquy – the lament – and the priest's advice, leads to a focal point which gives momentum to the issue of human existence in the form of yet another "antipodal" section: the compadre's satirical comments on marriage versus the widower's memory of his honorable wife. This quality of human existence is, of course, virtue (i.e., honor, not only as an innate condition of human dignity but also as a visible source of correct social integration) which becomes the motivating motif of the rest of the dramatic piece.

We will recall that, like Manrique, the priest noted the importance of man's existential condition in leading him to the state of glory ("gloria"): "sólo con memento mei, / son sus ánimas en gloria." This concept of the right ordering of secular existence in relation to the hereafter, in this case of socially acceptable norms of integration and interaction (family or otherwise), is, then, the prime source that shapes the plot structure of the *Comédia do Viúvo*. In imitating the stated action (to preserve family honor), Gil Vicente juxtaposes and contrasts dramatic segments of the plot that convey this idea of rewarding virtuous behavior through the contrastive use of these "antipodal" situations. The fact that the thematic material preferred in this revolutionary age – a secular perspective that was not divorced from theological concepts of virtue – does not respond to modern about man's existential dilemma, may account for the incoherence of plot design that some readers of this play have noted. Insofar as it imitates the action that was stated above, however, the *Comédia* obeys the system of structural coherence that can be considered "organic," for, as Aristotle stated, this concept depends on the unity of ideological magnitude:

> As, therefore, in the case of animate bodies and organisms a certain magnitude is necessary, and a magnitude which may be easily embraced in one view; so in the plot, a certain length is necessary, and a length can be easily embraced by the memory.... And to define the matter roughly, we may say that the proper magnitude is comprised within such limits that the sequence of events, according to the law of probability or necessity, will admit of a change from bad fortune to good, or from good fortune to bad (66).

The fact that, ideologically, the *Comédia* may appear strange to a modern reader not versed in the theological world of the early Renaissance does not mean that the plot design is incoherent, but rather that it responds to another type of thematic stimulus. We have been noting that the play, semiologically (i.e., in terms of a structured system of verbal signs and symbolic process of communication), reflects that thematic material. The "beauty" of the plot design, however, ultimately depends on the aesthetic and thematic preferences of the audience for which it was conceived. Beckerman notes that the dramatist's choice of thematic material depends on this audience response:

> As we receive the texts, they embody a distinctive formulation of experience. . . . Communicating it to be audience is relatively simple when a dramatist's conception of humanity is part of an audience's background. But when time has dissolved that bakground, it is necessary for the performer to build a bridge between the text and audience. Contemporary conception of evil, for instance, is radically different from the late medieval conception so prevalent in Elizabethan drama. . . . Only by deeply understanding the particular aspects of humanity realized by the text can the performer provide the links. (*Dynamics* 220-21)

These principles of aesthetic appreciation are here being considered because they are deemed necessary in defining the integrity of the *Comédia* under study. But, as we have been observing, only a structural investigation of its fictional components can uncover the real beauty of design. Aesthetic evaluation, therefore, should ideally depend on the perception of a work's structure as it relates to the ideological context of the author's world view. Whether or not that particular design is aesthetically pleasing to a given audience or critical perspective is a matter that depends on many variables (personal, cultural, historical, political, etc.), and should enter into the field of literary inquiry only tangentially, as a final appraisal of the semantic whole.

The sense of loss that the widower expresses and the priest tries to alleviate within a spiritual dimension, then, is the dramatic inspiration for the rest of the play. The obstacles that are placed before the preservation of a harmonious family relationship, now disrupted by death, constitutes the remaining segments of dramatic movement. We have already noted the widower's recognition of the priest's wise comments about life and death and how his recognition constitutes, at least for the moment, a feeling of consolation which could be considered the comic ending.

But how are the two daughters involved dramatically (i.e., actantially) by this personal expression of tragic loss? What motivates the dramatic action in terms of ideological expression? How, in fact, is the dramatic movement transferred to the widower's daughters who, after all, carry the dramatic rhythm to its felicitous conclusion? In answering these questions we must remember that the dramatic motivation for the action appears to be a direct expression of the Peninsular idea of "honra" at this time. As in the *Rubena*, the *Comédia do Viúdo* represents a "generational" concept of honor which may seem strange to the modern reader. In this respect, Hayes has observed that in Lope de Vega:

> The clan spirit was dominant. Any smudge on the honor of the member of the family stained all, even cousins. Men might "restore" honor in one of four ways: (1) an apology by one of the contending parties, which required guts; (2) a duel; (3) a marriage; (4) taking the life of the one on the distaff side who was under a cloud (93).

In the *Comédia do Viúvo* the loss of a virtuous wife does not imply the loss of honor, but rather, the loss of a role model for the two daughters to follow. Paula and Melicia's happiness in the future worrries the widower whose personal (i.e., family) honor rests on the two daughters' righteous behavior. The death of the widower's wife opens up the possibility of dishonor in the daughters since she is no longer around to set the correct example or lead them in making virtuous decisions.

We have already observed that the priest addressed the widower's daughters, commending them, in place of the absent mother, to a virtuous life: "Inclináos a toda cosa / virtuosa" The father of Paula and Melicia, however, had already been asked by the priest to console his daughters ("Vuestras hijas consolad") which he does almost immediately thus transferring the preceding action to the subsequent representation involving his daughters:

>> Ora, oídme, hijas mías:
>> la muerte, por mi ventura,
>> me llevó mis alegrías
>> porque no fuessen mis días

> más de quanto es la tristura.
> Lo que más desassegura
> mi holgura,
> temer daño que se os siga,
> esto haze mi fatiga
> más escura. (132)

Thus the widower, as primary agent of the dramatic action, by commenting on the only obstacle to this present consoled state ("holgura"), transmits the dramatic (i.e., actantial) responsibilty to the two dramatic agents – the daughters – who, like Cismena, will sustain and elaborate on the initial dramatic situation. We may observe in the comments of the widower a fearful anticipation of his daughter's precarious future which only honorable behavior can prevent:

> Porque esta vida engañosa
> en la tierna mocedad
> es tan peligrosa cosa
> que harto bien temerosa
> está mi seguridad.
> Acuérdeseos de la honestidad
> y claridad
> de vuestra madre defunta,
> y en tanta bondad junta
> contemplad. (132-33)

The end of this scene, then, completes and transfers the meaning of the dramatic action. Furthermore, it creates an intense and foreboding direction for the dramatic movement. In Beckerman's words, "the action is a working out of the pressures aroused by the precipitating events" (*Dynamics* 82). He adds:

> Projects [which in Beckerman's terminology approximates our term "dramatic action"] tend to be directed toward adjusting to the precipitating context or venting the repressed thoughts, feelings, or experiences released by the precipitating circumstances (85).

These events have been thoroughly and skillfully handled and defined by the dramatist at this point of the comic action. Not once but twice does the widower express his fear for his daughters' future; and the representation of this concern ("precipitating context") as they relate to *his* (thus the title of the play: *Comédia do Viúvo*) sadness or happiness *is* the comic mimesis of the play.

Immediately after the definition of his fear, the friend (i.e., the "compadre") drops by and presents the first obstacle to the widower's desire. In this scene, contrary to the former scene with the priest, an opposition to the stability of family life (i.e., marriage) is manifested in the dramatic activity of the ill-intended friend. His scornful views about marriage are in direct contrast to those of the widower and those of the priest. Gil Vicente delights in presenting contrastive situations that impel the dramatic movement and give it shape.

Paula and Melicia's reaction to the friend's comments are important for they become more and more involved in dialogue (for the first time), as agents of the dramatic action. At the end of this scene they are left alone to digest, as it were, the previous words of the friend. In that segment they come to the same recognition that their father had reached with the good counsel of the priest. Here again the situation is paradoxically exposed by a juxtaposing of elements:

    (Melicia)   Gran secreto es el morir.
    (Paula)   Mas es mucho declarado:
                  mayor secreto es bivir
                  y ser cierto de partir
                  y no estar aparejado.
                  Cada uno está engañado
                  y confiado
                  que tiene luenga la vía. (138)

The older and wiser Paula, who will be rewarded firts at the end of the *Comédia*, notes that there is greater philosophical depth ("secreto") in the enigmatic process of existence than in the mystery of death, for only right and virtuous choices, as the priest observed earlier, orients the individual toward spiritual rewards. Paula's words prove to be prophetic in the ensuing complication of the *Comédia's* plot because in that section of the play one can observe a dramatic presentation of the existential ordeals that are placed in the lives of these individuals. There (i.e., in the following act) we may note also the genuine meaning of Paula's statement ("mayor secreto es bivir") when D. Rosvel presents the opportunity for the widower's two daughters to make decisions that will safeguard their honor. Here, as we also noted in the *Rubena*, Gil Vicente has presented the concept of honor as a personal reward for reasoned behavior, not solely as an inherited status related to economic gain. This idea is given expressed support from D. Rosvel who, acting as a member of a privileged class, convinces his brother (D. Gilberto) to protect and honor ("Amparemos e honremos") the younger Melicia, for her virtuous integrity, not her social status: "Quien casa por sólo haver, / casamiento es temporal."

In the second act of the *Comédia*, which some critics have seen as unrelated to the first, Gil Vicente represents the complication and final resolution of the precipitating circumstances presented in the beginning segments. These generative segments of the first part of the play are here given dynamic impetus through the introduction of a character who will dramatically interact with the widower and his family in such a way as to test the integrity of the two dramatic agents and provide the means for a comic resolution. This comic resolution, as we shall observe, not only rewards the widower and his two daughters with personal satisfaction and social ascendency, but also provides, through the *deus ex machina* appearance of D. Gilberto, an interesting plot device that is structurally significant in Gil Vicente's concept of *Comédia*. Although D. Gilberto's fortuitous entry may appear contrived to the modern reader, an unskilled dramatic ploy intended to tie up all loose ends at the end of an equally loose performance text, there is a theological motivation that justifies this agent's entrance into scene as an instrument of final harmonization: the concept of divine providence which, in the adventitious comic *mythos*, shapes into a coherent design all of the elements that may appear, at first, irreconcilable. We will have occasion to observe, however, that this technique of comic resolution does not diminish the skill of the causally related segments of the first part, but rather that it is embedded within the structural pattern that defines the ideological focus of the Vicentine *comédia*.

The first scene of the second act begins, then, with the abrupt entrance of the disguised D. Rosvel who, acting as the peasant Juan de las Broças, immediately introduces a farcical sketch in which marriage is again satirized through the story of his family background. In contrast to Paula and Melicia's virtuous mother, Juan de las Broça's mother is not only alive but living sinfully with a monk. When asked about his life under those conditions, Juan recalls that he got tired of working for the monk and that, although engaged to be married, he abandoned them all after his fiancée fled. In these escapades of Juan, we can observe Gil Vicente's dramatic intent of juxtaposing diverse opinions that converge on the topic of matrimony. As in the case with the widower's friend, the Portuguese dramatist is attempting, through this process of contrastive parallelism, to call attention to the notions about marriage that are often taken for granted.

The widower's entrance allows D. Rosvel to further elaborate upon his fictional past. His picaresque escapades make the widower sympathize with him and he offers him work for a year. The pervasive motif of work is thus neatly woven into the fabric of the plot. It soon becomes apparent that D. Rosvel's disguise is more than just a trickery to gain dishonest access to the two girls. His willingness to "put in an honest day's work" is directly related to the increasing fondness that the widower and his family feel for the young man. With the elaboration of these unique qualities, the impetuous youth of the comic *mythos* becomes here a conscientious representative of his estate through the actual "working out" of his many ordeals, having by the end of the play proven his true worth and personal integrity without the support of any pre-established authority (i.e., the nobility to which he belongs).

The intrinsic need that the family has of this man is manifested in the widower's comparison, "Havémoslo menester / como el pan que nos mantiene," which is later re-inforced by the comparison of D. Rosvel's worth to gold. This same concern about Rosvel's opportune entry in the unfortunate household of the widower and his two daughters is repeated after Juan has performed his tasks well and is later sent out to continue his labor:

> (Viudo) Muy buena dicha nos vino.
> (Paula) Viénenos como hecho al torno.
> (Melic) Bien lo haze. (143)

This leads to a sententious commentary on the relationship of servant and master, a bit of dramatic irony since the remarks are displaced comments about a lover and his mistress, a courtly love motif.

>(Viudo) Sabed que el buen servidor,
>   que lo pesen a oro fino
>   es merecido.
>(Paula) A según fuere el señor,
>   ansí abrirá el camino
>   a ser servido.
>   . . . .
>(Viudo) El que es buen servidor,
>   siempre ha buen galardón
>   se atura.
>(Paula) Mas antes lo ha peor;
>   pues no usa de razón
>   la ventura. (143)

Interestingly enough, the work episodes of Don Rosvel dramatize the courtly-love metaphor that equates the medieval lady (i.e., the "señor" of the *cantigas de amor*) to the sinuous task required of the lover in seeking her favor. Gil Vicente was working so confidently within his underlying belief or value system that he does not take the trouble to spell out the courtly-love literary conventions within which he is writing. Everything is so obvious to him that he speaks in a kind of literary shorthand, never doubting the reader's ability to see the implications of the hints he tosses his way.

Paula's statement that fortune does not follow the laws of reason seem to contradict her father's remark that all good service sooner or later attains its just reward. This cautious attitude echoes her earlier warning to Melicia that "mayor secreto es bivir," for no one knows when fortune may strike: "Cada uno está engañado / y confiado / que tiene luenga la vida" (138). Rosvel, then, is the dramatic instrument by which Paula's pessimism will be upturned through the mechanism of divine reason, which is structurally represented in the play through the *deus ex machina* finale that allows for the felicitous double wedding ceremonies, thus proving the priest's conclusion that all human effort is dependent upon divine justice ("los secretos gloriosos") and not, as Paula fears, upon the chancy wheel of fortune.

It is not coincidence, for example, that D. Rosvel possesses the dignity of a self-made man. This is actantially depicted through the motif of arduous labor which not only proves him meritorious in the eyes of all, but also provides a metaphor well suited to the development of the plot. The metaphorical representation of D. Rosvel as a laborer (i.e., a shepherd) stresses his dramatic function through the social metamorphosis so often depicted by his contemporaries, the power of love motif: "el amor es tan podroso / que me truxo a la defensa / con cayado" (145).

More that just a static concept, a theatrical artifice to bring together two traditionally distinct social states, the metaphor is here represented dynamically and given realistic significance through dramatic depiction. The many tasks that D. Rosvel performs well, almost to exhaustion, is artistically interwoven with the worries that the widower announced when he voiced his earlier anxieties about his two daughters. There is no fear, however, for it becomes quite certain very early in the play's complication of the main action that, although D. Rosvel's obsession with the two girls is somewhat unconventional, his intentions are well within the virtuous parameters the widower envisioned. That is, his dramatic function as protector of the widower's property and livestock is a prophetic reflection of the actantial mission: To preserve the honor of the family.

The motif of the "buen servidor," a quality which, as we noted earlier, the family learned to admire in Juan, is observed throughout. In scene six, for example, after Juan happily returns from his daily tasks, this idea is developed extensively. The symbol of destruction (i.e., the rapacious "gavilán"), which in the *Comédia de Rubena* appears with a more clearly defined pernicious attribute (i.e., the deflowering – "caçar" – of the virgin "garça") is here more subtly introduced when D. Rosvel states "Asperá diré primero: / anduve trás un gavilán / y allá quedó" [144]). This level of intertextual reading (the coherence of elements within a sign system), however, is conditioned in the *Comédia do Viúvo* by a different contextual reality, for, unlike the impetuous Felicio (cf. Halcón = gavilán) of the *Rubena*, D. Rosvel proves himself champion of the girls' cause by eliminating this figurative obstruction to the disciplined ordering of his daily chores. As a symbolic extension of this reality, D. Rosvel also does away with the obstacle to Paula and Melicia's integrity.

The motif is further developed when Rosvel reassures the widower that the livestock remained intact, none was lost. It is important, however, that Rosvel attribute his extraordinary talent for protecting or guarding the animals to God:

>   (Viudo)   ¿Queda todo en el corral?
>   (Rosvel) ¿Quién, el ganado?
>   Bueno está, bendito Dios:
>   no se me perdió ni tal,
>   Él sea loado. (144)

The emphasis on God's will underscores the ideology that considers everything subordinated to God's divine governance, a philosophy which Paula must learn through the existential overcoming of her personal dilemma (i.e., the pessimistic attitude that sees fortune as the "primum mobile" of existence).

When the two girls are left alone with D. Rosvel and he finally uncovers his true identity, the motif of the protective shepherd is complete. It is here, amidst the conventional rhetoric of fire, that Rosvel confesses his desire for the two girls: "Soy quien arde en bivas llamas, / pastor muy bien empleado / en tal poder" (145). But, once again, in contrast to the all-consuming passion of Cismena's suitors in the *Comédia de Rubena*, D. Rosvel's amorous intent is checked by virtuous behavior and channeled into a protective (Platonic) notion of love:

> Pido a vuestra gran beldad
> que no os turbéis, señoras,
> por aquesto,
> que en guardar vuessa beldad
> yo seré a todas horas
> mucho presto. (145)

The idea of "guarding" the girl's virtue ("beldad") without hope of physical remedy is repeated when D. Rosvel expresses his subjugation to the power of love:

> Mándame ser alquilado:
> ansí lo tengo por gloria
> y lo quiero

> sin ser de vos remediado,
> ni querer nunca vitoria,
> ni la espero. (145)

That Rosvel's intentions are sincere (i.é., not a product of the "loco amor" that eliminated Cismena's flirtatious suitors from her careful choice) is revealed more concretely at the end of the play when, through the principle of poetic justice, harmony is achieved through the union of the two lovers. Yet Paula perceives D. Rosvel's expression of love as an absurdity that can only lead to dishonorable contact between their two unequal social groups:

> La merced que nos haréis,
> que somos huérfanas, señor,
> y sin madre,
> que os vais y nos dexéis;
> no matéis al pecador
> de mi padre
> Abatéis en vuesso estado,
> siendo noble en señoría
> per derecho,
> y queréis ser deshonrado
> por tan pequeña contía
> sin provecho. (146)

This hopeless attitude reflected in Paula's speech ("sin provecho"), therefore, emphasizes the absurd societal law that must be overcome if final harmony is to be achieved. The metamorphosis of nobleman to shepherd is the dramatic metaphorical technique that will dialectically (i.e., semiologically) bring about the upturn of this social dimension.

We may recall that the comic *mythos,* according to Frye, is based on this movement from an irrational law to the overturning of that law in a new social ordering that is reflected in comedy. Actantially, after Paula and Melicia decide not to marry in their own state, thus opposing their father's wish and the very law that Paula defended above, the main obstacle to social renewal in the *Viúvo* is represented through the numerical impossibility of matrimonial bond: The two girls can not marry D. Rosvel, for it would only solve a societal problem (i.e., the lack of social interaction between distinct groups) at the expense of moral and spiritual decay. We have already had occasion to notice, however, that D. Rosvel does not intend on breaking any social taboos. When the two girls voice their concern at this absurd desire, Rosvel is quick to quiet their worries: "No tengáis de mí sospecha / porque esso más pena ordena / a mi dolor."

His desire, therefore, is tempered by moral responsibility from the very beginning. The integrity that we have observed in his trustworthy nature, as protector of the family well-being, remains impeccable throughout his performance. It is here that the motif of honest labor gains its functional significance within the ideological focus of the Portuguese dramatist. The paradoxical change which D. Rosvel willingly undergoes for love's sake ("Que no quiero ser yo, no; / ya me troqué" and "don Rosvel no quiero ser / ni por sueño, / que otro soy desque os vi") is significant of that ideological dimension. More than just a juxtaposing of social levels, here the power of love motif orients the interaction of these two classes in such a way as to bring about a new social ordering, one which not only uses the conventional rhetoric of this social conflict, but also sets in representational motion the dialectical resolution of that conflict.

The widower's entrance at peak moments of dramatic activity serves to heighten the tension aroused by these precipitating circumstances. Such is the case in scene eight when, soon after the encounter with D. Rosvel, the girls are warned by their father that idleness can lead to dangerous consequences. The widower's exit from this scene leaves Paula and Melicia alone, discussing their unfortunate situation. Paula's rhetoric reproduces that of Rubena when, in the midst of her passion, she too saw no way out of her lamentable predicament. But, whereas Rubena had already transgressed her moral and spiritual responsibility, Paula's decision will determine her spiritual and temporal rewards:

> ¿Qué consejo tomaremos?
> Nosotras, si nos callamos,
> consentimos;
> estamos en dos estremos,
> porque a él también erramos
> si dezimos,
> Son dos estremos sin medio. (149)

We may observe here the typical Vicentine binary principle which, as we noted earlier, in the sequential ordering of the complication, re-duplicates the contrastive elements of the plot in variables of the number two. In this case, Paula notes the difficult position that she must confront: "Son dos estremos sin medio." At first, it might appear that the younger Melicia, playing with *medio* as middle and medio as *means*, finds the answer to their dilemma – "El medio es si nos dexasse" – but this would not be the type of comic resolution that finds harmony in conflictive entities. Paula identifies the apparent impasse of the problem when, in response to Melicia's facile solution, she replies that it would not change the situation: "¿Tú no ves que esso no lleva remedio? / Si comigo lo acabasse / ¡cierto es!" (149). The arduous work motif is once again brought into dramatic interplay when the girls metaphorically discuss D. Rosvel's just recompense for his labor:

(PAULA) Y pues, ¿quién le pagará
la grande soldada suya
norabuena?
(MELIC) Hermana, él se enhadará:
culpa no es mía ni tuya
de su pena. (149)

Paula's concern and Melicia's less than tolerant attitude with D. Rosvel's love pleas seem to orient the structure of the play to the moment of resolution when the prince will decide the fate of the two girls. Paula, of course, will receive D. Rosvel in marriage.

The following scene (scene ten) brings D. Rosvel and the two girls together again. This segment serves not only to provide dialectical confrontation of two opposing dramatic constituents (i.e., the juxtaposition of contrastive signs) but also to further advance the shepherd motif, a variation of the more comprehensive work motif that provides the axis for the development of the comic *mythos*. The development of the courtly-love motif is noted when Paula asks D. Rosvel why he toils in vain – "¿Porque en vano trabajais?" The disguised prince notes that the service (i.e., "lavor") he performs for them is a desired goal ("paraíso") and that it provides the only viable means for the disclosure of his true love:

> Pero este mi sudor
> amata las bivas llamas
> que amor quiso,
> y el afán de mi lavor
> por vos, muy hermosas damas,
> es paraíso. (150)

The technique of binary subdivision to increase dramatic tension is once again employed in D. Rosvel's answer to Paula's important question: "¿Por qual de nos lo havéis vós?" It is at this point that Rosvel expresses the perplexity of his sentiments, the resolution of which must come from a morally responsible judgement:

> Dos amores se ajuntaron
> contra mí;
> los males de dos en dos
> mi cuerpo y alma cercaron
> quando os vi.
> De dos en dos los dolores,
> dos saetas en mí siento
> y me hirieron.
> ¡Ay!, que juntos dos amores
> en uno solo pensamiento
> no se vieron.
>   Sofrir doble padecer,
> padecer doble passión
> qual me veis,
> no sé cómo puede ser,
> que mi fuerça y coraçón
> vos la tenéis:
> la una de vos bastara
> para que mi poder fuera
> consomido;
> la vida y alma gastara,
> no que mi querer podiera,
> ser perdido (151).

It is important, meanwhile, to emphasize D. Rosvel's statement in which he demonstrates an ethically directed opinion: "la una de vos bastara / para que mi poder fuera / consomido." The dramatic tension mounts to its peak when, in the next scene, the widower returns with the news that he has arranged a marriage for both daughters. Words and expressions such as "valles sombríos" and "tristoños" reveal Rosvel's reaction. The "ganado" which in scene ten symbolically approached an apocalyptic vision – "y el ganado que apaciento, / como a ángeles del cielo / los adoro" – here is reversed into the realm of the demonic:

> Quiero llevar el ganado
> a unos valles sombríos
> y tristoños,
> donde se harte el cuitado
> de oír los gritos míos
> muy medoños (152).

The infernal vision produced by Rosvel's loss of hope is complemented by the widower's command that he should clean the stables, thus compounding D. Rosvel's plight with symbols of wastage and deterioration. The dramatist focuses on the motif of high versus low social status: the discrepancy between nobility and those that must handle manure. These same symbols, especially with reference to fertilization, ironically contain an ideological premise: the germ for the comic *mythos* of seasonal renewal.

Paula and Melicia recognize that Rosvel's love is constant, however, ("Pues no es de los fengidos") and avow that they shall not marry until D. Rosvel is once again made happy. This "contract," as it were, is faithfully kept by both of them until the end of the play when, unkowingly, they alone will provide the means for the happy turn of events. The dramatic irony of this situation is complemented by the widower's departure from scene eleven when he leaves to pray that God may make his daughters happy through marriage: "Yo me voy ora a rezar / que Dios haga a tu contento / aquel marido." The demonstrative adjective "aquel" is dubious enough to allow for the necessary accommodation of the final stage reality: unknowingly the widower is blessing the union of Paula and D. Rosvel, for it is they who will be paired off at the end. D. Rosvel's return, in scene twelve, allows him to continue his lament and to invoke death as a solution; but not even death will help him in his sorrow – "tú te hazes sorda a mí" – and he tenaciously decides, instead, to continue his service as shepherd:

> que no dexaré el ganado
> aunque lo mandasse Dios,
> pues vuestro es.
>   Yo lo tomo por guarida;
> en pastor quiero servir
> y tener fe,
> y ésta será mi vida
> muy agena de este nombre,
> yo no sé (154).

The metaphorical relationship between the sheep and the two girls is here related when D. Rosvel states that he will not tire of guarding them: "No dexaré el ganado /.../ pues vuestro es," thus completing or rounding out the pastoral motif (i.e., the work motif) that was dramatized from the beginning of the second act. The design uncovered by the thematic relationship of this motif to the play's dramatic movement and final ideological unveiling allows us to confirm that D. Rosvel is, in fact, the most worthy of all possible suitors for Paula's hand. When Paula explains that his worries are unfounded because she and her sister will not marry, the sad rhythm of the play is reversed and the felicitous discovery produces an immediate response from the eager D. Rosvel:

> ¡Oh, preciosa mercé!
> ¿Quándo serviré yo esso,
> diesas mías?
>   Pues tan firme es mi querer,
> que de más en más se enciende,
> no por tema,
> dexaros no puedo hazer,
> y mirándoos más se enciende
> el que me quema.
> Con. dambas no puede ser
> casar yo, como sabéis:
> echad suertes,
> que quiero satisfazer
> la merced que me hazéis
> de mil muertes. (154)

It is at this point of the plot arrangement that the unraveling of the previous complication is initiated in the play's overall configuration. The thorny moral issue that is represented by the numerical impasse – the love triangle – is not so easily solved, however, and D. Rosvel's appeal to the two girls to cast lots is shocking, not only to Paula and Melicia, but also to the contemporary (and modern) audience. But as the only possible pragmatic solution it serves as proof of his truthfullness: he loves *both* girls equally. Casting lots, however unrealistic and ridiculous this may seem to us, is, nonetheless, a dramatic device that depends on a metaphysical authority for the resolution of a dilemma.

Notice how this reliance on a transcendental solution is on the same footing (or at least an equal footing) with the appeal to Prince João for a decision (since his decree would also represent an expression of transcendental judgement). Notice also how it is in harmony with the appearance of Don Gilberto whose appearance has signs of being miraculously motivated. Still, it is important to observe that, in his suggestion, D. Rosvel is acting within the moral limitations that are to him the only viable means of (comic) resolution: matrimony. The appeal to chance to orient him toward matrimony is followed by Rosvel's rejection of the pastoral disguise in favor of his true identity as he utters: "No quiero más ser pastor."

It would appear, then, that the sacrament of marriage, the spiritual and temporal union of man and woman, is the only acceptable means of social leveling and spiritual reward. Once the determination to integrate diverse social levels is made, the pastoral disguise can be rejected as the illusion it is. At this point, the absurd, static laws of social immobility and the chanciness of fortune are overthrown in favor of a final society in which temporal and spiritual qualities are renewed. The rejuvenated spirit that calls for festive ceremonies underscores this comic epiphany which is triggered in the *Viúvo* by the symbolic divesting of the comic hero. Northrop Frye explains the social revelation which finalizes the comic *mythos*:

> Thus the movement from *pistis* to *gnosis*, from a society controlled by habit, ritual bondage, arbitrary law and the older characters to a society controlled by youth and pragmatic freedom is fundamentally, as the Greek words suggest, a

movement from illusion to reality. Illusion is whatever is fixed or definable, and reality is best understood as its negation: whatever reality is, it is not *that*. Hence the importance of the theme of creating and dispelling illusion in comedy: the illusions caused by disguise, obsession, hypocrisy, or unknown parentage (169-70).

This new social reality finds royal support in scene fourteen where the stage illusion is broken in the *Comédia* and the fictional world blends with that of the real, as a member of the audience (i.e., the Prince D. João III, later to become King D. João III) is asked to determine which of the two girls will marry first. At this point in the story, the audience is not yet aware of the fortunate *deus ex machina* entrance that D. Gilberto, D. Rosvel's brother, will soon make. The performance text, that which constitutes the theatrical reality *per se*, reaches here a conclusive comic resolution represented by the young Prince's wise choice as the prettily pretended *vicarius Dei supra terram*.[2] Even Melicia prophetically acknowledges the benevolence of the Princes's judicious pick when, not being chosen first for marriage, she observes "En Paula cayó la suerte; / Dios se acordará de mí." These words are especially profound in view of the ideological focus of the work. We have already observed the importance of God's divine providence in the play's structure; how chance (i.e., "suerte") is, sooner or later, subjected to a divine will that structurally and ideologically demands the *deus ex machina* technique.

In this light, Melicia's presaging words can be interpreted as the causal-ideological motivation for D. Gilberto's fortunate entrance. This conditions the notion of the *deus ex machina* concept greatly, for instead of the gratuitous break in dramatic logic, the causal-chronological ordering of the incidents, we note here a more literal interpretation of the phrase, one which becomes part of the

---

[2] If the 1514 date is valid, D. João was twelve years old. Breaking this fictional on-stage reality to appeal to the young boy's judgement is an obvious bit of flattery, but, at the same time, being "cute," it creates a new fiction, one that pretends that the child is a worthy and a valid decision-maker. This pretense is based on the principle pointed out earlier: the King as God's vicar. The boy not yet consecrated as King by coronation is prettily invited to believe in his God-guided effectiveness. One can be sure, of course, since this is make-believe, or a play within a play, that the boy had been coached on the decision he was to make: the rest of the play depends on it!

work's immanent system of interlocking dramatic segmentation. Previously, we have noted how divine governance also conditioned D. Rosvel's concept of good works (cf. "ganado" motif). This notion will ultimately be manifested dramatically in the fertility ritual of matrimony that is contingent on God's assent (i.e., grace) for its final confirmation. The final scene of the play clarifies the importance of this theme of matrimony within the ideological perspectives dramatized in the *Comédia*:

> Este sancto sacramento,
> magníficos desposados,
> es precioso ayuntamiento.
> Dios mismo fue el instrumento
> de los primeros casados:
> por su boca son sagrados.
> Serán dos en carne una,
> benditos del sol y luna,
> en un amor conservados. (159)

Furthermore, we can not ascribe the actions of the dramatic agent totally to chance when, in scene fifteen, D. Gilberto miraculously meets with his long lost brother. The very first words point to the ideological focus observed above:

> ¡El Señor sea loado
> y toda la corte del cielo,
> pues mi hermano y mi consuelo
> tengo hallado! (155)

The theological orientation of these words reflects the play's dramatic impulse which can not be divorced from its global, structural design. This we note in the duality of connotative possibilities found in the use of the word *corte* above (i.e., God's realm = *corte*, where the temporal idea of "corte" is the metaphorical vehicle of comparison) which makes it quite clear that Prince D. João's judgment reflects God's divine ordering, thus giving further evidence that the prince's decision to marry off Paula first was not only wise or divinely inspired, but also a structural "necessity" reflecting the ideological orientation of the unfolding (causal) chain of dramatic events.

As for the late comer D. Gilberto, he too will share in his brother's good fortune through marriage. This idea is expressed by him when he refers to D. Rosvel as "mi consuelo." Actantially, the expression ("mi consuelo") simply refers, of course, to the emotive response to the encounter with his long lost brother, but on another level (i.e., a structural level of ironic design) it presents D. Rosvel as a dramatic instrument of his felicity. Thus, unknowingly, even D. Gilberto is destined to fulfill the integrative mission of the play's action: to protect the family's honor. We will recall here that the widower too was in need of "consolación" after his wife's death:

>   (Fraile)   La gloria y consolación
>   d'aquel que es padre eternal
>   sea en vuestro coraçón
>   porque tenéis gran razón
>   de llorardes vuestro mal. (130)

The Vicentine idea of harmonization carries with it the intention of restoring happiness to a potentially tragic situation. The word "consolación" is directly related to this notion, for it implies that retribution must be sought if comic resolution is desired. It is difficult, as we have mentioned, to see this medieval and early Renaissance concept of retribution because modern, existential philosophies of man are no longer colored by the theological tint that was prevalent at this early age of intellectual development. The motivating forces of modern man respond to an entirely different set of ethical patterns that reflect his scientific (i.e., secular) vision. The total separation of theology from temporal affairs was not a possibility seriously contemplated by the early Christian humanist. In this respect, the total secularization of society, one must not forget that the great mechanical discovery of the fifteenth century (i.e., the printing press) was, at first, used mainly for the sale of church indulgences! [3]

---

[3] Rice explains that: "These first printed books have a further, and curious, characteristic: their pages so closely resemble those of manuscript books as to be virtually indistinguishable to the unpracticed eye. Clearly the printers' technical, aesthetic, and commercial aim was to reproduce exactly the handwritten manuscript.... Their difficulty in freeing themselves from traditional conceptions is explained by the fact that although typography was the greatest invention of the Renaissance, its earliest development was shaped almost exclusively by clerical

The comic rhythm of the play is, once more, edged close to its denouement when, after the brotherly embraces, D. Rosvel convinces his brother to undertake the reputable task (i.e., "hazaña") of marrying the younger daughter, Melicia, as he had done with Paula. But the happy momentum leading to resolution is arrested again when the widower enters unaware of the honorable intentions of these two noblemen:

> Señores, ¿qué cosa es ésta?
> ¿Qué hazéis en mi posada,
> dolorida y quebrantada,
> descompuesta? (157)

The widower's unexpected surprise at seeing the two men hand in hand with his two daughters awaken in him the fears and anxieties that he had voiced much earlier, in scene two of the first act, when he confessed his misgivings about his two daughters' future safety after their mother's demise. We will remember that his worry at that time was clearly translated in terms of honor: "Acuérdeseos la honestidad / y claridad / de vuestra madre defunta" (133). These remarks are, dramatically considered, ironic to an extreme because the same men he is accusing of dishonorable conduct in scene sixteen of the second act will present the means by which all the family, including the widower [!], will be brought together in joyous unison. It is ironic, furthermore, that the two gentlemen should present their matrimonial actions in terms of glorious feats (cf. "hazaña") while the widower, on the other hand, perceives their apparent offense as a sign of their lack on manly valor: "Pues, ¿qué batallas vencistes? / ¿Qué gentes desbarataste?" (157).

The idea of custody or preservation of the family honor is best exemplified by the repeated use of the word "huérfanas" when

---

tastes and needs. Its geographical origins were far from Italy, the literary and artistic center of European culture in the fifteenth century. Printing first became a significant business enterprise in a provincial ecclesiastical capital with a population of about three thousand and meager intellectual distinction. Monasteries and cathedral chapters contracted for the Latin Bibles, missals, psalters, and antiphonaries which were the printers' more important productions. The ecclesiastical authorities dominated job printing; for example, a common order was for indulgence forms" (5-6).

referring to the widower's two daughters. This, of course, refers to their state of total vulnerability after their mother's death, a notion which carries with it the very pertinent idea that the loss of the girls' mother was, by the same token, the loss of an ideal pattern of behavior that they could emulate. This concept is further emphasized by the widower who, shocked by the evident manifestations of family disrepute, wonders why the two young men should not have protected (instead) the solitary orphans, especially coming from so privileged a class as theirs:

> ¡Qué cosa tan deshonesta
> para señores reales!
> Guardar las huérfanas tales,
> ¿qué os cuesta? (157)

This thematic focus becomes clear when Paula, noting (at last) the true and divine nature of their felicitous outcome, quiets her father's anxiety by observing that "Dios nos quiso amparar / y nos casó." The idea of divine ordination expressed in the repetition of the word "amparar," although in a different contextual reality, is also reflected in the intentions of the two young men who, acting as the dramatic agents or spokesmen of the privileged sector of society, had echoed these ideological notions of the monarch's responsibility, of the right secular ordering of man's world in accordance to a divine plan.

We may observe this idea in the section, noted previously, when the older Rosvel exhorts his brother to shelter the defenseless orphans: "Amparemos y honremos / huérfanas tan preciosas". A paradigmatic reading of the reiterated "huérfana" motif (i.e., the coinciding of the transitive verb, "amparar," on two distinct levels, the temporal and the spiritual) underscores a basic premise of humanist comedy in general and of the *Comédia do Viúvo* in particular: The ideological swing toward royal absolutism, the notion of the sovereign King (in this case the future King) as "Vicarius Dei supra terram." This political dimension, in turn, finds its source of inspiration in Catholic moral theology, basically Thomist, that underscores the *comedia*'s societal (i.e., medieval) ideal:

The state... is willed by God and has its God-given function. It was required because of the social nature of man. The state is not, for Aquinas, as it was for Augustine, a product of man's sinfulness. On the contrary, Aquinas says that even "in the state of innocence man would have lived in society." But even then, "a common life could not exist, unless there were someone in control, to attend to the common good." The state's function is to secure the common good by keeping the peace, organizing the activities of the citizens into harmonious pursuits, providing for the resources to sustain life, and preventing, as far as possible, obstacles to the good life.... Each government is faced with the task of fashioning specific statutes to regulate the behavior of its citizens under the particular circumstances of it own time and place. Lawmaking, however, must not be an arbitrary act but must be done under influence of the natural law, which is man's participation in God's eternal law. Positive laws must consist of particular rules derived from the general principles of natural law. Any postive human law that violates the natural law loses its character as law, is a "perversion of law," and loses its binding force in the consciences of men. The lawmaker has his authority to legislate from God, the source of all authority, and to God he is responsible. If the sovereign decrees an unjust law by violating God's divine law, such a law, says Aquinas, "must nowise be observed" (Stumpf 204-5).[4]

In the *Comédia do Viúvo* as well as the *Rubena*, we have observed a familiar pattern of dramatic design by Gil Vicente. It is hoped that the preceding examination concerning the concept and structure of the Vicentine comedy has demonstrated how that part of Gil Vicente's dramatic corpus, the *comédia* genre, is unique as an important contribution to the historical significance of later comic developments in the theater of the Iberian Peninsula.

---

[4] For St. Thomas Aquinas (1225-1274) "natural law" corresponds to the "human laws that are fashioned for the direction of the community's behavior.... these activities of preserving life, propagating the species, forming an ordered society under human laws, and pursuing the quest for truth... pertain to man at this natural level" (201). Human or "positive" laws are derived from natural laws, and are all subordinated to divine reason or eternal law. Aquinas parts company with Aristotle when he notes that divine law, in reflecting the eternal law, orients man toward the supernatural through "revelation and is found in the Scriptures" (203).

We have noted that this type of comic drama responds to a cyclical stimulus in which we can observe an archetypal movement toward societal renovation, a concept that Northrop Frye has termed the *mythos of spring*. This all important thrust, as is the case in Gil Vicente, is imitated in a dramatic action that brings about an ideal society, one which Gil Vicente's audience – the aristocratic court audience – could consider desirable.

We may recall that the *mythos of spring* commemorates the joy of instinctual impulse. This manifestation is at the very foundation of comic activity. The vital impulse towards euphoric exertion, however, is manifested in many ways and for many reasons. Its viability is projected, like any human myth, in terms of a desired ideal. In the cases we have examined, that ideal is channeled into a longing for secular reform that is not divorced from a theocentric paragon. These affinities between the instinctual level of the *mythos of spring* and socio-spiritual needs are succintly explained by Knutson, who notes that these archetypal activities can be further elucidated by Freudian principles:

> In real life, the pleasure principle motivating the id is gradually subdued and controlled by the reality principle resident in the ego. The impulse to immediate gratification tends to be asocial while the sense of practical limits endeavours in part to put the ego in tune with social realities. Curiously enough, however, we witness in comedy a kind of moral reversal. The superego, usually a voice of guilt, anxiety, even terror, is embodied in a ludicrous "barbon" whose authority is so diminished that he can be "berné" without a second thought. By the same token, the unruly is shown in a favourable light. We cannot but like the impulsive young hero of comedy as side with him in his struggle. The fundamental legitimacy of his impulse is confirmed by his victory at the end of the play, and by the unfavourable light in which his opponent is shown. Mauron explains that apparent contradiction by another notion of traditional psychology: wish-fulfilment or what the Frenchman call "une fantasie de triomphe." To quote one of the fundamental tenets of his comic theory: "la grande loi du genre comique, c'est que le principe de plaisir l'emporte" (12).

This justifies an interest in tracing, archetypically, the development of a specific national form of comic drama in the previous manifestations of that mythic projection, that is, those activities which shaped the developing comic impulse through autochthonous forms of comic expression: the *cantigas* and other forms noted earlier. Frye notes that in the *Tractatus Coislinianus*, the *dianoia* of comedy is divided between *pistis* (opinion) and *gnosis* (proof). Both of these parts of the comic ideal reflect the dualism that knutson described above, and they "correspond roughly to the usurping and the desirable societies respectively" (166).

In the comedies of Gil Vicente, the ascending movement that corresponds to this archetypal impulse (i.e., the *mythos of spring*) reflects an evolutionary notion of *opinion* to *proof* in two major modes of representation which are both projections of prevalent social ideals, conditioned by specific historical circumstances. These two major modes of comic expression are contained within the *mythos of spring* but point, as indicated earlier, to a dimension of wish-fulfillment very close to another archetype: the *mythos of Summer* or that of romance. Within these two extremes of ironic presentation and the dreamy world of romance, Gil Vicente set forth his secular notions of societal reform in which he clearly defined the usurpers and the triumphant elements of a social renaissance.

This entire secular cycle actually begins with the farce and ends with the two "tragicomedies" (*Don Duardos* and the *Amadís*), but it is in the two comedies examined here that the Portuguese dramatist enclosed his most poignant message of reform and supplied the most coherent formula for comic structure in the drama of the Iberian Peninsula. From the slap-stick domesticity of the farces to the fanciful world of magic and chivalric ideals, Gil Vicente never tired of castigating the moral and spiritual errors of his society. But whereas in his farces he focused the low mimetic world of peasantry and in his tragicomedies that of the superior beings of fictional narratives, it was in the two comedies that we have seen that he poured his most important message of harmonization, one in which both worlds, the ironic and the romantic, come together to form, in realistic terms, the very texture and design of his poetic expression.

Structurally, we have noted the binary pattern of this dimension, the comic and the romantic, which interact to present a final epiphany of spiritual triumph through social communion; we will recall that matrimony in these plays is a ceremonial synthesis of societal reform in which many levels of harmonization are effected. Spiritually, it presents God's special favor of the social miscegenation which is not seriously considered in the farces and statically presented in the tragicomedies. Socially, it represents an incorporation of new bloodlines (e.g., the merchant and the middle class in general) to that of the old aristocracy. This "democratic" inclination in the comedies of Gil Vicente, a sentiment included in his letter of 1531, will culminate in the social patterns of comic expression that were practiced by the Golden Age dramatists. These later playwrights also envisioned a new society in which the King was in unison with his people and they, as representatives of a lower station, with each other (cf. *Fuenteovejuna, El Alcalde de Zalamea, Peribáñez,* etc.).

These aspirations seem to reflect the ideological-spiritual-ethnic struggles of the Peninsular "edad conflictiva," the dawn of the modern era in the development of the *comédia* form. In this respect, it is interesting to note that Gil Vicente has dramatized in both *comédias* the Renaissance concept of the personal dignity of man in the face of inherited social status, a notion which would be especially pertinent to the social reality of the Iberian Peninsula in the fifteenth and sixteenth century.

As Américo Castro has observed, in the early Peninsular theater "... sale a luz la inquietud de quienes, salvados por la Natividad de Cristo y por el bautismo, se sentían socialmente en condición de inferioridad" (64). In fact, the duplicity of the period in question, when public opinion became the standard of honor, was compounded by the historical reality of the Iberian Peninsula, that is, by the struggle of three distinct social castes: Jews and Moslems against Christians. It is not surprising, then, to observe the relatively unimportant status given to the "learned" and often affected class in the theater of Gil Vicente (cf. Dario Ledo's "Ora anday gastando a vida / na escola"), nor of the wealthy (e.g., Crasto Liberal). Castro poignantly focuses the issues dramatized by these early dramatists when he observes that "La inquietud, el bullir en los negocios, el ejercitar la curiosidad mental, podían dar motivo a no ser tenido por hombre de limpia ascendencia" (174). Gil Vicente's concept of *comédia* preludes an era that will mirror the patterns and ideological focus of the past while depicting the social chaos of a decaying society.

WORKS CITED

Alfonso el Sabio. "Cantigas." *Antología general de la literatura española*. Ed. Angel Del Río and Amelia A. Del Río. New York: Holt, Rinehart and Winston, 1960. 50-51.
Almeida, Manuel Antônio de. *Memórias de um Sargento de Milícias*. 8th ed. São Paulo: Atica, 1978.
Andrews, J. Richard. "The Artistry in the Plays of Gil Vicente." Diss. Princeton U, 1953.
———. *Juan del Encina: Prometheus in Search of Prestige*. Berkeley: U of California P, 1959.
Baldwin, T. W. *Shakespeare's Five Act Structure*. Urbana: The U of Illinois P, 1963.
Barnes, Harry Elmer. *An Intellectual and Cultural History of the Western World*. New York: the Cordan Company, 1937.
Barthes, Roland. *Elements of Semiology*. Trans. Annette Lavers and Colin Smith. New York: Hill and Wang, 1968.
Beckerman, Bernard. *The Dynamics of Drama: Theory and Method of Analysis*. New York: Knopf, 1970.
———. *Shakespeare at the Globe*. New York: Macmillan, 1967.
———. *Berceo, Gonzalo de. Milagros de Nuestra Señora*. 6th ed. Madrid: Espasa-Calpe, 1973.
Bevington, David. *Medieval Drama*. Boston: Houghton, 1975.
Boethius. *The Consolation of Philosophy*. Trans. Richard Green. Indianapolis: Bobbs, 1962.
Bogin, Meg. *The Women Troubadours*. New York: Norton, 1976.
Braamcamp Freire, Anselmo. *Vida e Obras de Gil Vicente: Trovador, Mestre da Balança*. Lisbon: Revista Occidente, 1944.
Bragança, António. *Lições de Literatura Portuguesa*. 8th ed. Porto: Livraria Escolar Infantil, 1973.
Bremond, Claude. "The Logic of Narrative Possibilities." *New Literary History* 11 (1980): 387-411.
Brockett, Oscar G. *History of the Theater*. 3rd ed. Boston: Allyn, 1977.
Calderón de la Barca, Pedro. *El Alcalde de Zalamea*. Ed. Gabriel Espina. Zaragoza: Editorial Ebro, 1962.
Castro, Américo. *De la edad conflictiva*. Madrid: Taurus, 1961.
Chase, Gilbert. *The Music of Spain*. 2nd ed. New York: Dover Publications, 1959.
Cirlot. J. E. *A Dictionary of Symbols*. Trans. Jack Sage. New York: Philosophical Library, 1962.
Cooper, Lane. *An Aristotelian Theory of Comedy*. New York: Harcourt, 1922.

Curtius, Ernst Robert. *European Literature and the Latin Middle Ages.* New York: Harper, 1963.
Del Río, Angel and Amelia A. *Antología general de la literatura española.* 2 vols. New York: Holt, 1960.
Del Río, Angel. *Historia de la literatura española.* 2 vols. New York: Holt, 1963.
Dorsch, T. S. *Classical Literary Criticism.* London: Penguin, 1977.
Dronke, Peter. *The Medieval Lyric.* 2nd ed. Cambridge: Cambridge UP, 1977.
Durant, Will. *The Story of Civilization.* 6 vols. New York: Simon, 1957.
Elam, Keir. *The Semiotics of Theatre and Drama.* London: Methuen, 1980.
Fergusson, Francis. *The Idea of a Theater.* New York: Doubleday, 1953.
Frazer, James George. *The Golden Bough: A Study in Magic and Religion.* New York: Macmillan, 1951.
Frye, Northrop. *Anatomy of Criticism: Four Essays.* New York: Atheneum, 1966.
García Márquez, Gabriel. *Chronicle of a Death Foretold.* Trans. Gregory Rabassa. New York: Knopf, 1983.
Gillet, Joseph E. *Propalladia and Other Works of Bartolomé de Torrres Naharro.* 4 vols. Philadelphia: U of Philadelphia P, 1960.
Gilman, Stephen. *The Art of the Celestina.* Madison: U of Wisconsin P, 1956.
Gout, Donald Jay. *A History of Western Music.* New York: Norton, 1960.
Greimas, A.-J. *Structural Semantics: An Attempt at a Method.* Trans. Daniele McDowell, Ronald Schleifer, and Alan Velie. Lincoln: U of Nebraska P, 1983.
Hardison, O. B. *Christian Rite and Christian Drama in the Middle Ages.* Baltimore: Johns Hopkins UP, 1965.
Hayes, Francis C. *Lope de Vega.* New York: Twayne, 1967.
Herrick, Marion T. *Comic Theory in the Sixteenth Century.* Urbana: U of Illinois P, 1964.
Knutson, Harold C. *Molière: An Archetypal Approach.* Toronto: U of Toronto P, 1976.
Lagarde, André, and Lauren Michard. *Les Grands Auteurs Français.* Paris: Bordas, 1971.
Langer, Susanne K. *Feeling and Form: A Theory of Art.* New York: Scribner's, 1953.
Lauter, Paul. *Theories of Comedy.* New York: Doubleday, 1964.
Lázaro Carreter, Fernando. *Teatro medieval.* Valencia: Castalia, 1958.
Lewis, C. S. *The Discarded Image: An Introduction to Medieval and Renaissance Literature.* Cambridge: Cambridge UP, 1970.
Lindsay, W. M. *Isidori Hispalensis Episcopi: Etymologiarum Sive Originum.* 2 vols. Oxford: Oxford UP, 1911.
López Morales, Humberto. *Tradición y creación en los orígenes del teatro castellano.* Madrid: Alcalá, 1968.
Mandel, Oscar. *Five Comedies of Medieval France.* New York: Dutton, 1970.
Mayer, Frederick. *A History of Ancient and Medieval Philosophy.* New York: The American Book Company, 1950.
Menéndez Pidal, Ramón. *Poesía juglaresca y juglares.* 6th ed. Madrid: Espasa-Calpe, 1969.
Michaëlis de Vasconcelos, Carolina. *Notas Vicentinas.* Lisbon: Revista de Occidente, 1949.
Milburn, A. R. "Gil Vicente." *The Penguin Companion to European Literature.* Ed. Anthony Thorly. New York: McGraw, 1969.
Nugent, Georgia. "Ancient Theories of Comedy: The Treatises of Evanthius and Donatus." *Shakespearean Comedy.* Ed. Maurice Charney. New York Literary Forum, 1980. 259-280.

Parker, A. A. "The Approach of the Spanish of the Golden Age." *Tulane Drama Review* Sept. 1959: 42-59.
Parker, Jack Horace. *Gil Vicente*. New York: Twayne, 1967.
Picchio, Luciana Stegagno. *A Lição do Texto: Filologia e Literatura*. Lisbon: Edições 70, 1979.
Plato. "Timée." *Œuvres de Platon*. Trans. Victor Cousin. Paris: Rey et Gravier Libraries, 1834.
———. "Symposium." *The Great Dialogues of Plato*. Trans. W. H. E. Rouse. New York: The New American Library, 1964.
Pratt, Oscar de. *Gil Vicente: Notas e comentários*. Lisbon: Livraria Clássica, 1970.
Rebello, Luiz Francisco. *O Primitivo Teatro Português*. Lisbon: Instituto de Cultura Portuguesa, 1977.
Reckert, Stephen. *Gil Vicente: Espíritu y Letra*. Madrid: Gredos, 1977.
Reis, Carlos. *Técnicas de Análise Textual*. Coimbra: Livraria Almedina, 1978.
Révah, I. S. "La *Comédia* dans l'œuvre de Gil Vicente." *Etudes Portugaises* 4 (1975): 15-36.
———. "Manifestations Théâtrales Pré-Vicentines: Les 'momos' de 1500." *Bulletin d'Histoire du Théâtre Portugais* 3 (1952): 91-105.
Rice, Eugene F. *The Foundation of Early Modern Europe: 1460-1559*. New York: Norton, 1970.
Riggio, Edward A. "The Place of the Comic in the Theater of Gil Vicente." Diss. U. of Pittsburgh, 1969.
Robertson, D. W. *The Literature of Medieval England*. New York: McGraw, 1970.
Rocha, Andrée Crabbé. *García do Resende e o 'Cancioneiro Geral.'* Lisbon: Instituto de Cultura Portuguesa, 1979.
Roger, Jacques and Payen, Jean-Charles. *Histoire de la Littérature Française*. Paris: Librarie Armand Colin, 1969.
Rojas, Fernando de. *Celestina*. Ed. Julio Cejador y Frauca. Madrid: Espasa-Calpe, 1968.
Romera-Navarro, M. "Estudio de la *Comedia Himenea* de Torres Naharro." *Romanic Review* Jan.-Mar. 1921: 58-72.
Sánchez Escribano, Federico, and Alberto Porqueras Mayo. *Preceptiva dramática española del renacimiento*. Madrid: Gredos, 1965.
Saraiva, António José. "Gil Vicente e Bertolt Brecht." *Vértice* Sept. 1960: 465-475.
———. *Gil Vicente e o Fim do Teatro Medieval*. 3rd ed. Lisbon: Publicações Europa-América, 1979.
Saraiva, José Hermano. *História Concisa de Portugal*. 5th ed. Lisbon: Publicações Europa-América, 1979.
Scholes, Robert. *Structuralism in Literature*. New Haven: Yale UP, 1974.
Singleton, Charles S. *Dante Alighieri: The Divine Comedy*. New Jersey: Princeton UP, 1970.
Spingarn, J. E. *A History of Literary Criticism in the Renaissance*. 2nd ed. New York: Columbia UP, 1908.
St. Augustine. *Concerning the City of God Against the Pagans*. Trans. Henry Bettenson. New York: Penguin, 1977.
Stumpf, Samuel Enoch. *Socrates to Sartre: A History of Philosophy*. New York: McGraw, 1966.
Teyssier, Paul. *Gil Vicente: O autor e a obra*. Trans. Alvaro Salema. Lisbon: Instituto de Cultura e Língua Portuguesa, 1982.
Ticknor, George. *History of Spanish Literature*. New York: The Odyssey P. 1965.
Todorov, Tzvetan. *The Fantastic: A Structural Approach to a Literary Genre*. Trans. Richard Howard. New York: Cornell UP, 1975.

Tydeman, William. *The Theatre in the Middle Ages.* Cambridge: Cambridge UP, 1978.
Udall, Nicholas. "Ralph Roister Doister." *Medieval and Tudor Drama.* E. John Gassner. New York: Bantam, 1971.
Vicente, Gil. *Comédia de Rubena.* Ed. Giuseppe Tavani. Rome: Edizioni dell'Ateneo, 1965.
——. "Comédia del viudo." *Gil Vicente: Obras dramáticas castellanas.* Ed. Thomas Hart. Madrid: Espasa-Calpe, 1968.
——. *Copilaçam de todalas obras de Gil Vicente.* Lisbon, 1562.
Wardropper, Bruce W. "The dramatization of figurative language in the Spanish theatre." *Yale French Studies* 47 (1972): 189-198.
Webber, Edwin J. "The Literary Reputation of Terence and Plautus in Medieval and Pre-Renaissance Spain." *Hispanic Review* 24 (1956): 191-206.
Wilson, Margaret. *Spanish Drama of the Golden Age.* Oxford: Pergamon, 1969.
Young, Karl. *The Drama of the Medieval Church.* Oxford: Clarendon, 1933.

NORTH CAROLINA STUDIES IN THE ROMANCE LANGUAGES AND LITERATURES

I.S.B.N. Prefix 0-8078-

Recent Titles

"THE CORT D'AMOR". A THIRTEENTH-CENTURY ALLEGORICAL ART OF LOVE, by Lowanne E. Jones. 1977. (No. 185). *-9185-1.*
PHYTONYMIC DERIVATIONAL SYSTEMS IN THE ROMANCE LANGUAGES: STUDIES IN THEIR ORIGIN AND DEVELOPMENT, by Walter E. Geiger. 1978. (No. 187). *-9187-8.*
LANGUAGE IN GIOVANNI VERGA'S EARLY NOVELS, by Nicholas Patruno. 1977. (No. 188). *-9188-6.*
BLAS DE OTERO EN SU POESÍA, by Moraima de Semprún Donahue. 1977. (No. 189). *-9189-4.*
LA ANATOMÍA DE "EL DIABLO COJUELO": DESLINDES DEL GÉNERO ANATOMÍSTICO, por C. George Peale. 1977. (No. 191). *-9191-6.*
RICHARD SANS PEUR, EDITED FROM "LE ROMANT DE RICHART" AND FROM GILLES CORROZET'S "RICHART SANS PAOUR", by Denis Joseph Conlon. 1977. (No. 192). *-9192-4.*
MARCEL PROUST'S GRASSET PROOFS. *Commentary and Variants,* by Douglas Alden. 1978. (No. 193). *-9193-2.*
MONTAIGNE AND FEMINISM, by Cecile Insdorf. 1977. (No. 194). *-9194-0.*
SANTIAGO F. PUGLIA, AN EARLY PHILADELPHIA PROPAGANDIST FOR SPANISH AMERICAN INDEPENDENCE, by Merle S. Simmons. 1977. (No. 195). *-9195-9.*
BAROQUE FICTION-MAKING. A STUDY OF GOMBERVILLE'S "POLEXANDRE", by Edward Baron Turk. 1978. (No. 196). *-9196-7.*
THE TRAGIC FALL: DON ÁLVARO DE LUNA AND OTHER FAVORITES IN SPANISH GOLDEN AGE DRAMA, by Raymond R. MacCurdy. 1978. (No. 197). *-9197-5.*
A BAHIAN HERITAGE. An Ethnolinguistic Study of African Influences on Bahian Portuguese, by William W. Megenney. 1978. (No. 198). *-9198-3.*
"LA QUERELLE DE LA ROSE": Letters and Documents, by Joseph L. Baird and John R. Kane. 1978. (No. 199). *-9199-1.*
TWO AGAINST TIME. *A Study of the Very Present Worlds of Paul Claudel and Charles Péguy,* by Joy Nachod Humes. 1978. (No. 200). *-9200-9.*
TECHNIQUES OF IRONY IN ANATOLE FRANCE. Essay on *Les Sept Femmes de la Barbe-Bleue,* by Diane Wolfe Levy. 1978. (No. 201). *-9201-7.*
THE PERIPHRASTIC FUTURES FORMED BY THE ROMANCE REFLEXES OF "VADO (AD)" PLUS INFINITIVE, by James Joseph Champion. 1978. (No. 202). *-9202-5.*
THE EVOLUTION OF THE LATIN /b/-/ṷ/ MERGER: A Quantitative and Comparative Analysis of the *B-V* Alternation in Latin Inscriptions, by Joseph Louis Barbarino. 1978. (No. 203). *-9203-3.*
METAPHORIC NARRATION: THE STRUCTURE AND FUNCTION OF METAPHORS IN "A LA RECHERCHE DU TEMPS PERDU", by Inge Karalus Crosman. 1978. (No. 204). *-9204-1.*
LE VAIN SIECLE GUERPIR. A Literary Approach to Sainthood through Old French Hagiography of the Twelfth Century, by Phyllis Johnson and Brigitte Cazelles. 1979. (No. 205). *-9205-X.*
THE POETRY OF CHANGE: A STUDY OF THE SURREALIST WORKS OF BENJAMIN PÉRET, by Julia Field Costich. 1979. (No. 206). *-9206-8.*
NARRATIVE PERSPECTIVE IN THE POST-CIVIL WAR NOVELS OF FRANCISCO AYALA "MUERTES DE PERRO" AND "EL FONDO DEL VASO", by Maryellen Bieder. 1979. (No. 207). *-9207-6.*
RABELAIS: HOMO LOGOS, by Alice Fiola Berry. 1979. (No. 208). *-9208-4.*
"DUEÑAS" AND "DONCELLAS": A STUDY OF THE "DOÑA RODRÍGUEZ" EPISODE IN "DON QUIJOTE", by Conchita Herdman Marianella. 1979. (No. 209). *-9209-2.*

When ordering please cite the *ISBN Prefix* plus the last four digits for each title.

Send orders to: University of North Carolina Press
P.O. Box 2288
CB# 6215
Chapel Hill, NC 27515-2288
U.S.A.

NORTH CAROLINA STUDIES IN THE ROMANCE LANGUAGES AND LITERATURES

I.S.B.N. Prefix 0-8078-

Recent Titles

PIERRE BOAISTUAU'S "HISTOIRES TRAGIQUES": A STUDY OF NARRATIVE FORM AND TRAGIC VISION, by Richard A. Carr. 1979. (No. 210). *-9210-6.*
REALITY AND EXPRESSION IN THE POETRY OF CARLOS PELLICER, by George Melnykovich. 1979. (No. 211). *-9211-4.*
MEDIEVAL MAN, HIS UNDERSTANDING OF HIMSELF, HIS SOCIETY, AND THE WORLD, by Urban T. Holmes, Jr. 1980. (No. 212). *-9212-2.*
MÉMOIRES SUR LA LIBRAIRIE ET SUR LA LIBERTÉ DE LA PRESSE, introduction and notes by Graham E. Rodmell. 1979. (No. 213). *-9213-0.*
THE FICTIONS OF THE SELF. THE EARLY WORKS OF MAURICE BARRES, by Gordon Shenton. 1979. (No. 214). *-9214-9.*
CECCO ANGIOLIERI. A STUDY, by Gifford P. Orwen. 1979. (No. 215). *-9215-7.*
THE INSTRUCTIONS OF SAINT LOUIS: A CRITICAL TEXT, by David O'Connell. 1979. (No. 216). *-9216-5.*
ARTFUL ELOQUENCE, JEAN LEMAIRE DE BELGES AND THE RHETORICAL TRADITION, by Michael F. O. Jenkins. 1980. (No. 217). *-9217-3.*
A CONCORDANCE TO MARIVAUX'S COMEDIES IN PROSE, edited by Donald C. Spinelli. 1979. (No. 218). 4 volumes, *-9218-1* (set); *-9219-X* (v. 1); *-9220-3* (v. 2); *-9221-1* (v. 3); *-9222-X* (v. 4).
ABYSMAL GAMES IN THE NOVELS OF SAMUEL BECKETT, by Angela B. Moorjani. 1982. (No. 219). *-9223-8.*
GERMAIN NOUVEAU DIT HUMILIS: ÉTUDE BIOGRAPHIQUE, par Alexandre L. Amprimoz. 1983. (No. 220). *-9224-6.*
THE "VIE DE SAINT ALEXIS" IN THE TWELFTH AND THIRTEENTH CENTURIES: AN EDITION AND COMMENTARY, by Alison Goddard Elliot. 1983. (No. 221). *-9225-4.*
THE BROKEN ANGEL: MYTH AND METHOD IN VALÉRY, by Ursula Franklin. 1984. (No. 222). *-9226-2.*
READING VOLTAIRE'S "CONTES": A SEMIOTICS OF PHILOSOPHICAL NARRATION, by Carol Sherman. 1985. (No. 223). *-9227-0.*
THE STATUS OF THE READING SUBJECT IN THE "LIBRO DE BUEN AMOR", by Marina Scordilis Brownlee. 1985. (No. 224). *-9228-9.*
MARTORELL'S "TIRANT LO BLANCH": A PROGRAM FOR MILITARY AND SOCIAL REFORM IN FIFTEENTH-CENTURY CHRISTENDOM, by Edward T. Aylward. 1985. (No. 225). *-9229-7.*
NOVEL LIVES: THE FICTIONAL AUTOBIOGRAPHIES OF GUILLERMO CABRERA INFANTE AND MARIO VARGAS LLOSA, by Rosemary Geisdorfer Feal. 1986. (No. 226). *-9230-0.*
SOCIAL REALISM IN THE ARGENTINE NARRATIVE, by David William Foster. 1986. (No. 227). *-9231-9.*
HALF-TOLD TALES: DILEMMAS OF MEANING IN THREE FRENCH NOVELS, by Philip Stewart. 1987. (No. 228). *-9232-7.*
POLITIQUES DE L'ECRITURE BATAILLE/DERRIDA: le sens du sacré dans la pensée française du surréalisme à nos jours, par Jean-Michel Heimonet. 1987. (No. 229). *-9233-5.*
GOD, THE QUEST, THE HERO: THEMATIC STRUCTURES IN BECKETT'S FICTION, by Laura Barge. 1988. (No. 230). *-9235-1.*
THE NAME GAME. WRITING/FADING WRITER IN "DE DONDE SON LOS CANTANTES", by Oscar Montero. 1988. (No. 231). *-9236-X.*
GIL VICENTE AND THE DEVELOPMENT OF THE COMEDIA, by René Pedro Garay. 1988. (No. 232). *-9234-3.*

When ordering please cite the *ISBN Prefix* plus the last four digits for each title.

Send orders to: University of North Carolina Press
P.O. Box 2288
CB# 6215
Chapel Hill, NC 27515-2288
U.S.A.

The Department of Romance Studies Digital Arts and Collaboration Lab at the University of North Carolina at Chapel Hill is proud to support the digitization of the North Carolina Studies in the Romance Languages and Literatures series.

www.ingramcontent.com/pod-product-compliance
Lightning Source LLC
Chambersburg PA
CBHW030619230426
43661CB00053B/2061